Contri

Peter ˙

Ray S

Micha

Consu

Dave ˙

Dale J

Pam N

Wiley Publishing, Inc.

Author's Acknowledgements
I would like to thank Peter Z. Orton for his valuable assistance and contributions and Michele Spence for her patience (the manuscript took a year longer than expected) and fine editing. I would also like to thank my family: my wife, Susan, daughter Jennifer Lynn, son, Adam Michael, and newest addition, Jonathan Matthew, for their wonderful diversions during the writing process (and overall moral support).

Publisher's Acknowledgments
Production
  Wiley Publishing Indianapolis Composition Services

Cliffs Math Review For Standardized Tests

Published by:
Wiley Publishing, Inc.
909 Third Avenue
New York, NY 10022
www.wiley.com

ISBN: 0-8220-2033-5

Printed in the United States of America
10 9 8

For general information on our other products and services or to obtain technical support, please contact our Customer Care Department within the U.S. at 800-762-2974, outside the U.S. at 317-572-3993, or fax 317-572-4002.

Wiley also publishes its books in a variety of electronic formats. Some content that appears in print may not be available in electronic books.

CONTENTS

PART I: INTRODUCTION

PART II: BASIC SKILLS REVIEW

PART III: STRATEGIES AND PRACTICE

Part I: Introduction

Why You Need This Guide

Are you planning to take the . . .

GRE   SAT   GMAT   NTE

CBEST   PSAT   ACT   PPST

or any other standardized test with a math section?

During the author's fourteen years of offering test preparation programs at over thirty universities, the most requested supplementary aid has been a text, guide, or wonder drug to help give candidates a "fighting chance" on the math questions encountered on standardized tests. *Math Review for Standardized Tests* is designed specifically to review, refresh, reintroduce, diagnose, and, in effect, give you that "fighting chance" by focusing squarely on a test-oriented review.

This is the *most unique math guide available today*. Not only is it clear, concise, and easy to use, but its *focus by test-preparation experts on standardized tests* gives insight on problem types. Our unique approach will bring back memories of mathematical rules and concepts once learned but since forgotten through lack of use or understanding. Throughout this guide, language will be nontechnical but consistent with the terminology used on most standardized tests.

What This Guide Contains

Math Review for Standardized Tests provides an excellent and extensive overview of the areas of concern for most test takers:

- Arithmetic
- Algebra
- Geometry
- Word Problems
- Strategies for Common Problem Types
- Unique Test-Type Problems
    Math Ability
    Quantitative Comparison
    Data Sufficiency

3

Each review section includes a diagnostic test, explanations of rules and concepts with examples, practice problems with complete explanations, a review test, and a glossary.

If you're taking the GRE, GMAT, SAT, PSAT, ACT, CBEST, NTE, PPST, or any other exam with a math section, this book was designed for YOU.

Range of Difficulty and Scope

The range of difficulty and scope of problem types on standardized tests vary significantly, depending upon which exam is taken. For example . . .

The ACT includes math problems drawing from arithmetic, algebra I, geometry, and algebra II.

The GMAT includes math problems from only arithmetic, algebra I, and geometry, but it is heavily laden with word problems. It also includes a section or two of data sufficiency, a unique problem type.

The SAT, PSAT, and GRE include math problems from arithmetic, algebra I, and geometry. They also include a problem type called quantitative comparison, unfamiliar to many test takers.

The NTE, CBEST, and PPST include problems from basic arithmetic to simple algebra I concepts and basic geometry. Although these tests draw upon the more basic mathematical concepts, procedure problems are quite common. (Procedure problems do not ask for a final numerical answer but rather "how" a problem should be worked to be solved.)

A General Guideline

From a strictly mathematical perspective, the ACT requires the greatest range and highest level of math skills of the exams mentioned. Although the GMAT does not require algebra II, its problems tend to be more complex, more rigorous, and more demanding of insights and techniques than, say, the NTE, CBEST, or PPST. The SAT, PSAT, and GRE would probably fall in the middle category of difficulty, as their questions tend to be less difficult than the ACT and GMAT, but more difficult than the NTE, CBEST, and PPST.

As you work through this book, keep in mind which questions will be appropriate for you. The practice problems in each area are generally arranged so that the first few are easiest and the last few are most difficult. Therefore, an ACT or GMAT candidate should work all the practice problems, whereas an NTE candidate will probably not have to be concerned with the most difficult in each set. Be sure to check the Cliffs Guide for the specific exam you will take to determine the level of difficulty for your math questions. Make use of the informational bulletins from the test makers. *Review the appropriate level of math. Use your time effectively!*

How to Use This Guide

1. Review the materials concerning your test provided by the testing company. This information is usually available at no charge and will detail the areas and question types for your particular exam.
2. Take the diagnostic test in arithmetic.
3. Check your answers on the diagnostic arithmetic test. If your results warrant extensive arithmetic study, then—
4. Work through the arithmetic review and practice problems.
5. If your results on the arithmetic diagnostic test do not warrant extensive arithmetic review but you still have some weakness in that area, *skip step 4* but concentrate on the review sections pertinent to your weaknesses. (The diagnostic test answers are keyed to appropriate review pages.)
6. Take the arithmetic review test.
7. Based on your results on the review test, review any sections still requiring improvement.
8. Follow the same procedure (steps 2 through 7) for each review section (algebra, geometry, word problems).
9. Notice that the final section of this guide includes chapters on test strategies and special problem types appearing on some exams—math ability, quantitative comparison, and data sufficiency. The particular exam you are taking will determine which of these areas are important to you. These questions will help "fine tune" your general math review and improve your problem-solving skills for your test.

10. Even if a unique problem type (say, quantitative comparison or data sufficiency) will not appear on your exam, you should also work these practice problems in the final section of this guide. These will help broaden your understanding of the particular math skill and give insight which may help solve the question types found on the test you will take.

Part II: Basic Skills Review

Each review section includes:
- A diagnostic test to assess your strengths and weaknesses.
- Explanations of rules and concepts to demonstrate important mathematical processes.
- Practice problems with complete explanations to enable you to apply the rules and concepts.
- A review test to help you focus on areas still needing improvement.
- A glossary to assist in your understanding of mathematical terms used in problems and explanations.

Areas covered include:
- Arithmetic
- Algebra
- Geometry
- Word Problems

ARITHMETIC

ARITHMETIC DIAGNOSTIC TEST

Questions

1. Which of the following are integers? $\frac{1}{2}$, -2, 0, 4, 3.2

2. Which of the following are rational numbers?
   5.8, 6, $\frac{1}{4}$, $\sqrt{4}$, $\sqrt{7}$, π

3. Is 37 prime?

4. Which of the following are perfect cubes? $1, 6, 8, 9, 27$

5. The commutative property of addition is represented by
   (A) $2 + (3 + 4) = (2 + 3) + 4$
   (B) $2 + (-2) = 0$
   (C) $3 + 5 = 5 + 3$

6. $(6 \times 10^4) + (3 \times 10^2) + (4 \times 10^{-1}) =$

7. Simplify $3[3^2 + 2(4 + 1)]$.

8. Round 4.4584 to the nearest thousandth.

9. $-4 + 8 =$

10. $-12 - 6 =$

11. $(-6)(-8) =$

12. 2,730 is divisible by which of the following? $3, 4, 8$

13. Change $5\frac{3}{4}$ to an improper fraction.

14. Change $\frac{32}{6}$ to a mixed number in lowest terms.

15. $\frac{2}{7} + \frac{3}{5} =$

16. $1\frac{3}{8} + 2\frac{5}{6} =$

17. $11 - \frac{2}{3} =$

18. $6\frac{1}{8} - 3\frac{3}{4} =$

19. $-\frac{7}{8} - \frac{5}{9} =$

20. $-\frac{1}{6} \times \frac{1}{3} =$

21. $2\frac{3}{8} \times 1\frac{5}{6} =$

22. $-\frac{1}{4} \div \frac{9}{14} =$

23. $2\frac{3}{7} \div 1\frac{1}{4} =$

24. $\dfrac{1}{3 + \dfrac{2}{1 + \frac{1}{3}}} =$

25. $.08 + 1.3 + .562 =$

26. $.45 - .003 =$

27. $8.001 \times 2.4 =$

28. $.147 \div .7 =$

29. Change $\frac{3}{20}$ to a decimal.

30. Change 7% to a decimal.

31. 79% of 64 =

32. 40% of what is 20?

33. Change $\frac{1}{8}$ to a percent.

34. What is the percent increase of a rise in temperature from 80° to 100°?

35. Express .00000023 in scientific notation.

36. $(3.2 \times 10^3)(2.4 \times 10^8) =$

37. $(5.1 \times 10^6) \div (1.7 \times 10^2) =$

38. $8^3 \times 8^7 =$

39. $9^5 \div 9^2 =$

40. $(5^3)^2 =$

41. Approximate $\sqrt{30}$ to the nearest tenth.

42. Simplify $\sqrt{80}$.

43. $-\sqrt{9} =$

44. $\sqrt[3]{64}$ =

45. What is the probability of rolling two dice so they total 9?

46. In how many ways can the letters TEAM be arranged?

47. A scientist is trying to select three members for his research team from six possible applicants. How many possible combinations are there, assuming all applicants are qualified?

48. Find the arithmetic mean, mode, median, and range of the following group of numbers: 6, 4, 4, 2, 5, 9

49. Find the next number in the series: 2, 5, 11, 23, 47, _____

50. If 1 kilometer equals .6 mile, then 25 kilometers equal how many miles?

Answers

Page numbers following each answer refer to the review section applicable to this problem type.

1. −2, 0, 4 (p. 13)

2. 5.8, 6, ¼, $\sqrt{4}$ ($\sqrt{4}$ = 2) (p. 13)

3. yes (p. 13)

4. 1, 8, 27 (p. 13)

5. (C) (p. 14)

6. 60,300.4 (p. 17)

7. 57 (p. 18)

8. 4.458 (p. 20)

9. 4 (p. 22)

10. −18 (p. 23)

11. 48 (p. 24)

12. 3 (p. 25)

13. ²³⁄₄ (p. 28)

14. 5²⁄₆ = 5⅓ (p. 28)

15. ³¹⁄₃₅ (p. 34)

16. 4⁵⁄₂₄ (p. 39)

17. 10⅓ (p. 41)

18. 2⅜ (p. 41)

19. − ¹⁰³⁄₇₂ = −1³¹⁄₇₂ (p. 38)

20. − ¹⁄₁₈ (p. 42)

21. ²⁰⁹⁄₄₈ = 4¹⁷⁄₄₈ (p. 43)

22. − ⁷⁄₁₈ (p. 44)

23. ⁶⁸⁄₃₅ = 1³³⁄₃₅ (p. 46)

24. ²⁄₉ (p. 47)

25. 1.942 (p. 49)

26. .447 (p. 49)

27. 19.2024 (p. 50)

28. .21 (p. 51)

29. .15 (p. 51)

30. .07 (p. 53)

31. 50.56 (p. 55)

32. 50 (p. 55)

33. $12\frac{1}{2}\%$ or 12.5% (p. 53)

34. 25% (p. 59)

35. 2.3×10^{-7} (p. 60)

36. 7.68×10^{11} (p. 61)

37. 3×10^{4} (p. 62)

38. 8^{10} (p. 65)

39. 9^{3} (p. 65)

40. 5^{6} (p. 65)

41. 5.5 (p. 67)

42. $4\sqrt{5}$ (p. 69)

43. -3 (p. 66)

44. 4 (p. 66)

45. $\frac{4}{36} = \frac{1}{9}$ (p. 70)

46. 24 (p. 73)

47. 20 (p. 73)

48. mean = 5 (p. 76)
     mode = 4 (p. 78)
     median = $4\frac{1}{2}$ or 4.5 (p. 78)
     range = 7 (p. 79)

49. 95 (p. 80)

50. 15 miles (p. 83)

ARITHMETIC REVIEW

You should already be familiar with the fundamentals of addition, subtraction, multiplication, and division of whole numbers (0, 1, 2, 3, ...). The following is a review of signed numbers, fractions, decimals, and important additional topics from arithmetic.

Preliminaries

Groups of Numbers

- In doing arithmetic and algebra, we work with several groups of numbers.

NATURAL or COUNTING NUMBERS: The numbers 1, 2, 3, 4, ... are called natural or counting numbers.

WHOLE NUMBERS: The numbers 0, 1, 2, 3, ... are called whole numbers.

INTEGERS: The numbers ... −2, −1, 0, 1, 2, ... are called integers.

NEGATIVE INTEGERS: The numbers ... −3, −2, −1 are called negative integers.

POSITIVE INTEGERS: The natural numbers are sometimes called the positive integers.

RATIONAL NUMBERS: Fractions, such as $\frac{3}{2}$ or $\frac{7}{8}$, are called rational numbers. Since a number such as 5 may be written as $\frac{5}{1}$, all *integers* are *rational numbers*.

IRRATIONAL NUMBERS: Another type of number is an irrational number. Examples of irrational numbers are $\sqrt{3}$ and π.

REAL NUMBERS: Real numbers consist of all *rational* and *irrational numbers*. Typically most standardized exams use only real numbers, which are the numbers you are used to using.

PRIME NUMBERS: A prime number is a number that can be evenly divided by only itself and 1. For example, 19 is a prime number because it can be evenly divided only by 19 and 1, but 21 is not a prime number because 21 can be evenly divided by other numbers (3 and 7). The only even prime number is 2; thereafter, any even number may be divided evenly by 2. Zero and 1 are *not* prime numbers. The first ten prime numbers are 2, 3, 5, 7, 11, 13, 17, 19, 23, and 29.

ODD NUMBERS: Odd numbers are whole numbers not divisible by 2: 1, 3, 5, 7, ...

EVEN NUMBERS: Even numbers are numbers divisible by 2: 0, 2, 4, 6, . . .

COMPOSITE NUMBERS: A composite number is a number divisible by more than just 1 and itself: 4, 6, 8, 9, 10, 12, 14, 15, . . .

SQUARES: Squares are the result when numbers are multiplied by themselves: $(2 \cdot 2 = 4)$, $(3 \cdot 3 = 9)$; 1, 4, 9, 16, 25, 36 . . .

CUBES: Cubes are the result when numbers are multiplied by themselves twice: $(2 \cdot 2 \cdot 2 = 8)$, $(3 \cdot 3 \cdot 3 = 27)$; 1, 8, 27 . . .

Ways to Show Multiplication

● There are several ways to show multiplication. They are

$$4 \times 3 = 12 \qquad\qquad 4(3) = 12$$
$$4 \cdot 3 = 12 \qquad\qquad (4)3 = 12$$
$$(4)(3) = 12$$

Common Math Symbols

● Symbol references:

= is equal to	≥ is greater than or equal to
≠ is not equal to	≤ is less than or equal to
> is greater than	‖ is parallel to
< is less than	⊥ is perpendicular to

Properties of Basic Mathematical Operations

Some Properties (Axioms) of Addition

● *Closure* is when all answers fall into the original set. If you add two even numbers, the answer is still an even number; therefore the set of even numbers *is closed* under addition (has closure). $(2 + 4 = 6)$ If you add two odd numbers, the answer is not an odd number; therefore the set of odd numbers is *not closed* under addition (no closure). $(3 + 5 = 8)$

● *Commutative* means that the *order* does not make any difference.

$$2 + 3 = 3 + 2$$
$$a + b = b + a$$

Note: Commutative does *not* hold for subtraction.

$$3 - 1 \neq 1 - 3$$
$$a - b \neq b - a$$

- *Associative* means that the *grouping* does not make any difference.

$$(2 + 3) + 4 = 2 + (3 + 4)$$
$$(a + b) + c = a + (b + c)$$

The grouping has changed (parentheses moved), but the sides are still equal.
Note: Associative does *not* hold for subtraction.

$$4 - (3 - 1) \neq (4 - 3) - 1$$
$$a - (b - c) \neq (a - b) - c$$

- The *identity element* for addition is 0. Any number added to 0 gives the original number

$$3 + 0 = 3$$
$$a + 0 = a$$

- The *additive inverse* is the opposite (negative) of the number. Any number plus its additive inverse equals 0 (the identity).

$$3 + (-3) = 0; \text{ therefore 3 and } -3 \text{ are inverses}$$
$$-2 + 2 = 0; \text{ therefore } -2 \text{ and 2 are inverses}$$
$$a + (-a) = 0; \text{ therefore a and } -a \text{ are inverses}$$

Some Properties (Axioms) of Multiplication

- *Closure* is when all answers fall into the original set. If you multiply two even numbers, the answer is still an even number; therefore the set of even numbers *is closed* under multiplication (has closure). ($2 \times 4 = 8$). If you multiply two odd numbers, the answer is an odd number; therefore the set of odd numbers *is closed* under multiplication (has closure). ($3 \times 5 = 15$)

- *Commutative* means that the *order* does not make any difference.

$$2 \times 3 = 3 \times 2$$
$$a \times b = b \times a$$

Note: Commutative does *not* hold for division.

$$2 \div 4 \neq 4 \div 2$$

- *Associative* means that the *grouping* does not make any difference.

$$(2 \times 3) \times 4 = 2 \times (3 \times 4)$$
$$(a \times b) \times c = a \times (b \times c)$$

The grouping has changed (parentheses moved) but the sides are still equal.
Note: Associative does *not* hold for division.

$$(8 \div 4) \div 2 \neq 8 \div (4 \div 2)$$

- The *identity element* for multiplication is 1. Any number multiplied by 1 gives the original number.

$$3 \times 1 = 3$$
$$a \times 1 = a$$

- The *multiplicative inverse* is the reciprocal of the number. Any number multiplied by its reciprocal equals 1.

$$2 \times \tfrac{1}{2} = 1; \text{ therefore 2 and } \tfrac{1}{2} \text{ are inverses}$$
$$a \times \tfrac{1}{a} = 1; \text{ therefore a and } \tfrac{1}{a} \text{ are inverses}$$

A Property of Two Operations

- The *distributive property* is the process of distributing the number on the outside of the parentheses to each term on the inside.

$$2(3 + 4) = 2(3) + 2(4)$$
$$a(b + c) = a(b) + a(c)$$

Note: You cannot use the distributive property with only one operation.

$$3(4 \times 5 \times 6) \neq 3(4) \times 3(5) \times 3(6)$$
$$a(bcd) \neq a(b) \times a(c) \times a(d) \text{ or } (ab)(ac)(ad)$$

Place Value

- Each position in any number has *place value*. For instance, in the number 485, the 4 is in the hundreds place, 8 is in the tens place, and 5 is in the ones place. Thus, place value is as follows:

Practice: Place Value Problems

1. Which digit is in the tens place in 483?
2. In 36,548, which digit is in the thousands place?
3. The digit 7 is in which place in 45,328.769?
4. Which digit is in the hundredths place in 25.0671?
5. Which digit is in the ten millions place in 867,451,023.79?

Answers: Place Value Problems

1. 8   2. 6   3. tenths   4. 6   5. 6

Expanded Notation

- Sometimes numbers are written in *expanded notation* to point out the place value of each digit. For example, 345 can be written

$$300 + 40 + 5$$
$$(3 \times 100) + (4 \times 10) + (5 \times 1)$$
$$(3 \times 10^2) + (4 \times 10^1) + (5 \times 10^0)$$

These last two are the more common forms of expanded notation, one with exponents, one without exponents. Notice that in these, the digit is multiplied times its place value—1's, 10's, 100's, etc.

Another example: 43.25 can be written

$$40 + 3 + .2 + .05$$
$$(4 \times 10) + (3 \times 1) + (2 \times \frac{1}{10}) + (5 \times \frac{1}{100})$$
$$(4 \times 10^1) + (3 \times 10^0) + (2 \times 10^{-1}) + (5 \times 10^{-2})$$

Notice that the tenths place is 10^{-1} and the hundredths place is 10^{-2}, and so on.

Practice: Expanded Notation Problems

Write in expanded notation using exponents.

1. 576   2. 1,489   3. 3.581   4. 302,400

Answers: Expanded Notation Problems

1. $(5 \times 10^2) + (7 \times 10^1) + (6 \times 10^0)$
2. $(1 \times 10^3) + (4 \times 10^2) + (8 \times 10^1) + (9 \times 10^0)$
3. $(3 \times 10^0) + (5 \times 10^{-1}) + (8 \times 10^{-2}) + (1 \times 10^{-3})$
4. $(3 \times 10^5) + (0 \times 10^4) + (2 \times 10^3) + (4 \times 10^2) + (0 \times 10^1) +$
   (0×10^0) *or* $(3 \times 10^5) + (2 \times 10^3) + (4 \times 10^2)$

Grouping Symbols: Parentheses, Brackets, Braces

Parentheses ( )

- *Parentheses* are used to group numbers or variables. Everything inside parentheses must be done before any other operations. *For example:*

$$50(2 + 6) = 50(8) = 400$$

When a parenthesis is preceded by a minus sign, to remove the parentheses, change the sign of each term within the parentheses. *For example:*

$$6 - (-3 + a - 2b + c) =$$
$$6 + 3 - a + 2b - c = 9 - a + 2b - c$$

Brackets [ ] *and Braces* { }

- *Brackets* and *braces* are also used to group numbers or variables. Technically, they are used after parentheses. Parentheses are to be used first, then brackets, then braces: $\{[()]\}$ Sometimes, instead of brackets or braces, you will see the use of larger parentheses.

$$\left((3 + 4) \cdot 5\right) + 2$$

A number using all three grouping symbols would look like this

$$2\{1 + [4(2 + 1) + 3]\}$$

and simplified as follows (notice that you work from the inside out):

$$2\{1 + [4(2 + 1) + 3]\} =$$
$$2\{1 + [4(3) + 3]\} =$$
$$2\{1 + [12 + 3]\} =$$
$$2\{1 + [15]\} =$$
$$2\{16\} =$$
$$32$$

Order of Operations

- If multiplication, division, powers, addition, parentheses, etc., are all contained in one problem, the *order of operations* is as follows.

1. parentheses
2. powers and square roots
3. multiplication ⎤
4. division ⎦ whichever comes first left to right

5. addition ⎤
6. subtraction ⎦ whichever comes first left to right

Examples:

1. $6 + 4 \times 3 =$
   $6 + 12 =$ (multiplication)
   18 (then addition)

2. $10 - 3 \times 6 + 10^2 + (6 + 1) \times 4 =$
   $10 - 3 \times 6 + 10^2 + (7) \times 4 =$ (parentheses first)
   $10 - 3 \times 6 + 100 + (7) \times 4 =$ (powers next)
   $10 - 18 + 100 + 28 =$ (multiplication)
   $-8 + 100 + 28 =$ (addition/subtraction left to right)
   $92 + 28 = 120$

An easy way to remember the order of operations *after parentheses* is: **P**lease **M**y **D**ear **A**unt **S**arah (**P**owers, **M**ultiplication, **D**ivision, **A**ddition, **S**ubtraction).

Practice: Order of Operations Problems

Simplify:

1. $6 + 4 \times 3^2$
2. $3^2 + 6(4 + 1)$
3. $12 - 2(8 + 2) + 5$
4. $8[3(3^2 - 8) + 1]$

5. $6\{4[2(3 + 2) - 8] - 8\}$
6. $6(12 + 8) \div 2 + 1$

Answers: Order of Operations Problems

1. $6 + 4 \times 3^2 =$
   $6 + 4 \times 9 =$
   $6 + 36 =$
   42

2. $3^2 + 6(4 + 1) =$
   $9 + 6(5) =$
   $9 + 30 =$
   39

3. $12 - 2(8 + 2) + 5 =$
   $12 - 2(10) + 5 =$
   $12 - 20 + 5 =$
   $-8 + 5 =$
   -3

4. $8[3(3^2 - 8) + 1] =$
   $8[3(9 - 8) + 1] =$
   $8[3(1) + 1] =$
   $8[3 + 1] =$
   $8[4] =$
   32

5. $6\{4[2(3 + 2) - 8] - 8\} =$
   $6\{4[2(5) - 8] - 8\} =$
   $6\{4[10 - 8] - 8\} =$
   $6\{4[2] - 8\} =$
   $6\{8 - 8\} =$
   $6\{0\} =$
   0

6. $6(12 + 8) \div 2 + 1 =$
   $6(20) \div 2 + 1 =$
   $120 \div 2 + 1 =$
   $60 + 1 =$
   61

Rounding Off

- To *round off* any number:

  1. Underline the place value to which you're rounding off.
  2. Look to the immediate right (one place) of your underlined place value.
  3. Identify the number (the one to the right). If it is 5 or higher,

round your underlined place value up 1. If the number (the one to the right) is 4 or less, leave your underlined place value as it is and change all the other numbers to its right to zeros. *For example:* Round to the nearest thousand:

$$345,\underline{6}78 \text{ becomes } 346,000$$
$$92\underline{8},499 \text{ becomes } 928,000$$

This works with decimals as well. Round to the nearest hundredth:

$$3.4\underline{6}78 \text{ becomes } 3.47$$
$$298,435.0\underline{8}3 \text{ becomes } 298,435.08$$

Notice that the numbers to the right of the rounded digit are dropped when working with decimals.

Practice: Rounding Off Problems

1. Round off 137 to the nearest ten.
2. Round off 4,549 to the nearest hundred.
3. Round off .4758 to the nearest hundredth.
4. Round off 99.483 to the nearest one.
5. Round off 6,278.38512 to the nearest thousandth.

Answers: Rounding Off Problems

1. 140   2. 4,500   3. .48   4. 99   5. 6,278.385

Signed Numbers (Positive Numbers and Negative Numbers)

Number Lines

● On a *number line,* numbers to the right of 0 are positive. Numbers to the left of 0 are negative, as follows.

Given any two numbers on a number line, the one on the right is always larger, regardless of its sign (positive or negative). Note that fractions may also be placed on a number line.
For example:

etc. $\dashv\!\!\!-\!\!\!+\!\!\!-\!\!\!+\!\!\!-\!\!\!+\!\!\!-\!\!\!+\!\!\!-\!\!\!+\!\!\!-\!\!\!+\!\!\!-\!\!\!+\!\!\!-\!\!\!\vdash$ etc.
$-2\frac{1}{2}$ $-1\frac{1}{2}$ $-\frac{1}{2}$ $\frac{1}{2}$ $1\frac{1}{2}$ $2\frac{1}{2}$
-3 -2 -1 0 $+1$ $+2$ $+3$

Practice: Number Line Problems

Complete the number line below, and then locate

1. $+2$ 2. -3 3. $+1\frac{1}{2}$ 4. $-\frac{1}{2}$ 5. $+3\frac{1}{4}$

Answers: Number Line Problems

1. F   2. A   3. E   4. C   5. G

Addition of Signed Numbers

● When *adding two numbers with the same sign* (either both positive or both negative), add the numbers and keep the same sign.
For example:

$$
\begin{array}{r} +5 \\ +\ +7 \\ \hline +12 \end{array}
\qquad
\begin{array}{r} -8 \\ +\ -3 \\ \hline -11 \end{array}
$$

When *adding two numbers with different signs* (one positive and one negative), subtract the numbers and keep the sign from the larger one. *For example:*

$$
\begin{array}{r} +5 \\ +\ -7 \\ \hline -2 \end{array}
\qquad
\begin{array}{r} -59 \\ +\ +72 \\ \hline +13 \end{array}
$$

Signed numbers may also be added "horizontally." *For example:*

$$+9 + 6 = +15$$
$$-12 + 9 = -3$$
$$8 + (-5) = 3$$

Practice: Addition of Signed Numbers Problems

1. $+25 + 8 =$

2. $-10 + 15 =$

3. $\quad -7$
    $\underline{+\ -3}$

4. $\quad -82$
    $\underline{+\ +60}$

5. $-18 + (+5) =$

Answers: Addition of Signed Numbers Problems

1. $+33$ 2. $+5$ 3. -10 4. -22 5. -13

Subtraction of Signed Numbers

● To *subtract positive and/or negative numbers,* just change the sign of the number being subtracted and then add. *For example:*

$+12$	-14	-19	$+20$
$\underline{-\ +4}$	$\underline{-\ -4}$	$\underline{-\ +6}$	$\underline{-\ -3}$

$+12$	-14	-19	$+20$
$+\ -4$	$+\ +4$	$+\ -6$	$+\ +3$
$\overline{+8}$	$\overline{-10}$	$\overline{-25}$	$\overline{+23}$

This may also be done "horizontally." *For example:*

$$+12 - (+4) = +12 + (-4) = 8$$
$$+16 - (-6) = +16 + (+6) = 22$$
$$-20 - (+3) = -20 + (-3) = -23$$
$$-5 - (-2) = -5 + (+2) = -3$$

Practice: Subtraction of Signed Numbers Problems

1. $\quad +9$
    $\underline{-\ +3}$

2. $\quad +25$
    $\underline{-\ -9}$

3. $+36 - (-5) =$

4. $-27 - (+4) =$

5. $-30 - (-2) =$

Answers: Subtraction of Signed Numbers Problems

1. $+6$ 2. $+34$ 3. $+41$ 4. -31 5. -28

Minus Preceding Parenthesis

● If a *minus precedes a parenthesis,* it means everything within the parentheses is to be subtracted. Therefore, using the same rule as in subtraction of signed numbers, simply change every sign within the parentheses to its opposite, and then add.

Examples:

1. $9 - (+3 - 5 + 7 - 6) =$
   $9 + (-3 + 5 - 7 + 6) =$
   $9 + (+1) =$
   10

2. $20 - (+35 - 50 + 100) =$
   $20 + (-35 + 50 - 100) =$
   $20 + (-85) =$
   -65

Practice: Minus Preceding Parenthesis Problems

1. $-(+5 - 3) =$
2. $6 - (+8 - 5 + 10) =$
3. $10 - (-12 - 5 + 3) =$
4. $25 - (-4 + 7 - 8 - 5 + 6) =$

Answers: Minus Preceding Parenthesis Problems

1. $2 - (+2) = 2 + (-2) = 0$
2. $6 - (+13) = 6 + (-13) = -7$
3. $10 - (-14) = 10 + (+14) = 24$
4. $25 - (-4) = 25 + (+4) = 29$

Multiplying and Dividing Signed Numbers

● To *multiply or divide signed numbers,* treat them just like regular numbers but remember this rule: An odd number of negative signs will produce a negative answer. An even number of negative signs will produce a positive answer. *For example:*

$$(-3)(+8)(-5)(-1)(-2) = +240$$
$$(-3)(+8)(-1)(-2) = -48$$

$$\frac{-64}{-2} = +32$$

$$\frac{-64}{+2} = -32$$

Practice: Multiplying and Dividing Signed Number Problems

1. $(-3)(+9) =$

2. $-8 \div -2 =$

3. $(-8)(+3)(-2) =$

4. $\dfrac{-10}{+5} =$

5. $\dfrac{(-4)(+2)(-6)}{-12} =$

Answers: Multiplying and Dividing Signed Number Problems

1. -27 2. $+4$ 3. $+48$ 4. -2 5. -4

Multiplying and Dividing Using Zero

● Zero times any number equals zero. *For example:*

$$0 \times 5 = 0$$
$$0 \times (-3) = 0$$
$$8 \times 9 \times 3 \times (-4) \times 0 = 0$$

● Likewise, zero divided by any number is zero. *For example:*

$$0 \div 5 = 0$$

$$\frac{0}{3} = 0$$

$$0 \div (-6) = 0$$

Important Note: Dividing by zero is "undefined" and is **not** permitted. *For example:*

$$\frac{6}{0} \text{ is not permitted}$$

because there is no such answer. The answer *is not* zero.

Divisibility Rules

● The following set of rules can help you save time in trying to check the divisibility of numbers.

A NUMBER IS DIVISIBLE BY	IF
2	it ends in 0, 2, 4, 6, or 8
3	the total of its digits is divisible by 3
4	the number formed by the last two digits is divisible by 4
5	if it ends in 0 or 5
6	if it is divisible by 2 and 3 (use the rules for both)
7	(no simple rule)
8	the number formed by the last three digits is divisible by 8
9	the total of its digits is divisible by 9

Examples: Divisibility Rules

1. Is 126 divisible by 3? Total of digits = 9. Since 9 is divisible by 3, 126 is divisible by 3.
2. Is 1,648 divisible by 4? Since 48 is divisible by 4, then 1,648 is divisible by 4.
3. Is 186 divisible by 6? Since 186 ends in 6, it is divisible by 2. Total of digits = 15. Since 15 is divisible by 3, 186 is divisible by 3. 186 is divisible by 2 and 3; therefore it is divisible by 6.
4. Is 2,488 divisible by 8? Since 488 is divisible by 8, then 2,488 is divisible by 8.
5. Is 2,853 divisible by 9? Total of digits = 18. Since 18 is divisible by 9, then 2,853 is divisible by 9.

Practice: Divisibility Problems

1. 4,620 is divisible by which of the following numbers?
   2, 3, 4, 5, 6, 7, 8, 9
2. 13,131 is divisible by which of the following numbers?
   2, 3, 4, 5, 6, 7, 8, 9

Answers: Divisibility Problems

1. 2, 3, 4, 5, 6, 7

   2—the number is even
   3—the digits total 12, which is divisible by 3
   4—the number formed by the last two digits, 20, is divisible by 4
   5—the number ends in 0
   6—the number is divisible by 2 and 3
   7—divide 4,620 by 7 and you get 660
   8̸—the number formed by the last three digits, 620, is not divisible by 8
   9̸—the total of the digits is 12, which is not divisible by 9

2. 3, 9

   2̸—the number is not even
   3—the digits total 9, which is divisible by 3
   4̸—the number is not even
   5̸—the number does not end in 0 or 5
   6̸—the number is not even
   7̸—divide and you will see that there is a remainder
   8̸—the number is not even
   9—the digits total 9, which is divisible by 9

Common Fractions

Numerator and Denominator

- Fractions consist of two numbers: a *numerator* (which is above the line) and a *denominator* (which is below the line).

$$\frac{1}{2} \frac{numerator}{denominator} \quad \text{or } numerator\ 1/2\ denominator$$

The denominator lets us know the number of equal parts into which something is divided. The numerator tells us how many of these equal parts are being considered. Thus, if the fraction is ⅗ of a pie, then the denominator 5 tells us that the pie has been divided into 5 equal parts, of which 3 (numerator) are in the fraction. Sometimes it helps to think of the dividing line (in the middle of a fraction) as meaning "out of." In other words, ⅗ would also mean 3 "out of" 5 equal pieces from the whole pie. All rules for signed numbers also apply to fractions.

Negative Fractions

- Fractions may be *negative* as well as positive. (See number line on p. 22.) However, negative fractions are typically written

$$-\frac{3}{4} \quad \text{not} \quad \frac{-3}{4} \quad \text{or} \quad \frac{3}{-4} \quad \text{(although they are all equal)}$$

$$-\frac{3}{4} = \frac{-3}{4} = \frac{3}{-4}$$

Proper Fractions and Improper Fractions

- A fraction like ³⁄₅, where the numerator is smaller than the denominator, is less than one. This kind of fraction is called a *proper fraction*. But sometimes a fraction may be more than one. This is when the numerator is larger than the denominator.

Thus, ¹²⁄₇ is more than one. This is called an *improper fraction*.

Examples of proper fractions: ⁴⁄₇, ²⁄₅, ¹⁄₉, ¹⁰⁄₁₂

Examples of improper fractions: ⁷⁄₄, ³⁄₂, ¹⁰⁄₃, ¹⁶⁄₁₅

Mixed Numbers

- When a term contains both a whole number (3, 8, 25, etc.) and a fraction (½, ¼, ¾, etc.), it is called a *mixed number*. For instance, 5¼ and 290¾ are both mixed numbers. To change an improper fraction to a mixed number, you divide the denominator into the numerator. *For example:*

$$\frac{18}{5} = 3\tfrac{3}{5} \qquad\qquad 5\overline{)\overset{3}{18}} \atop \underline{15} \atop 3$$

To change a mixed number to an improper fraction, you multiply the denominator times the whole number, add in the numerator, and put the total over the original denominator. *For example:*

$$4\tfrac{1}{2} = \tfrac{9}{2} \qquad\qquad 2 \times 4 + 1 = 9$$

Practice: Mixed Number Problems

Change the following improper fractions to mixed numbers.

1. $\frac{3}{2}$ 2. $\frac{7}{4}$ 3. $\frac{10}{3}$ 4. $\frac{16}{5}$ 5. $\frac{23}{4}$

Change the following mixed numbers to improper fractions.

6. $1\frac{3}{4}$ 7. $4\frac{1}{2}$ 8. $5\frac{3}{4}$ 9. $21\frac{3}{4}$ 10. $8\frac{4}{5}$

Answers: Mixed Number Problems

1. $1\frac{1}{2}$ 5. $5\frac{3}{4}$ 9. $\frac{87}{4}$
2. $1\frac{3}{4}$ 6. $\frac{7}{4}$ 10. $\frac{44}{5}$
3. $3\frac{1}{3}$ 7. $\frac{9}{2}$
4. $3\frac{1}{5}$ 8. $\frac{23}{4}$

Equivalent Fractions

Reducing Fractions

● A fraction must be *reduced* to *lowest terms*. This is done by dividing both the numerator and denominator by the largest number that will divide evenly into both. For example, $\frac{10}{25}$ is reduced to $\frac{2}{5}$ by dividing both numerator and denominator by 5. *Other examples:*

$$\frac{30}{50} = \frac{30 \div 10}{50 \div 10} = \frac{3}{5}$$

$$\frac{8}{40} = \frac{8 \div 8}{40 \div 8} = \frac{1}{5}$$

$$\frac{9}{15} = \frac{9 \div 3}{15 \div 3} = \frac{3}{5}$$

Practice: Reducing Fractions Problems

Reduce the following fractions.

1. $\frac{6}{8}$ 2. $\frac{15}{20}$ 3. $\frac{18}{36}$ 4. $\frac{40}{90}$ 5. $\frac{75}{30}$

Answers: Reducing Fractions Problems

1. ¾   2. ¾   3. ½   4. ⁴⁄₉   5. ⁵⁄₂

Enlarging Denominators

- The *denominator* of a fraction may be *enlarged* by multiplying both the numerator and the denominator by the same number. *For example:*

$$\frac{1}{2} = \frac{1 \times 5}{2 \times 5} = \frac{5}{10}$$

$$\frac{3}{4} = \frac{3 \times 10}{4 \times 10} = \frac{30}{40}$$

Practice: Enlarging Denominators Problems

1. Change ⅗ to tenths.
2. Express ¾ as eighths.
3. ⁵⁄₇ = ?⁄₂₁
4. ²⁄₁₅ = ?⁄₄₅
5. Change the fraction ⅜ to an equivalent fraction with a denominator of 24.

Answers: Enlarging Denominators Problems

1. ⁶⁄₁₀   2. ⁶⁄₈   3. ¹⁵⁄₂₁   4. ⁶⁄₄₅   5. ⁹⁄₂₄

Factors

- *Factors* of a number are those whole numbers which when multiplied together yield the number. *For example:* What are the factors of 8?

$$8 = 2 \times 4$$
$$8 = 1 \times 8$$

Therefore, the factors of 8 are 4 and 2 because $4 \times 2 = 8$ and 1 and 8 because $1 \times 8 = 8$.

What are the factors of 24?

$$24 = 1 \times 24$$
$$= 2 \times 12$$
$$= 3 \times 8$$
$$= 4 \times 6$$

Therefore, the factors of 24 are 1, 2, 3, 4, 6, 8, 12, and 24.

Practice: Factor Problems

Find the factors of

1. 6   2. 9   3. 12   4. 48

Answers: Factor Problems

1. 1, 2, 3, and 6   3. 1, 2, 3, 4, 6, and 12
2. 1, 3, and 9   4. 1, 2, 3, 4, 6, 8, 12, 16, 24, and 48

Common Factors

● *Common factors* are those factors which are the same for two or more numbers. For example: What are the common factors of 6 and 8?

6: ⟨1⟩ ⟨2⟩ 3, 6
8: ⟨1⟩ ⟨2⟩ 4, 8

1 and 2 are common factors of 6 and 8. *Note:* Some numbers may have many common factors. *For example:* What are the common factors of 24 and 36?

24: ⟨1⟩⟨2⟩⟨3⟩⟨4⟩⟨6⟩ 8, ⟨12⟩ 24
36: ⟨1⟩⟨2⟩⟨3⟩⟨4⟩⟨6⟩ 9, ⟨12⟩ 18, 36

Thus the common factors of 24 and 36 are 1, 2, 3, 4, 6, and 12.

Practice: Common Factor Problems

Find the common factors of

1. 10 and 30   3. 6 and 15
2. 12 and 18   4. 70 and 80

Answers: Common Factor Problems

1. 1, 2, 5, and 10
2. 1, 2, 3, and 6

3. 1 and 3
4. 1, 2, 5, and 10

Greatest Common Factor

- The *greatest common factor* is the largest factor common to two or more numbers. *For example:* What is the greatest common factor of 12 and 30?

$$12\ \textcircled{1}\ \textcircled{2}\ \textcircled{3},\ 4\ \textcircled{6},\ 12$$
$$30\ \textcircled{1}\ \textcircled{2}\ \textcircled{3},\ 5\ \textcircled{6},\ 10,\ 15,\ 30$$

Notice that while, 1, 2, 3, and 6 are all common factors of 12 and 30, only 6 is the greatest common factor.

Practice: Greatest Common Factor Problems

Find the greatest common factor of

1. 6 and 12
2. 24 and 40

3. 24 and 60
4. 40 and 100

Answers: Greatest Common Factor Problems

1. 6   2. 8   3. 12   4. 20

Multiples

- *Multiples* of a number are found by multiplying that number by 1, by 2, by 3, by 4, by 5, etc. *For example:*

Multiples of 3 are: 3, 6, 9, 12, 15, 18, 21, etc.
Multiples of 4 are: 4, 8, 12, 16, 20, 24, 28, 32, etc.
Multiples of 7 are: 7, 14, 21, 28, 35, 42, 49, 56, etc.

Practice: Multiples Problems

Name the first seven multiples of

1. 2   2. 5   3. 6   4. 8   5. 10

Answers: Multiples Problems

1. 2, 4, 6, 8, 10, 12, 14
2. 5, 10, 15, 20, 25, 30, 35
3. 6, 12, 18, 24, 30, 36, 42

4. 8, 16, 24, 32, 40, 48, 56
5. 10, 20, 30, 40, 50, 60, 70

Common Multiples

- *Common multiples* are those multiples which are the same for two or more numbers. *For example:* What are the common multiples of 2 and 3?

$$2 \rightarrow 2 \quad 4 \quad \boxed{6} \quad 8 \quad 10 \quad \boxed{12} \quad 14 \quad 16 \quad \boxed{18} \text{ etc.}$$
$$3 \rightarrow 3 \quad \boxed{6} \quad 9 \quad \boxed{12} \quad 15 \quad \boxed{18} \text{ etc.}$$

Notice that common multiples may go on indefinitely.

Practice: Common Multiples Problems

Find the first three common multiples of

1. 2 and 6   2. 3 and 4   3. 4 and 6

Answers: Common Multiples Problems

1. 6, 12, 18   2. 12, 24, 36   3. 12, 24, 36

Least Common Multiple

- The *least common multiple* is the smallest multiple which is common to two or more numbers. *For example:* What is the least common multiple of 2 and 3?

$$2 \rightarrow 2 \quad 4 \quad \boxed{6} \quad 8 \quad 10 \quad \boxed{12} \text{ etc.}$$
$$3 \rightarrow 3 \quad \boxed{6} \quad 9 \quad \boxed{12} \text{ etc.}$$

6 is the smallest multiple common to both 2 and 3. *Another example:* What is the least common multiple of 2, 3, and 4?

$$2 \rightarrow 2 \quad 4 \quad 6 \quad 8 \quad 10 \quad \boxed{12} \quad \text{etc.}$$
$$3 \rightarrow 3 \quad\quad 6 \quad\quad 9 \quad\quad 12 \quad \text{etc.}$$
$$4 \rightarrow \quad\quad 4 \quad\quad 8 \quad\quad\quad 12 \quad \text{etc.}$$

12 is the least common multiple of 2, 3, and 4.

Practice: Least Common Multiple Problems

Find the least common multiple of

1. 3 and 4   2. 4 and 6   3. 3, 4, and 5

Answers: Least Common Multiple Problems

1. 12   2. 12   3. 60

Adding and Subtracting Fractions

Adding Fractions

● To *add fractions* you must first change all denominators to their *lowest common denominator* (LCD)—the lowest number that can be divided evenly by all the denominators in the problem. When you have all the denominators the same, you may add fractions by simply adding the numerators (the denominator remains the same). *For example:*

$$\frac{3}{8} = \frac{3}{8}$$
$$+\frac{1}{2} = \frac{4}{8} \leftarrow \begin{cases} \text{one-half is} \\ \text{changed to} \\ \text{four-eighths} \end{cases}$$
$$\frac{7}{8}$$

$$\frac{1}{4} = \frac{3}{12}$$
$$+\frac{1}{3} = \frac{4}{12} \quad \begin{cases} \text{change both} \\ \text{fractions to} \\ \text{LCD of 12} \end{cases}$$
$$\frac{7}{12}$$

In the first example, we changed the ½ to ⅘ because 8 is the lowest common denominator, and then we added the numerators 3 and 4 to get ⅞. In the second example, we had to change both fractions to get the lowest common denominator of 12, and then we added the numerators to get $\frac{7}{12}$. Of course, if the denominators are already the same, just add the numerators. *For example:*

$$\begin{array}{r} \dfrac{6}{11} \\[2ex] + \ \dfrac{3}{11} \\[1ex] \hline \dfrac{9}{11} \end{array}$$

Note that fractions may be added across, as well. *For example:*

$$\tfrac{1}{2} + \tfrac{1}{3} = \tfrac{3}{6} + \tfrac{2}{6} = \tfrac{5}{6}$$

Practice: Adding Fractions Problems

1. $\frac{1}{4} + \frac{3}{8} =$

2. $$\begin{array}{r} \dfrac{1}{2} \\[2ex] + \ \dfrac{3}{10} \\[1ex] \hline \end{array}$$

3. $\frac{7}{8} + \frac{3}{10}$

4. $$\begin{array}{r} \dfrac{4}{15} \\[2ex] + \ \dfrac{2}{5} \\[1ex] \hline \end{array}$$

Answers: Adding Fractions Problems

1. $\frac{1}{4} + \frac{3}{8} = \frac{2}{8} + \frac{3}{8} = \frac{5}{8}$
2. $\frac{1}{2} + \frac{3}{10} = \frac{5}{10} + \frac{3}{10} = \frac{8}{10} = \frac{4}{5}$
3. $\frac{7}{8} + \frac{3}{10} = \frac{35}{40} + \frac{12}{40} = \frac{47}{40}$ or $1\frac{7}{40}$
4. $\frac{4}{15} + \frac{2}{5} = \frac{4}{15} + \frac{6}{15} = \frac{10}{15} = \frac{2}{3}$

Adding Positive and Negative Fractions

● The rules for signed numbers (p. 21) apply to fractions as well. *For example:*

1. $-\dfrac{1}{2} + \dfrac{1}{3} = -\dfrac{3}{6} + \dfrac{2}{6} = -\dfrac{1}{6}$

2. $$\begin{array}{rcr} +\dfrac{3}{4} & = & +\dfrac{9}{12} \\[2ex] + \ -\dfrac{1}{3} & = & + \ -\dfrac{4}{12} \\[1ex] \hline & & +\dfrac{5}{12} \end{array}$$

Practice: Adding Positive and Negative Fractions Problems

1. $+\dfrac{4}{5}$

$\underline{-\dfrac{1}{10}}$

2. $-\dfrac{9}{10}$

$\underline{+\dfrac{4}{15}}$

3. $+\dfrac{3}{4} + \left(-\dfrac{1}{2}\right) =$

4. $\left(-\dfrac{3}{4}\right) + \dfrac{1}{3} + \left(-\dfrac{1}{6}\right) =$

Answers: Adding Positive and Negative Fractions Problems

1. $+\dfrac{4}{5} = +\dfrac{8}{10}$

$\underline{-\dfrac{1}{10} = -\dfrac{1}{10}}$

$\dfrac{7}{10}$

2. $-\dfrac{9}{10} = -\dfrac{27}{30}$

$\underline{+\dfrac{4}{5} = +\dfrac{8}{30}}$

$-\dfrac{19}{30}$

3. $+\dfrac{3}{4} + \left(-\dfrac{1}{2}\right) = +\dfrac{3}{4} + \left(-\dfrac{2}{4}\right) = \dfrac{1}{4}$

4. $\left(-\dfrac{3}{4}\right) + \left(\dfrac{1}{3}\right) + \left(-\dfrac{1}{6}\right) =$

$\left(-\dfrac{9}{12}\right) + \left(\dfrac{4}{12}\right) + \left(-\dfrac{2}{12}\right) = -\dfrac{7}{12}$

Subtracting Fractions

- To *subtract fractions,* the same rule (find the LCD) given on p. 34 applies, except that you subtract the numerators. *For example:*

$$\frac{7}{8} = \frac{7}{8}$$

$$\frac{3}{4} = \frac{9}{12}$$

$$-\frac{1}{4} = \frac{2}{8}$$

$$-\frac{1}{3} = \frac{4}{12}$$

$$\frac{5}{8}$$

$$\frac{5}{12}$$

Again, a subtraction problem may be done across, as well as down:

$$+\frac{5}{8} - \left(+\frac{3}{8}\right) = +\frac{2}{8} = +\frac{1}{4}$$

Practice: Subtracting Fractions Problems

1. $\frac{3}{4}$

   $-\frac{1}{2}$

2. $\frac{5}{6}$

   $-\frac{1}{3}$

3. $\frac{3}{8}$

   $-\frac{1}{9}$

4. $\frac{5}{12} - \frac{2}{5} =$

Answers: Subtracting Fractions Problems

1. $\frac{3}{4} = \frac{3}{4}$

   $-\frac{1}{2} = -\frac{2}{4}$

   $\frac{1}{4}$

2. $\frac{5}{6} = \frac{5}{6}$

   $-\frac{1}{3} = -\frac{2}{6}$

   $\frac{3}{6} = \frac{1}{2}$

3. $\dfrac{3}{8} = \dfrac{27}{72}$

    $\dfrac{-\dfrac{1}{9} = -\dfrac{8}{72}}{\dfrac{19}{72}}$

4. $\dfrac{5}{12} - \dfrac{2}{5} = \dfrac{25}{60} - \dfrac{24}{60} = \dfrac{1}{60}$

Subtracting Positive and Negative Fractions

● The rule for subtracting signed numbers (p. 23) applies to fractions as well. *For example:*

1. $+\dfrac{9}{10} = \quad +\dfrac{9}{10} = +\dfrac{9}{10}$

    $\dfrac{- -\dfrac{1}{5} = \quad + +\dfrac{1}{5} = +\dfrac{2}{10}}{\quad\quad\quad +\dfrac{11}{10} = 1\dfrac{1}{10}}$

2. $+\dfrac{2}{3} - \left(-\dfrac{1}{5}\right) = \dfrac{10}{15} - \left(-\dfrac{3}{15}\right) = \dfrac{10}{15} + \dfrac{3}{15} = \dfrac{13}{15}$

3. $+\dfrac{1}{3} - \dfrac{3}{4} = +\dfrac{4}{12} - \dfrac{9}{12} = +\dfrac{4}{12} + \left(-\dfrac{9}{12}\right) = -\dfrac{5}{12}$

Practice: Subtracting Positive and Negative Fractions Problems

1. $+\dfrac{3}{4}$

    $\dfrac{-\quad\dfrac{1}{3}}{}$

2. $+\dfrac{1}{6} - \left(-\dfrac{1}{3}\right) =$

3. $-\dfrac{1}{4} - \left(+\dfrac{2}{3}\right) =$

4. $-\dfrac{7}{12} - \left(+\dfrac{5}{6}\right) =$

Answers: Subtracting Positive and Negative Fractions Problems

1.
$$+\frac{3}{4} = +\frac{9}{12}$$
$$-\frac{1}{3} = -\frac{4}{12}$$
$$\overline{\qquad +\frac{5}{12}}$$

2. $+\frac{1}{6} - \left(-\frac{1}{3}\right) = +\frac{1}{6} - \left(-\frac{2}{6}\right) = +\frac{1}{6} + \frac{2}{6} = \frac{3}{6} = \frac{1}{2}$

3. $-\frac{1}{4} - \left(+\frac{2}{3}\right) = -\frac{3}{12} - \left(+\frac{8}{12}\right) = -\frac{3}{12} + \left(-\frac{8}{12}\right) = -\frac{11}{12}$

4. $-\frac{7}{12} - \left(+\frac{5}{6}\right) = -\frac{7}{12} - \left(+\frac{10}{12}\right) = -\frac{7}{12} + \left(-\frac{10}{12}\right) = -\frac{17}{12}$ or $-1\frac{5}{12}$

Adding and Subtracting Mixed Numbers

Adding Mixed Numbers

- To *add mixed numbers,* the same rule (find the LCD) shown on p. 34 applies, but make sure that you always add the whole numbers to get your final answer. *For example:*

$$2\frac{1}{2} = 2\frac{2}{4} \leftarrow \begin{cases} \text{one-half is changed} \\ \text{to two-fourths} \end{cases}$$
$$\underline{+\ 3\frac{1}{4} = 3\frac{1}{4}}$$
$$5\frac{3}{4} \quad \begin{cases} \text{remember to add the} \\ \text{whole numbers} \end{cases}$$

Sometimes you may end up with a mixed number which includes an improper fraction. In that case, you must change the improper fraction to a mixed number and combine it with the sum of the integers. *For example:*

$$2\frac{1}{2} = 2\frac{2}{4}$$
$$+ 5\frac{3}{4} = 5\frac{3}{4}$$
$$7\frac{5}{4}$$

And since $\frac{5}{4} = 1\frac{1}{4}$

$$7\frac{5}{4} = 7 + 1\frac{1}{4} = 8\frac{1}{4}$$

Remember, the rules for adding signed numbers (p. 22) apply for mixed numbers as well.

Practice: Adding Mixed Numbers Problems

1. $3\frac{1}{2}$
   $+ 1\frac{2}{6}$

2. $4\frac{3}{5}$
   $+ 2\frac{1}{10}$

3. $+4\frac{5}{6} + (-2\frac{1}{3}) =$

4. $- 14\frac{3}{4}$
   $+ 21\frac{7}{8}$

Answers: Adding Mixed Numbers Problems

1. $3\frac{1}{2} = \quad 3\frac{3}{6}$
   $+ 1\frac{2}{6} = + 1\frac{2}{6}$
   $\quad\quad\quad\quad 4\frac{5}{6}$

2. $4\frac{3}{5} = \quad 4\frac{6}{10}$
   $+ 2\frac{1}{10} = + 2\frac{1}{10}$
   $\quad\quad\quad\quad 6\frac{7}{10}$

3. $+ 4\frac{5}{6} + (-2\frac{1}{3}) = +4\frac{5}{6} + (-2\frac{2}{6}) = + 4\frac{5}{6} - 2\frac{2}{6} = 2\frac{3}{6} = 2\frac{1}{2}$

4. $- 14\frac{3}{4} = -14\frac{6}{8}$
   $+ 21\frac{7}{8} = +21\frac{7}{8}$
   $\quad\quad\quad\quad 7\frac{1}{8}$

Subtracting Mixed Numbers

- When you subtract mixed numbers, sometimes you may have to "borrow" from the whole number, just like you sometimes borrow from the next column when subtracting ordinary numbers. *For example:*

$$
\begin{array}{r}
6\overset{4}{\cancel{3}}\overset{11}{1} \\
- 129 \\
\hline
522
\end{array}
\qquad
\begin{array}{r}
\overset{3\%}{\cancel{4}}\overset{1\%}{} \\
- 2\frac{5}{6} \\
\hline
1\frac{2}{6} = 1\frac{1}{3}
\end{array}
$$

| you borrowed 1 from the 10's column | you borrowed one in the form $\frac{6}{6}$ from the 1's column |

To subtract a mixed number from a whole number, you have to "borrow" from the whole number. *For example:*

$$
\begin{array}{r}
6 \;\; = 5\frac{5}{5} \\
- \, 3\frac{1}{5} = 3\frac{1}{5} \\
\hline
2\frac{4}{5}
\end{array}
$$

$\leftarrow$ borrow one in the form of $\frac{5}{5}$ from the 6

remember to subtract the remaining whole numbers

Remember that the rules for signed numbers (p. 23) apply here also and that subtracting can be done across as well as down.

Practice: Subtracting Mixed Numbers Problems

1. $\quad 3\frac{7}{8}$
   $-\, 1\frac{2}{8}$

2. $4\frac{3}{4} - 1\frac{1}{2} =$

3. $\quad 15\frac{1}{4}$
   $-\, 6\frac{1}{2}$

4. $24\frac{1}{8} - 16\frac{3}{4} =$

5. $\quad\quad 102\frac{3}{6}$
   $-\, -53\frac{1}{2}$

Answers: Subtracting Mixed Numbers Problems

1. $\quad 3\frac{7}{8}$
   $-\, 1\frac{2}{8}$
   $\quad\; 2\frac{5}{8}$

2. $4\frac{3}{4} - 1\frac{1}{2} = 4\frac{3}{4} - 1\frac{2}{4} = 3\frac{1}{4}$

3. $\quad 15\frac{1}{4} = \quad 15\frac{1}{4} = \quad 1\overset{4\frac{5}{4}}{\cancel{5}\frac{1}{4}}$
   $\quad -\ 6\frac{1}{2} = -\ 6\frac{2}{4} = -\ 6\frac{2}{4}$
   $\qquad\qquad\qquad\qquad\qquad\qquad 8\frac{3}{4}$

4. $24\frac{1}{8} - 16\frac{3}{4} = 24\frac{1}{8} - 16\frac{6}{8} = 2\overset{3\frac{9}{8}}{\cancel{4}\frac{1}{8}} - 16\frac{6}{8} = 7\frac{3}{8}$

5. $\qquad 102\frac{3}{6} = \qquad 102\frac{3}{6} = \quad 102\frac{3}{6}$
   $\quad -\ -53\frac{1}{2} = - \quad -53\frac{3}{6} = +\ 53\frac{3}{6}$
   $\qquad\qquad\qquad\qquad\qquad\qquad\qquad 155\frac{6}{6} = 156$

Multiplying Fractions and Mixed Numbers

Multiplying Fractions

- To *multiply fractions,* simply multiply the numerators, then multiply the denominators. Reduce to lowest terms if necessary. *For example:*

$$\frac{2}{3} \times \frac{5}{12} = \frac{10}{36} \qquad \text{reduce } \tfrac{10}{36} \text{ to } \tfrac{5}{18}$$

This answer had to be reduced as it wasn't in lowest terms. Since whole numbers can also be written as fractions ($3 = \frac{3}{1}$, $4 = \frac{4}{1}$, etc.), the problem $3 \times \frac{3}{8}$ would be worked by changing 3 to $\frac{3}{1}$.

- *Canceling when multiplying fractions:* You could first have "canceled." That would have eliminated the need to reduce your answer. To cancel, find a number that divides evenly into one numerator and one denominator. In this case, 2 will divide evenly into 2 in the numerator (it goes in one time) and 12 in the denominator (it goes in 6 times). *Thus:*

$$\frac{\overset{1}{\cancel{2}}}{3} \times \frac{5}{\underset{6}{\cancel{12}}} = \frac{5}{18}$$

Remember, you may cancel only when *multiplying* fractions. The rules for multiplying signed numbers hold here too (p. 24). *For example:*

$$\frac{1}{4} \times \frac{2}{7} = \frac{1}{\underset{2}{\cancel{4}}} \times \frac{\overset{1}{\cancel{2}}}{7} = \frac{1}{14} \quad \text{and} \quad \left(-\frac{\overset{1}{\cancel{3}}}{\underset{2}{\cancel{8}}}\right) \times \left(-\frac{\overset{1}{\cancel{4}}}{\underset{3}{\cancel{9}}}\right) = +\frac{1}{6}$$

Practice: Multiplying Fractions Problems

1. $\dfrac{3}{5} \times \dfrac{1}{2} =$

2. $\dfrac{7}{8} \times \dfrac{2}{3} =$

3. $-\dfrac{4}{7} \times \dfrac{14}{3} =$

4. $\dfrac{7}{10} \times \dfrac{5}{6} \times \dfrac{1}{3} =$

5. $7 \times \dfrac{2}{14} =$

Answers: Multiplying Fractions Problems

1. $\dfrac{3}{5} \times \dfrac{1}{2} = \dfrac{3}{10}$

2. $\dfrac{7}{8} \times \dfrac{2}{3} = \dfrac{7}{\overset{}{\underset{4}{8}}} \times \dfrac{\overset{1}{2}}{3} = \dfrac{7}{12}$

3. $-\dfrac{4}{7} \times \dfrac{14}{3} = -\dfrac{4}{\underset{1}{7}} \times \dfrac{\overset{2}{14}}{3} = -\dfrac{8}{3}$

4. $\dfrac{7}{10} \times \dfrac{5}{6} \times \dfrac{1}{3} = \dfrac{7}{\underset{2}{10}} \times \dfrac{\overset{1}{5}}{6} \times \dfrac{1}{3} = \dfrac{7}{36}$

5. $7 \times \dfrac{2}{14} = \dfrac{7}{1} \times \dfrac{2}{\underset{2}{14}} = \dfrac{2}{2} = 1$

Multiplying Mixed Numbers

- To *multiply mixed numbers*, first change any mixed number to an improper fraction. Then multiply as previously shown (p. 42).

$$3\tfrac{1}{3} \times 2\tfrac{1}{4} = \tfrac{10}{3} \times \tfrac{9}{4} = \tfrac{90}{12} = 7\tfrac{6}{12} = 7\tfrac{1}{2}$$

or

$$\dfrac{\overset{5}{10}}{\underset{1}{3}} \times \dfrac{\overset{3}{9}}{\underset{2}{4}} = \dfrac{15}{2} = 7\tfrac{1}{2}$$

Change the answer, if in improper fraction form, back to a mixed number and reduce if necessary. Remember, the rules for multiplication of signed numbers apply here as well (p. 24).

Practice: Multiplying Mixed Numbers Problems

1. $2\tfrac{1}{2} \times 3\tfrac{1}{4} =$
2. $3\tfrac{1}{5} \times 6\tfrac{1}{2} =$

3. $-5\tfrac{1}{4} \times 3\tfrac{3}{7} =$
4. $(-4\tfrac{9}{10}) \times (-3\tfrac{3}{7}) =$

Answers: Multiplying Mixed Numbers Problems

1. $2\frac{1}{2} \times 3\frac{1}{4} = \frac{5}{2} \times \frac{13}{4} = \frac{65}{8} = 8\frac{1}{8}$

2. $3\frac{1}{5} \times 6\frac{1}{2} = \frac{16}{5} \times \frac{13}{2} = \frac{\overset{8}{\cancel{16}}}{5} \times \frac{13}{\underset{1}{\cancel{2}}} = \frac{104}{5} = 20\frac{4}{5}$

3. $-5\frac{1}{4} \times 3\frac{3}{7} = -\frac{21}{4} \times \frac{24}{7} = -\frac{\overset{3}{\cancel{21}}}{\underset{1}{\cancel{4}}} \times \frac{\overset{6}{\cancel{24}}}{\underset{1}{\cancel{7}}} = -18$

4. $(-4\frac{9}{10}) \times (-3\frac{3}{7}) = \left(-\frac{49}{10}\right) \times \left(-\frac{24}{7}\right) = \left(\frac{\overset{7}{\cancel{49}}}{\underset{5}{\cancel{10}}}\right) \times \left(\frac{\overset{12}{\cancel{24}}}{\underset{1}{\cancel{7}}}\right) = \frac{84}{5} = 16\frac{4}{5}$

Dividing Fractions and Mixed Numbers

Dividing Fractions

● To *divide fractions,* invert (turn upside down) the second fraction (the one "divided by") and multiply. Then reduce, if necessary. *For example:*

$$\frac{1}{6} \div \frac{1}{5} = \frac{1}{6} \times \frac{5}{1} = \frac{5}{6} \qquad \frac{1}{6} \div \frac{1}{3} = \frac{1}{\underset{2}{\cancel{6}}} \times \frac{\overset{1}{\cancel{3}}}{1} = \frac{1}{2}$$

Here too the rules for division of signed numbers apply (p. 24).

Practice: Dividing Fractions Problems

1. $\frac{1}{2} \div \frac{1}{3} =$

2. $\frac{3}{4} \div \frac{1}{2} =$

3. $\frac{3}{7} \div \frac{3}{14} =$

4. $\frac{3}{4} \div \left(-\frac{5}{8}\right) =$

Answers: Dividing Fractions Problems

1. $\frac{1}{2} \div \frac{1}{3} = \frac{1}{2} \times \frac{3}{1} = \frac{3}{2} = 1\frac{1}{2}$

2. $\frac{3}{4} \div \frac{1}{2} = \frac{3}{\underset{2}{\cancel{4}}} \times \frac{\overset{1}{\cancel{2}}}{1} = \frac{3}{2} = 1\frac{1}{2}$

3. $\dfrac{3}{7} \div \dfrac{3}{14} = \dfrac{\overset{1}{\cancel{3}}}{\cancel{7}} \times \dfrac{\overset{2}{\cancel{14}}}{\cancel{3}} = \dfrac{2}{1} = 2$

4. $\dfrac{3}{4} \div \left(-\dfrac{5}{8}\right) = \dfrac{3}{4} \times \left(-\dfrac{8}{5}\right) = \dfrac{3}{\cancel{4}} \times \left(-\dfrac{\overset{2}{\cancel{8}}}{5}\right) = -\dfrac{6}{5} = -1\frac{1}{5}$

Dividing Complex Fractions

- Sometimes a division of fractions problem may appear in this form (these are called *complex fractions*).

$$\dfrac{\dfrac{3}{4}}{\dfrac{7}{8}}$$

If so, consider the line separating the two fractions to mean "divided by." Therefore, this problem may be rewritten as

$$\dfrac{3}{4} \div \dfrac{7}{8} =$$

Now, follow the same procedure as shown on p. 44.

$$\dfrac{3}{4} \div \dfrac{7}{8} = \dfrac{3}{\cancel{4}} \times \dfrac{\overset{2}{\cancel{8}}}{7} = \dfrac{6}{7}$$

Practice: Dividing Complex Fractions Problems

1. $\dfrac{\dfrac{3}{4}}{\dfrac{1}{2}}$ 　　　 2. $\dfrac{\dfrac{5}{6}}{\dfrac{1}{3}}$ 　　　 3. $\dfrac{\dfrac{1}{2}}{\dfrac{3}{8}}$ 　　　 4. $\dfrac{\dfrac{7}{8}}{\dfrac{1}{2}}$

Answers: Dividing Complex Fractions Problems

1. $\dfrac{\dfrac{3}{4}}{\dfrac{1}{2}} = \dfrac{3}{4} \div \dfrac{1}{2} = \dfrac{3}{\cancel{4}} \times \dfrac{\overset{1}{\cancel{2}}}{1} = \dfrac{3}{2} = 1\dfrac{1}{2}$

2. $\dfrac{\dfrac{5}{6}}{\dfrac{1}{3}} = \dfrac{5}{6} \div \dfrac{1}{3} = \dfrac{5}{\overset{}{\underset{2}{6}}} \times \dfrac{\overset{1}{\cancel{3}}}{1} = \dfrac{5}{2} = 2\dfrac{1}{2}$

3. $\dfrac{\dfrac{1}{2}}{\dfrac{3}{8}} = \dfrac{1}{2} \div \dfrac{3}{8} = \dfrac{1}{\underset{1}{\cancel{2}}} \times \dfrac{\overset{4}{\cancel{8}}}{3} = \dfrac{4}{3} = 1\dfrac{1}{3}$

4. $\dfrac{\dfrac{7}{8}}{\dfrac{1}{2}} = \dfrac{7}{8} \div \dfrac{1}{2} = \dfrac{7}{\underset{4}{\cancel{8}}} \times \dfrac{\overset{1}{\cancel{2}}}{1} = \dfrac{7}{4} = 1\dfrac{3}{4}$

Dividing Mixed Numbers

- To *divide mixed numbers,* first change them to improper fractions (p. 28). Then follow the rule for dividing fractions (p. 44). *For example:*

1. $3\tfrac{3}{5} \div 2\tfrac{2}{3} = \dfrac{18}{5} \div \dfrac{8}{3} = \dfrac{\overset{9}{\cancel{18}}}{5} \times \dfrac{3}{\underset{4}{\cancel{8}}} = \dfrac{27}{20} = 1\tfrac{7}{20}$

2. $2\tfrac{1}{5} \div 3\tfrac{1}{10} = \dfrac{11}{5} \div \dfrac{31}{10} = \dfrac{11}{\underset{1}{\cancel{5}}} \times \dfrac{\overset{2}{\cancel{10}}}{31} = \dfrac{22}{31}$

Notice that after you invert and have a multiplication of fractions problem, you may then cancel tops with bottoms when appropriate.

Practice: Dividing Mixed Numbers Problems

1. $3\tfrac{1}{2} \div \tfrac{3}{4} =$

2. $1\tfrac{1}{6} \div 4\tfrac{1}{2} =$

3. $(-5\tfrac{4}{5}) \div (2\tfrac{1}{2}) =$

4. $(-3\tfrac{1}{5}) \div (-3\tfrac{1}{3}) =$

Answers: Dividing Mixed Numbers Problems

1. $3\tfrac{1}{2} \div \tfrac{3}{4} = \dfrac{7}{2} \div \dfrac{3}{4} = \dfrac{7}{\underset{1}{\cancel{2}}} \times \dfrac{\overset{2}{\cancel{4}}}{3} = \dfrac{14}{3} = 4\tfrac{2}{3}$

2. $1\frac{1}{6} \div 4\frac{1}{2} = \frac{7}{6} \div \frac{9}{2} = \frac{7}{\cancel{6}_3} \times \frac{\cancel{2}^1}{9} = \frac{7}{27}$

3. $(-5\frac{4}{5}) \div (2\frac{1}{2}) = \left(-\frac{29}{5}\right) \div \left(\frac{5}{2}\right) = \left(-\frac{29}{5}\right) \times \left(\frac{2}{5}\right) = -\frac{58}{25} = -2\frac{8}{25}$

4. $(-3\frac{1}{5}) \div (-3\frac{1}{3}) = \left(-\frac{16}{5}\right) \div \left(-\frac{10}{3}\right) = \left(-\frac{\cancel{16}^8}{5}\right) \times \left(-\frac{3}{\cancel{10}_5}\right) = \frac{24}{25}$

Simplifying Fractions and Complex Fractions

● If either numerator or denominator consists of several numbers, these numbers must be combined into one number. Then reduce if necessary. *For example:*

1. $\dfrac{28 + 14}{26 + 17} = \dfrac{42}{43}$

2. $\dfrac{\frac{1}{4} + \frac{1}{2}}{\frac{1}{3} + \frac{1}{4}} = \dfrac{\frac{1}{4} + \frac{2}{4}}{\frac{4}{12} + \frac{3}{12}} = \dfrac{\frac{3}{4}}{\frac{7}{12}} = \frac{3}{4} \div \frac{7}{12} = \frac{3}{\cancel{4}_1} \times \frac{\cancel{12}^3}{7} = \frac{9}{7} = 1\frac{2}{7}$

3. $\dfrac{2 + \frac{1}{2}}{3 + \frac{1}{4}} = \dfrac{2\frac{1}{2}}{3\frac{1}{4}} = \dfrac{\frac{5}{2}}{\frac{13}{4}} = \frac{5}{2} \div 13\frac{1}{4} = \frac{5}{\cancel{2}_1} \times \frac{\cancel{4}^2}{13} = \frac{10}{13}$

4. $\dfrac{3 - \frac{3}{4}}{-4 + \frac{1}{2}} = \dfrac{2\frac{1}{4}}{-3\frac{1}{2}} = \dfrac{\frac{9}{4}}{-\frac{7}{2}} = \frac{9}{4} \div -\frac{7}{2} = \frac{9}{\cancel{4}_2} \times -\frac{\cancel{2}^1}{7} = -\frac{9}{14}$

5. $\dfrac{1}{1 + \dfrac{1}{1 + \frac{1}{4}}} = \dfrac{1}{1 + \dfrac{1}{\frac{5}{4}}} = \dfrac{1}{1 + (1 \div \frac{5}{4})} = \dfrac{1}{1 + (1 \times \frac{4}{5})} = \dfrac{1}{1 + \frac{4}{5}} =$

$\dfrac{1}{1\frac{4}{5}} = \dfrac{1}{\frac{9}{5}} = 1 \div \frac{9}{5} = 1 \times \frac{5}{9} = \frac{5}{9}$

Practice: Simplifying Fractions and Complex Fractions Problems

1. $\dfrac{-3-2}{-6+5} =$

3. $\dfrac{2 - \frac{7}{8}}{1 + \frac{3}{4}} =$

2. $\dfrac{3 + \frac{1}{2}}{5 + \frac{5}{6}} =$

4. $\dfrac{1 + \dfrac{1}{2 + \frac{1}{2}}}{3} =$

Answers: Simplifying Fractions and Complex Fractions Problems

1. $\dfrac{-3-2}{-6+5} = \dfrac{-5}{-1} = 5$

2. $\dfrac{3 + \frac{1}{2}}{5 + \frac{5}{6}} = \dfrac{3\frac{1}{2}}{5\frac{5}{6}} = \dfrac{7}{2} \div \dfrac{35}{6} = \dfrac{\overset{1}{7}}{\underset{1}{2}} \times \dfrac{\overset{3}{\cancel{6}}}{\underset{5}{\cancel{35}}} = \dfrac{3}{5}$

3. $\dfrac{2 - \frac{7}{8}}{1 + \frac{3}{4}} = \dfrac{1\frac{1}{8}}{1\frac{3}{4}} = \dfrac{9}{8} \div \dfrac{7}{4} = \dfrac{9}{\underset{2}{\cancel{8}}} \times \dfrac{\overset{1}{\cancel{4}}}{7} = \dfrac{9}{14}$

4. $\dfrac{1 + \dfrac{1}{2 + \frac{1}{2}}}{3} = \dfrac{1 + \dfrac{1}{\frac{5}{2}}}{3} = \dfrac{1 + \left(1 \div \frac{5}{2}\right)}{3} = \dfrac{1 + \left(1 \times \frac{2}{5}\right)}{3} =$

$\dfrac{1 + \left(\frac{2}{5}\right)}{3} = \dfrac{1\frac{2}{5}}{3} = \dfrac{\frac{7}{5}}{3} = \dfrac{7}{5} \div \dfrac{3}{1} = \dfrac{7}{5} \times \dfrac{1}{3} = \dfrac{7}{15}$

Decimals

Changing Decimals to Fractions

- *Fractions* may also be written in *decimal* form (decimal fractions) by using a symbol called a *decimal point*. All numbers to the left of the decimal point are whole numbers. All numbers to the right of the decimal point are fractions with denominators of only 10, 100, 1,000, 10,000, etc. *For example:*

$$.6 = \frac{6}{10} = \frac{3}{5} \qquad .0007 = \frac{7}{10,000}$$

$$.7 = \frac{7}{10} \qquad .00007 = \frac{7}{100,000}$$

$$.07 = \frac{7}{100} \qquad .25 = \frac{25}{100} = \frac{1}{4}$$

$$.007 = \frac{7}{1,000}$$

Read it: .8   Write it: $\frac{8}{10}$ Reduce it: $\frac{4}{5}$

All rules for signed numbers also apply to decimals.

Practice: Changing Decimals to Fractions Problems

Change the following decimals to fractions. Reduce if necessary.

1. .4   2. .09   3. .75   4. .062

Answers: Changing Decimals to Fractions Problems

1. $.4 = \frac{4}{10} = \frac{2}{5}$ 3. $.75 = \frac{75}{100} = \frac{3}{4}$

2. $.09 = \frac{9}{100}$ 4. $.062 = \frac{62}{1,000} = \frac{31}{500}$

Adding and Subtracting Decimals

● To *add or subtract decimals,* just line up the decimal points and then add or subtract in the same manner you would add or subtract regular numbers. *For example:*

$$23.6 + 1.75 + 300.002 = \begin{array}{r} 23.6 \\ 1.75 \\ 300.002 \\ \hline 325.352 \end{array}$$

Adding in zeros can make the problem easier to work:

$$
\begin{array}{r}
23.600 \\
1.750 \\
300.002 \\
\hline
325.352
\end{array}
$$

and
$$54.26 - 1.1 = \quad
\begin{array}{r}
54.26 \\
- \ 1.10 \\
\hline
53.16
\end{array}$$

and
$$78.9 - 37.43 = \quad
\begin{array}{r}
78.\overset{8}{9}{}^{1}0 \\
-37.4\ 3 \\
\hline
41.4\ 7
\end{array}$$

A whole number has an understood decimal point to its right. *For example:*

$$17 - 8.43 = \quad
\begin{array}{r}
1\overset{6}{7}.\overset{9}{\emptyset}{}^{1}0 \\
- \ 8.4\ 3 \\
\hline
8.5\ 7
\end{array}$$

Practice: Adding and Subtracting Decimals Problems

1. $19.6 + 5.02 =$ 3. $.16 - .043 =$

2. $108 + 71.04 =$ 4. $12 - .061 =$

Answers: Adding and Subtracting Decimals Problems

1. 24.62   2. 179.04   3. .117   4. 11.939

Multiplying Decimals

● To *multiply decimals*, just multiply as usual. Then count the total number of digits above the line which are to the right of all decimal points. Place your decimal point in your answer so there is the same number of digits to the right of it as there was above the line. *For example:*

$$
\begin{array}{r}
40.012 \leftarrow 3 \text{ digits} \\
\times \quad 3.1 \leftarrow 1 \text{ digit} \\
\hline
40012 \\
120036 \\
\hline
124.0372 \leftarrow 4 \text{ digits}
\end{array}
$$

$\left\{\begin{array}{l}\text{total of 4 digits above the line} \\ \text{that are to the right of the decimal point}\end{array}\right.$

$\left\{\begin{array}{l}\text{decimal point placed so there is} \\ \text{same number of digits to the right} \\ \text{of the decimal point}\end{array}\right.$

Practice: Multiplying Decimals Problems

1. 30.1
    ×2.65

2. 30 × 9.061 =

3. (.906) × (−.1) =

4. (−.012) × (−.003) =

Answers: Multiplying Decimals Problems

1. 79.765   2. 271.83   3. −.0906   4. .000036

Dividing Decimals

● *Dividing decimals* is the same as dividing other numbers, except that if the divisor (the number you're dividing by) has a decimal, move it to the right as many places as necessary until it is a whole number. Then move the decimal point in the dividend (the number being divided into) the same number of places. Sometimes you may have to add zeros to the dividend (the number inside the division sign). *For example:*

$$1.25\overline{)5.} = 125\overline{)500.}^{\,4.}$$

or

$$0.002\overline{)26.} = 2\overline{)26000.}^{\,13000.}$$

Practice: Dividing Decimals Problems

1. Divide 8 by .4

2. .2)6.84

3. Divide 30.6 by .05

4. 90.804)181.608

Answers: Dividing Decimals Problems

1. 20   2. 34.2   3. 612   4. 2

Changing Fractions to Decimals

● To *change a fraction to a decimal,* simply do what the operation says. In other words, $^{13}/_{20}$ means 13 divided by 20. So do just that (insert decimal points and zeros accordingly). *For example:*

$$20\overline{)13.00}^{.65} = .65 \qquad 5/8 = 8\overline{)5.000}^{.625} = .625$$

Practice: Changing Fractions to Decimals

Change each fraction to a decimal.

1. $\frac{1}{4}$ 2. $\frac{3}{10}$ 3. $\frac{3}{8}$ 4. $\frac{7}{11}$

Answers: Changing Fractions to Decimals

1. .25   2. .3   3. .375   4. .6363 . . .
                                   (sometimes written $.\overline{63}$)

Percentage

- A fraction whose denominator is 100 is called a *percent*. The word *percent* means hundredths (per hundred). *For example:*

$$37\% = {}^{37}/_{100}$$

Changing Decimals to Percents

- To change decimals to percents:
    1. Move the decimal point two places to the right.
    2. Insert a percent sign.

For example:

.75 = 75%   1.85 = 185%   .003 = .3%
.05 = 5%   20.3 = 2,030%

Practice: Changing Decimals to Percents Problems

Change each decimal to percent.

1. .32   2. .8   3. .006   4. 1.75

Answers: Changing Decimals to Percents Problems

1. 32%   2. 80%   3. .6%   4. 175%

Changing Percents to Decimals

- To *change percents to decimals:*
  1. Eliminate the percent sign.
  2. Move the decimal point two places to the left (sometimes adding zeros will be necessary).

  For example:

  $75\% = .75$ $23\% = .23$ $5\% = .05$ $.2\% = .002$

Practice: Changing Percents to Decimals Problems

Change each percent to a decimal.

1. 25%   2. 80%   3. 2%   4. .4%   5. 300%

Answers: Changing Percents to Decimals Problems

1. .25   2. .80 or .8   3. .02   4. .004   5. 3.00 or 3

Changing Fractions to Percents

- To *change a fraction to a percent:*
  1. Change to a decimal.
  2. Change the decimal to a percent.

  For example:

  $\frac{1}{2} = .5 = 50\%$ $\frac{5}{2} = 2.5 = 250\%$
  $\frac{2}{5} = .4 = 40\%$ $\frac{1}{20} = .05 = 5\%$

Practice: Changing Fractions to Percents Problems

Change each fraction to a percent.

1. $\frac{1}{4}$ 2. $\frac{3}{8}$ 3. $\frac{7}{20}$ 4. $\frac{7}{2}$

Answers: Changing Fractions to Percents Problems

1. 25%   2. 37½% or 37.5%   3. 35%   4. 350%

Changing Percents to Fractions

● To *change percents to fractions:*
  1. Drop the percent sign.
  2. Write over one hundred.
  3. Reduce if necessary.

For example:

$$60\% = {}^{60}/_{100} = {}^{3}/_{5} \qquad 230\% = {}^{230}/_{100} = {}^{23}/_{10} \qquad 13\% = {}^{13}/_{100}$$

Practice: Changing Percents to Fractions Problems

Change each percent to a fraction.

1. 30%   2. 5%   3. 125%   4. 19%

Answers: Changing Percents to Fractions Problems

1. $30\% = \dfrac{30}{100} = \dfrac{3}{10}$ 3. $125\% = \dfrac{125}{100} = \dfrac{5}{4}$

2. $5\% = \dfrac{5}{100} = \dfrac{1}{20}$ 4. $19\% = \dfrac{19}{100}$

Important Equivalents That Can Save You Time

● Memorizing the following can eliminate unnecessary computations.

$\frac{1}{100} = .01 = 1\%$ $\frac{1}{3} = .33\frac{1}{3} = 33\frac{1}{3}\%$

$\frac{1}{10} = .1 = 10\%$ $\frac{2}{3} = .66\frac{2}{3} = 66\frac{2}{3}\%$

$\frac{1}{5} = \frac{2}{10} = .2 = .20 = 20\%$ $\frac{1}{8} = .125 = .12\frac{1}{2} = 12\frac{1}{2}\%$

$\frac{3}{10} = .3 = .30 = 30\%$ $\frac{3}{8} = .375 = .37\frac{1}{2} = 37\frac{1}{2}\%$

$\frac{2}{5} = \frac{4}{10} = .4 = .40 = 40\%$ $\frac{5}{8} = .625 = .62\frac{1}{2} = 62\frac{1}{2}\%$

$\frac{1}{2} = \frac{5}{10} = .5 = .50 = 50\%$ $\frac{7}{8} = .875 = .87\frac{1}{2} = 87\frac{1}{2}\%$

$\frac{3}{5} = \frac{6}{10} = .6 = .60 = 60\%$ $\frac{1}{6} = .16\frac{2}{3} = 16\frac{2}{3}\%$

$\frac{7}{10} = .7 = .70 = 70\%$ $\frac{5}{6} = .83\frac{1}{3} = 83\frac{1}{3}\%$

$\frac{4}{5} = \frac{8}{10} = .8 = .80 = 80\%$ $1 = 1.00 = 100\%$

$\frac{9}{10} = .9 = .90 = 90\%$ $2 = 2.00 = 200\%$

$\frac{1}{4} = {}^{25}/_{100} = .25 = 25\%$ $3\frac{1}{2} = 3.5 = 3.50 = 350\%$

$\frac{3}{4} = {}^{75}/_{100} = .75 = 75\%$

Finding Percent of a Number

● To *determine percent of a number,* change the percent to a fraction or decimal (whichever is easier for you) and multiply. Remember, the word *of* means multiply. *For example:*

What is 20% of 80?

$^{20}/_{100} \times 80 = {}^{1600}/_{100} = 16$ or $.20 \times 80 = 16.00 = 16$

What is 12% of 50?

$^{12}/_{100} \times 50 = {}^{600}/_{100} = 6$ or $.12 \times 50 = 6.00 = 6$

What is ½% of 18?

$\dfrac{1/2}{100} \times 18 = {}^{1}/_{200} \times 18 = {}^{18}/_{200} = {}^{9}/_{100}$ or $.005 \times 18 = .09$

Practice: Finding Percent of a Number Problems

1. What is 10% of 30?   3. What is ¼% of 1,000?
2. What is 70% of 20?   4. What is 250% of 12?

Answers: Finding Percent of a Number Problems

1. $x = (.10)(30) = 3$ 3. $x = (.0025)(1,000) = 2.5$
2. $x = (.70)(20) = 14$ 4. $x = (2.50)(12) = 30$

Other Applications of Percent

● Turn the question word-for-word into an equation. For *what* substitute the letter *x;* for *is* substitute an *equal sign;* for *of* substitute a *multiplication sign.* Change percents to decimals or fractions, whichever you find easier. Then solve the equation. *For example:*

18 is what percent of 90? $18 = x(90)$
$^{18}/_{90} = x$
$^{1}/_{5} = x$
$20\% = x$

10 is 50% of what number? $10 = .50(x)$
$^{10}/_{.50} = x$
$20 = x$

What is 15% of 60? $x = {}^{15}\!/_{100} \times 60 = {}^{90}\!/_{10} = 9$
   or $.15(60) = 9$

Practice: Other Applications of Percent Problems

1. 20 is what percent of 80?   3. 18 is what percent of 45?
2. 15 is 20% of what number?   4. What is 65% of 20?

Answers: Other Applications of Percent Problems

1. $20 = x(80)$

    $\dfrac{20}{80} = x$

    $\dfrac{1}{4} = x$

    $x = 25\%$

2. $15 = (.20)x$

    $\dfrac{15}{.20} = x$

    $x = 75$

3. $18 = x(45)$

    $\dfrac{18}{45} = x$

    $\dfrac{2}{5} = x$

    $x = 40\%$

4. $x = (.65)20$

    $x = 13$

Percent—Proportion Method

● Another simple method commonly used to solve percent problems is the *proportion* or *is/of method*. First set up a blank proportion and then fill in the empty spaces by using the following steps.

$$\frac{?}{?} = \frac{?}{?}$$

30 is what percent of 50?

1. What is next to the percent(%) is put over 100. (The word *what* is the unknown, or x.)

$$\frac{x}{100} = \frac{?}{?}$$

2. Whatever comes immediately after the word *of* goes on the bottom of one side of the proportion.

$$\frac{x}{100} = \frac{?}{50}$$

3. Whatever is left (comes next to the word *is*) goes on top, on one side of the proportion.

$$\frac{x}{100} = \frac{30}{50}$$

4. Then solve the proportion.

$$\frac{x}{100} = \frac{30}{50}$$

(In this particular instance, it can be observed that $\frac{30}{50} = \frac{60}{100}$, so the answer is 60%. Solving mechanically on this problem would not be time effective.)

This method works for the three basic types of percent questions.

1. 30 is what percent of 50?
2. 30 is 20% of what number?
3. What number is 30% of 50? (In this type it is probably easier to simply multiply the numbers.)

Practice: Percent—Proportion Method Problems

1. 40 is what percent of 200?
2. What percent of 25 is 10?
3. What number is 15% of 30?
4. 60 is 20% of what number?
5. 70% of what number is 35?

Answers: Percent—Proportion Method Problems

1. 20%.
   40 is what percent of 200?

$$\frac{x}{100} = \frac{40}{200}$$

Since $\frac{40}{200}$ can be reduced to $\frac{20}{100}$, x = 20. (This particular problem does not need to be solved mechanically.)

2. 40%
What percent of 25 is 10?

$$\frac{x}{100} = \frac{10}{25}$$

$$25x = 1,000$$

$$\frac{\cancel{25}x}{\cancel{25}} = \frac{\cancel{1,000}^{40}}{\cancel{25}}$$

$$x = 40$$

(You might have solved this by observing that $4 \times 25 = 100$, therefore $^{40}/_{100} = {}^{10}/_{25}$.)

3. 4.5
What number is 15% of 30?

$$\frac{15}{100} = \frac{x}{30}$$

$$450 = 100x$$

$$\frac{450}{100} = \frac{\cancel{100}x}{\cancel{100}}$$

$$x = 4.5$$

4. 300
60 is 20% of what number?

$$\frac{20}{100} = \frac{60}{x} \qquad \text{or} \qquad \frac{20}{100} = \frac{60}{x}$$

$$20x = 6,000 \qquad\qquad \frac{1}{5} = \frac{60}{x}$$

$$\frac{\cancel{20}x}{\cancel{20}} = \frac{6,000}{20}$$

$$x = 300 \qquad\qquad\qquad x = 300$$

5. 50
70% of what number is 35?

$$\frac{70}{100} = \frac{35}{x} \quad \text{or} \quad \frac{70}{100} = \frac{35}{x}$$

$$70x = 3,500 \qquad\qquad \frac{7}{10} = \frac{35}{x}$$

$$\frac{\cancel{70}x}{\cancel{70}} = \frac{3,500}{70} \qquad\qquad 7x = 350$$

$$x = 50 \qquad\qquad\qquad x = 50$$

(Again, this problem could have been solved by observing that $^{70}/_{100}$ can be reduced to $^{35}/_{50}$.)

Finding Percent Increase or Percent Decrease

● To find the *percent change* (increase or decrease), use this formula:

$$\frac{\text{change}}{\text{starting point}} = \text{percent change}$$

For example:

What is the percent decrease of a $500 item on sale for $400?

Change: $500 - 400 = 100$

$$\frac{\text{change}}{\text{starting point}} = \frac{100}{500} = \frac{1}{5} = 20\% \text{ decrease}$$

What is the percent increase of Jon's salary if it went from $150 a month to $200 a month?

Change: $200 - 150 = 50$

$$\frac{\text{change}}{\text{starting point}} = \frac{50}{150} = \frac{1}{3} = 33\tfrac{1}{3}\% \text{ increase}$$

Note that the terms *percentage rise, percentage difference,* and *percentage change* are the same as *percent change.*

Practice: Finding Percent Increase or Percent Decrease Problems

1. Find the percent decrease from 200 to 180.
2. What is the percent difference between a first month's rent of $250 and a second month's rent of $300?

3. What is the percent increase in rainfall from January (2.5 inches) to February (4.0 inches)?
4. What is the percent change from 2,100 to 1,890?

Answers: Finding Percent Increase or Percent Decrease Problems

1. $\dfrac{\text{change}}{\text{starting point}} = \dfrac{20}{200} = \dfrac{1}{10} = 10\%$

2. $\dfrac{\text{change}}{\text{starting point}} = \dfrac{50}{250} = \dfrac{1}{5} = 20\%$

3. $\dfrac{\text{change}}{\text{starting point}} = \dfrac{1.5}{2.5} = \dfrac{15}{25} = \dfrac{3}{5} = 60\%$

4. $\dfrac{\text{change}}{\text{starting point}} = \dfrac{210}{2,100} = \dfrac{1}{10} = 10\%$

Scientific Notation

- Very large or very small numbers are sometimes written in *scientific notation*. A number written in scientific notation is a number between 1 and 10 and multiplied by a power of 10. *For example:*

1. 2,100,000 written in scientific notation is 2.1×10^6.
   Simply place the decimal point to get a number between 1 and 10 and then count the digits to the right of the decimal to get the power of 10.

   2.100,000.   *moved 6 digits to the left*

2. .0000004 written in scientific notation is 4×10^{-7}.
   Simply place the decimal point to get a number between 1 and 10 and then count the digits from the original decimal point to the new one.

   .0000004,   *moved 7 digits to the right*

Notice that whole numbers have positive exponents and fractions have negative exponents.

Practice: Scientific Notation Problems

Change the following to scientific notation.

1. 35,000   2. 1,112,000,000   3. .00047   4. .00000000327

Change the following from scientific notation.

5. 2.6×10^4 6. 3.11×10^7 7. 6.1×10^{-4} 8. 7.22×10^{-6}

Answers: Scientific Notation Problems

1. 3.5×10^4 5. 26,000
2. 1.112×10^9 6. 31,100,000
3. 4.7×10^{-4} 7. .00061
4. 3.27×10^{-9} 8. .00000722

Multiplication in Scientific Notation

- To *multiply* numbers in *scientific notation,* simply multiply the numbers together to get the first number and add the powers of ten to get the second number. *For example:*

1. $(2 \times 10^2)(3 \times 10^4) =$

$$(2 \times 10^2)(3 \times 10^4) = 6 \times 10^6$$

2. $(6 \times 10^5)(5 \times 10^7) =$

$$(6 \times 10^5)(5 \times 10^7) = 30 \times 10^{12}$$

This answer must be changed to scientific notation (first number from 1 to 9).

$$30 \times 10^{12} = 3.0 \times 10^{13}$$

3. $(4 \times 10^{-4})(2 \times 10^5) =$

$$(4 \times 10^{-4})(2 \times 10^5) = 8 \times 10^1$$

Practice: Multiplication in Scientific Notation Problems

1. $(3 \times 10^5)(2 \times 10^7) =$ 4. $(6 \times 10^8)(4 \times 10^{-2}) =$
2. $(3.5 \times 10^2)(2.1 \times 10^4) =$ 5. $(2 \times 10^2)(4 \times 10^4)(5 \times 10^6) =$
3. $(5 \times 10^4)(9 \times 10^2) =$ 6. $(1.6 \times 10^{-3})(4.2 \times 10^{-4}) =$

Answers: Multiplication in Scientific Notation Problems

1. 6×10^{12} 4. $24 \times 10^6 = \underline{2.4 \times 10^7}$
2. 7.35×10^6 5. $40 \times 10^{12} = \underline{4.0 \times 10^{13}}$
3. $45 \times 10^6 = \underline{4.5 \times 10^7}$ 6. 6.72×10^{-7}

Division in Scientific Notation

- To *divide* numbers *in scientific notation*, simply divide the numbers to get the first number and subtract the powers of ten to get the second number. *For example:*

1. $(8 \times 10^5) \div (2 \times 10^2) =$

$$(8 \times 10^5) \div (2 \times 10^2) = 4 \times 10^3$$

2. $\dfrac{7 \times 10^9}{4 \times 10^3} = 1.75 \times 10^6$

3. $(6 \times 10^7) \div (3 \times 10^9) =$

$$(6 \times 10^7) \div (3 \times 10^9) = 2 \times 10^{-2}$$

4. $(2 \times 10^4) \div (5 \times 10^2) =$

$$(2 \times 10^4) \div (5 \times 10^2) = .4 \times 10^2$$

This answer must be changed to scientific notation.

$.4 \times 10^2 = 4 \times 10^1$

5. $(8.4 \times 10^5) \div (2.1 \times 10^{-4}) =$

$$(8.4 \times 10^5) \div (2.1 \times 10^{-4}) = 4 \times 10^{5-(-4)} = 4 \times 10^9$$

Practice: Division in Scientific Notation Problems

1. $(8 \times 10^7) \div (4 \times 10^3) =$

2. $\dfrac{9.3 \times 10^8}{3.1 \times 10^5} =$

3. $(7.5 \times 10^{12}) \div (1.5 \times 10^{15}) =$
4. $(1.2 \times 10^5) \div (4 \times 10^3) =$
5. $(9 \times 10^2) \div (2 \times 10^8) =$
6. $(6 \times 10^4) \div (2 \times 10^{-3}) =$

Answers: Division in Scientific Notation Problems

1. 2×10^4 4. $.3 \times 10^2 = \underline{3 \times 10^1}$
2. 3×10^3 5. 4.5×10^{-6}
3. 5×10^{-3} 6. 3×10^7 (exponents: $4 - (-3) = 4 + 3 = 7$)

Powers and Exponents

● An *exponent* is a positive or negative number placed above and to the right of a quantity. It expresses the power to which the quantity is to be raised or lowered. In 4^3, 3 is the exponent. It shows that 4 is to be used as a factor three times. $4 \times 4 \times 4$ (multiplied by itself twice). 4^3 is read as *four to the third power* (or *four cubed* as discussed below). *Some examples:*

$$2^4 = 2 \times 2 \times 2 \times 2 = 16$$
$$3^2 = 3 \times 3 = 9$$
$$3^5 = 3 \times 3 \times 3 \times 3 \times 3 = 243$$

Remember that $x^1 = x$ and $x^0 = 1$ when x is any number (other than 0).

For example: $2^1 = 2$ $2^0 = 1$
                        $3^1 = 3$ $3^0 = 1$
                        $4^1 = 4$ $4^0 = 1$

- If the exponent is negative, such as 3^{-2}, then the number and exponent may be dropped under the number 1 in a fraction to remove the negative sign. The number can be simplified as follows:

$$3^{-2} = \frac{1}{3^2} = \frac{1}{9}$$

A few more examples:

$$2^{-3} = \frac{1}{2^3} = \frac{1}{8}$$

$$3^{-4} = \frac{1}{3^4} = \frac{1}{81}$$

$$4^{-2} = \frac{1}{4^2} = \frac{1}{16}$$

Squares and Cubes

- Two specific types of powers should be noted, *squares and cubes.* To *square a number* just multiply it by itself (exponent would be 2). For example, 6 squared (written 6^2) is 6×6, or 36. 36 is called a perfect square (the square of a whole number). Following is a list of perfect squares:

$0^2 = 0$	$5^2 = 25$	$9^2 = 81$
$1^2 = 1$	$6^2 = 36$	$10^2 = 100$
$2^2 = 4$	$7^2 = 49$	$11^2 = 121$
$3^2 = 9$	$8^2 = 64$	$12^2 = 144$ etc.
$4^2 = 16$		

To *cube a number* just multiply it by itself twice (exponent would be 3). For example, 5 cubed (written 5^3) is $5 \times 5 \times 5$, or 125. 125 is called a perfect cube (the cube of a whole number). Following is a list of perfect cubes:

$0^3 = 0$	$4^3 = 64$
$1^3 = 1$	$5^3 = 125$
$2^3 = 8$	$6^3 = 216$
$3^3 = 27$	$7^3 = 343$ etc.

Practice: Powers and Exponents Problems

Give each answer without exponents.

1. $5^4 =$
2. $2^5 =$
3. $6^1 =$

4. $7^0 =$
5. $5^{-2} =$

Answers: Powers and Exponents Problems

1. $5^4 = 5 \times 5 \times 5 \times 5 = 625$
2. $2^5 = 2 \times 2 \times 2 \times 2 \times 2 = 32$
3. $6^1 = 6$

4. $7^0 = 1$

5. $5^{-2} = \dfrac{1}{5^2} = \dfrac{1}{25}$

Operations with Powers and Exponents

- To *multiply* two numbers with exponents, *if the base numbers are the same,* simply keep the base number and add the exponents. *For example:*

1. $2^3 \times 2^5 = 2^8$ $(2 \times 2 \times 2) \times (2 \times 2 \times 2 \times 2 \times 2) = 2^8$
2. $3^2 \times 3^4 = 3^6$
3. $5^4 \times 5^3 = 5^7$

- To *divide* two numbers with exponents, *if the base numbers are the same,* simply keep the base number and subtract the second exponent from the first. *For example:*

1. $3^4 \div 3^2 = 3^2$ 2. $4^8 \div 4^5 = 4^3$ 3. $\dfrac{9^6}{9^2} = 9^4$

- To *multiply or divide* numbers with exponents, *if the base numbers are different,* you must simplify each number with an exponent first and then perform the operation. *For example:*

1. $3^2 \times 2^2 = 9 \times 4 = 36$
2. $6^2 \div 2^3 = 36 \div 8 = 4\frac{4}{8} = 4\frac{1}{2}$

(Some shortcuts are possible.)

- To *add or subtract* numbers with exponents, *whether the base numbers are the same or different,* you must simplify each number with an exponent first and then perform the indicated operation.

For example:

1. $3^2 - 2^3 = 9 - 8 = 1$ 2. $4^3 + 3^2 = 64 + 9 = 73$

- If a *number with an exponent is taken to another power* $(4^2)^3$, simply keep the original base number and multiply the exponents. *For example:*

1. $(4^2)^3 = 4^6$ 2. $(3^3)^2 = 3^6$

Practice: Operations with Powers and Exponents Problems

Simplify, but leave with a number and one exponent when possible.

1. $2^4 \times 2^7 =$ 5. $4^6 \div 4^2 =$ 9. $(4^2)^4 =$
2. $3^6 \times 3^4 =$ 6. $5^2 \div 5^4 =$ 10. $(5^3)^5 =$
3. $5^3 \times 5 =$ 7. $4^2 \times 3^3 =$ 11. $(3^4)^3 =$
4. $2^9 \div 2^4 =$ 8. $2^4 \div 3^2 =$ 12. $(6^2)^3 =$

Answers: Operations with Powers and Exponents Problems

1. 2^{11} 7. $432 (16 \times 27)$
2. 3^{10} 8. $1\frac{7}{9} (16 \div 9)$
3. $5^4 (5^3 \times 5 = 5^3 \times 5^1 = 5^4)$ 9. 4^8
4. 2^5 10. 5^{15}
5. 4^4 11. 3^{12}
6. 5^{-2} or $\dfrac{1}{5^2}$ 12. 6^6

Square Roots and Cube Roots

- Note that square and cube roots and operations with them are often included in algebra sections, and the following will be discussed further in that section.

Square Roots

- To find the *square root* of a number, you want to find some number that when multiplied by itself gives you the original number. In other words, to find the square root of 25, you want to find the number that when multiplied by itself gives you 25. The square root of 25, then, is 5. The symbol for square root is $\sqrt{}$. Following is a list of perfect (whole number) square roots:

$$\sqrt{0} = 0 \qquad \sqrt{16} = 4 \qquad \sqrt{64} = 8$$
$$\sqrt{1} = 1 \qquad \sqrt{25} = 5 \qquad \sqrt{81} = 9$$
$$\sqrt{4} = 2 \qquad \sqrt{36} = 6 \qquad \sqrt{100} = 10 \quad \text{etc.}$$
$$\sqrt{9} = 3 \qquad \sqrt{49} = 7$$

- Other roots are similarly defined and identified by the index given. *Special Note:* If no sign (or a positive sign) is placed in front of the square root, then the positive answer is required. Only if a negative sign is in front of the square root is the negative answer required. This notation is used on most standardized exams and will be adhered to in this book. *For example:*

1. $\sqrt{9} = 3$ 2. $\sqrt{16} = 4$

   $-\sqrt{9} = -3$ $-\sqrt{16} = -4$

Cube Roots

- To find the *cube root* of a number, you want to find some number that when multiplied by itself twice gives you the original number. In other words, to find the cube root of 8, you want to find the number that when multiplied by itself twice gives you 8. The cube root of 8, then, is 2, since $2 \times 2 \times 2 = 8$. Notice that the symbol for cube root is the square root sign with a small three (called the index) above and to the left $\sqrt[3]{}$. (In square root, an index of two is understood and usually not written.) Following is a list of perfect (whole number) cube roots:

$$\sqrt[3]{0} = 0 \qquad \sqrt[3]{27} = 3$$
$$\sqrt[3]{1} = 1 \qquad \sqrt[3]{64} = 4$$
$$\sqrt[3]{8} = 2 \qquad \sqrt[3]{125} = 5$$

Approximating Square Roots

- To find the square root of a number that is not an exact square, it will be necessary to find an approximate answer by using the procedure explained below.

1. Approximate $\sqrt{42}$.

   The $\sqrt{42}$ is between $\sqrt{36}$ and $\sqrt{49}$. $\sqrt{36} < \sqrt{42} < \sqrt{49}$

$$\sqrt{36} = 6$$
$$\sqrt{49} = 7$$

Therefore, $6 < \sqrt{42} < 7$, and since 42 is halfway between 36 and 49, $\sqrt{42}$ is halfway between $\sqrt{36}$ and $\sqrt{49}$. To check, multiply: $6.5 \times 6.5 = 42.25$, or about 42.

Square roots of nonperfect squares can be approximated or looked up in tables. You may wish to keep these two in mind:

$$\sqrt{2} \simeq 1.414 \qquad \sqrt{3} \simeq 1.732$$

Practice: Approximating Square Root Problems

1. $\sqrt{22}$ 2. $\sqrt{71}$ 3. $\sqrt{13}$ 4. $\sqrt{\dfrac{400}{24}}$

Answers: Approximating Square Root Problems

1. 4.7   Check:

$\sqrt{16} < \sqrt{22} < \sqrt{25}$ 4.7
$4 < \sqrt{22} < 5$ $\times$ 4.7
$4 < 4.7 < 5$ 329
                                      188
                                      $\overline{22.09} \simeq 22$

2. 8.4   Check:

$\sqrt{64} < \sqrt{71} < \sqrt{81}$ 8.4
$8 < \sqrt{71} < 9$ $\times$ 8.4
$8 < 8.4 < 9$ 336
                                      672
                                      $\overline{70.56} \simeq 71$

3. 3.6   Check:

$\sqrt{9} < \sqrt{13} < \sqrt{16}$ 3.6
$3 < \sqrt{13} < 4$ $\times$ 3.6
$3 < 3.6 < 4$ 216
                                      108
                                      $\overline{12.96} \simeq 13$

4. 4.1   Check:

$$\sqrt{\frac{400}{24}} = \sqrt{16.7}$$

$$\sqrt{16} < \sqrt{16.7} < \sqrt{25}$$

$$4 < \sqrt{16.7} < 5$$

$$4 < 4.1 < 5$$

$$\begin{array}{r} 4.1 \\ \times\ \ 4.1 \\ \hline 41 \\ 164 \\ \hline 16.81 \approx 16.7 \end{array}$$

Simplifying Square Roots

● Sometimes you will have to simplify square roots or write them in simplest form. In fractions, $2/4$ can be reduced to $1/2$. In square roots, $\sqrt{32}$ can be simplified to $4\sqrt{2}$. To *simplify a square root,* first factor the number under the $\sqrt{\ }$ into a counting number times the largest perfect square number that will divide into the number without leaving a remainder. (Perfect square numbers are 1, 4, 9, 16, 25, 36, 49 . . .). *For example:*

$$\sqrt{32} = \sqrt{16 \times 2}$$

Then take the square root of the perfect square number.

$$\sqrt{16 \times 2} = \sqrt{16} \times \sqrt{2} = 4 \times \sqrt{2}$$

and finally write as a single expression: $4\sqrt{2}$

Remember that most square roots cannot be simplified, as they are already in simplest form, such as $\sqrt{7}$, $\sqrt{10}$, $\sqrt{15}$.

Practice: Simplifying Square Roots Problems

Simplify the following.

1. $\sqrt{18}$ 2. $\sqrt{75}$ 3. $\sqrt{96}$ 4. $\sqrt{50}$

Answers: Simplifying Square Roots Problems

1. $3\sqrt{2}$
$$\begin{aligned} \sqrt{18} &= \sqrt{9 \times 2} \\ &= \sqrt{9} \times \sqrt{2} \\ &= 3 \times \sqrt{2} \\ &= 3\sqrt{2} \end{aligned}$$

2. $5\sqrt{3}$
$$\begin{aligned} \sqrt{75} &= \sqrt{25 \times 3} \\ &= \sqrt{25} \times \sqrt{3} \\ &= 5 \times \sqrt{3} \\ &= 5\sqrt{3} \end{aligned}$$

3. $4\sqrt{6}$

$\sqrt{96} = \sqrt{16 \times 6}$
$\phantom{\sqrt{96}} = \sqrt{16} \times \sqrt{6}$
$\phantom{\sqrt{96}} = 4 \times \sqrt{6}$
$\phantom{\sqrt{96}} = 4\sqrt{6}$

4. $5\sqrt{2}$

$\sqrt{50} = \sqrt{25 \times 2}$
$\phantom{\sqrt{50}} = \sqrt{25} \times \sqrt{2}$
$\phantom{\sqrt{50}} = 5 \times \sqrt{2}$
$\phantom{\sqrt{50}} = 5\sqrt{2}$

Probability

- *Probability* is the numerical measure of the chance of an outcome or event occurring. *When all outcomes are equally likely to occur,* the probability of the occurrence of a given outcome can be found by using the following formula:

$$\text{probability} = \frac{\text{number of favorable outcomes}}{\text{number of possible outcomes}}$$

Examples:

1. Using the spinner below, what is the probability of spinning a 6 in one spin?

    Since there is only *one* 6 on the spinner out of *ten* numbers and all the numbers are equally spaced, the probability is $\frac{1}{10}$.

2. Using the spinner above, what is the probability of spinning either a 3 or a 5 in one spin?
    Since there are *two favorable outcomes* out of *ten possible outcomes,* the probability is $\frac{2}{10}$, or $\frac{1}{5}$.

- *When two events are independent of each other,* you need to multiply to find the favorable and/or possible outcomes.

3. What is the probability that both spinners below will stop on a 3 on the first spin?

 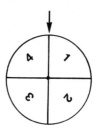

Since the probability that the first spinner will stop on the number 3 is ⅕ and the probability that the second spinner will stop on the number 3 is ¼, and since each event is independent of the other, simply multiply.

$$\tfrac{1}{5} \times \tfrac{1}{4} = \tfrac{1}{20}$$

4. What is the probability that on two consecutive rolls of a die the numbers will be 2 and then 3?
Since the probability of getting a 2 on the first roll is ⅙ and the probability of getting a 3 on the second roll is ⅙, and since the rolls are independent of each other, simply multiply.

$$\tfrac{1}{6} \times \tfrac{1}{6} = \tfrac{1}{36}$$

5. What is the probability of tossing heads three consecutive times with a two-sided fair coin?
Since each toss is independent and the odds are ½ for each toss, the probability would be $\tfrac{1}{2} \times \tfrac{1}{2} \times \tfrac{1}{2} = \tfrac{1}{8}$.

6. What is the probability of rolling two dice in one toss so that they total 5?
Since there are six possible outcomes on each die, the total possible outcomes for two dice is 6 × 6 = 36. The favorable outcomes are (1 + 4), (4 + 1), (2 + 3), and (3 + 2). These are all the ways of tossing a total of 5 on two dice. Thus there are four favorable outcomes, which gives the probability of throwing a five as

$$\frac{4}{36} = \frac{1}{9}$$

7. Three green marbles, two blue marbles, and five yellow marbles are placed in a jar. What is the probability of selecting at random a green marble on the first draw?
Since there are ten marbles (total possible outcomes) and three green marbles (favorable outcomes), the probability is ³⁄₁₀.

Practice: Probability Problems

1. Using the equally spaced spinner above, what is the probability of spinning a 4 or greater in one spin?

2. Using the equally spaced spinner above, what is the probability of spinning either a 2 or a 5 on one spin?

3. What is the probability of rolling two dice in one toss so that they total 7?

4. What is the probability of tossing tails four consecutive times with a two-sided fair coin?

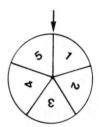

5. What is the probability that each equally spaced spinner above will stop on a 2 on its first spin?

6. In a regular deck of fifty-two cards, what is the probability of drawing a heart on the first draw? (13 hearts in a deck)

Answers: Probability Problems

1. Since there are five numbers that are 4 or greater out of the eight numbers and all the numbers are equally spaced, the probability is $\frac{5}{8}$.

2. Since there are two favorable outcomes out of eight possible outcomes, the probability is $\frac{2}{8}$, or $\frac{1}{4}$.

3. Since there are six ways to total 7 on two dice—$(1 + 6)$, $(6 + 1)$, $(2 + 5)$, $(5 + 2)$, $(3 + 4)$, $(4 + 3)$—out of a possible 36 outcomes (6×6), the probability is $\frac{6}{36}$, or $\frac{1}{6}$.

4. Since each toss is independent and the odds are $\frac{1}{2}$ for each toss, the probability would be $\frac{1}{2} \times \frac{1}{2} \times \frac{1}{2} \times \frac{1}{2} = \frac{1}{16}$.

5. Since the probability that the first spinner will stop on the number 2 is $\frac{1}{3}$ and the probability that the second spinner will stop on the number 2 is $\frac{1}{5}$, and since each event is independent of the other, simply multiply.

$$\frac{1}{3} \times \frac{1}{5} = \frac{1}{15}$$

6. Since there are thirteen favorable outcomes out of fifty-two possible outcomes, the probability is $\frac{13}{52}$, or $\frac{1}{4}$.

Combinations and Permutations

- If there are a *number of successive choices* to make and the choices are *independent of each other* (order makes no difference), the total number of possible choices (*combinations*) is the product of each of the choices at each stage. *For example:*

  1. How many possible combinations of shirts and ties are there if there are five different color shirts and three different color ties?

     To find the total number of possible combinations, simply multiply the number of shirts times the number of ties.

     $$5 \times 3 = 15$$

- If there are a *number of successive choices* to make and the choices are *affected by the previous choice or choices* (dependent upon order), then *permutations* are involved.

2. How many ways can you arrange the letters S, T, O, P in a row?

number of choices *for the first letter*		*number of choices* *for second letter*		*number of choices* *for third letter*		*number of choices* *for fourth letter*
4	×	3	×	2	×	1

$$4! = 4 \times 3 \times 2 \times 1 = 24$$

The product $4 \times 3 \times 2 \times 1$ can be written 4! (read *4 factorial* or *factorial 4*). Thus there are twenty-four different ways to arrange four different letters.

Following is a more difficult type of combination involving permutations.

3. If, from among five people, three executives are to be selected, how many possible combinations of executives are there? (Notice that the order of selection makes no difference.) The symbol used to denote this situation is C(n, r), which is read *the number of combinations of n things taken r at a time*. The formula used is

$$C(n, r) = \frac{n!}{r!(n - r)!}$$

Since $n = 5$ and $r = 3$ (five people taken three at a time), then the equation is as follows:

$$\frac{5!}{3!(5 - 3)!}$$

Now solve:

$$\frac{5 \cdot 4 \cdot 3 \cdot 2 \cdot 1}{3 \cdot 2 \cdot 1 \,(2)!} = \frac{5 \cdot \cancel{4}^2 \cdot \cancel{3} \cdot \cancel{2} \cdot 1}{\cancel{3} \cdot \cancel{2} \cdot 1 \,(\cancel{2} \cdot 1)} = 10$$

If the problem involves very few possibilities, you may wish to actually list the possible combinations.

Practice: Combinations and Permutations Problems

1. How many possible outfits could Tim wear if he has three different color shirts, four different types of slacks, and two pairs of shoes?

2. A combination lock has three settings, each of which contains numbers from 0 to 9. How many different possible combinations exist on the lock?

3. How many different ways are there to arrange three jars in a row on a shelf?

4. A coach is selecting a starting lineup for her basketball team. She must select from among nine players to get her starting lineup of five. How many possible starting lineups could she have?

5. How many possible combinations of a, b, c, and d taken two at a time are there?

Answers: Combinations and Permutations Problems

1. To find the total number of possible combinations, simply multiply the numbers together.

$$3 \times 4 \times 2 = 24$$

2. Note that each setting is independent of the others; thus, since each has ten possible settings, $10 \times 10 \times 10 = 1{,}000$ possible combinations.

3. Since the order of the items is affected by the previous choice(s), the number of different ways equals 3!, or $3 \times 2 \times 1 = 6$ different ways.

4. Since n = 9 and r = 5 (nine players taken five at a time), the equation is as follows:

$$\frac{9!}{5!(9-5)!}$$

$$\frac{9 \cdot 8 \cdot 7 \cdot 6 \cdot 5 \cdot 4 \cdot 3 \cdot 2 \cdot 1}{5 \cdot 4 \cdot 3 \cdot 2 \cdot 1(4)!} = \frac{9 \cdot 8^2 \cdot 7 \cdot 6^{2^1} \cdot 5 \cdot 4 \cdot 3 \cdot 2 \cdot 1}{5 \cdot 4 \cdot 3 \cdot 2 \cdot 1(4 \cdot 3 \cdot 2 \cdot 1)} = 126$$

5. Since n = 4 and r = 2 (four letters taken two at a time), the equation is as follows:

$$\frac{4!}{2!(4-2)!} = \frac{4!}{2!(2)!} = \frac{4^2 \cdot 3 \cdot 2 \cdot 1}{2 \cdot 1(2 \cdot 1)} = 6$$

You might simply have listed the possible combinations as ab, ac, ad, bc, bd, and cd.

Statistics

Some Basics: Measures of Central Tendencies

- Any measure indicating a center of a distribution is called a *measure of central tendency*. The three basic measures of central tendency are

    mean (or arithmetic mean)
    median
    mode

Mean

- The *mean* (arithmetic mean) is what is usually called the average. The arithmetic mean is the most frequently used measure of central tendency. It is generally reliable, easy to use, and is more stable than the median. To determine the arithmetic mean, simply total the items and then divide by the number of items. *For example:*

1. What is the arithmetic mean of 0, 12, 18, 20, 31, and 45?

    $0 + 12 + 18 + 20 + 31 + 45 = 126$
    $126 \div 6 = 21$
    The arithmetic mean is 21.

2. What is the arithmetic mean of 25, 27, 27, and 27?

    $25 + 27 + 27 + 27 = 106$
    $106 \div 4 = 26\frac{1}{2}$
    The arithmetic mean is $26\frac{1}{2}$.

3. What is the arithmetic mean of 20 and -10?

    $20 + (-10) = +10$
    $10 \div 2 = 5$
    The arithmetic mean is 5.

Practice: Arithmetic Mean Problems

1. Find the arithmetic mean of 3, 6, and 12.
2. Find the arithmetic mean of 2, 8, 15, and 23.
3. Find the arithmetic mean of 26, 28, 36, and 40.
4. Find the arithmetic mean of 3, 7, -5, and -13.

Answers: Arithmetic Mean Problems

1. 7 $(21 \div 3)$ 3. $32\frac{1}{2}$ $(130 \div 4)$
2. 12 $(48 \div 4)$ 4. -2 $(-8 \div 4)$

Weighted Mean

● When one or a number of items is used several times, those items have more "weight." This establishment of relative importance or weighting is used to compute the *weighted mean. For example:*

What is the mean of three tests averaging 70% plus seven tests averaging 85%?

In effect you have here ten exams, three of which score 70% and seven of which score 85%. Rather than adding all ten scores, to determine the above "weighted mean," simply multiply 3 times 70% to find the total of those items (210); then multiply 7 times 85% to find their total (595). Now add the two totals (805) and divide by the number of items overall (10). The weighted mean is thus 80.5%.

Practice: Weighted Mean Problems

1. For the first nine months of the year, the average monthly rainfall was two inches. For the last three months of that year, rainfall averaged four inches per month. What was the mean monthly rainfall for the entire year?

2. Six students averaged 90% on a class test. Four other students averaged 70% on the test. What was the mean score of all ten students?

Answers: Weighted Mean Problems

1. $9 \times 2'' = 18''$
   $\underline{3 \times 4'' = 12''}$
   Total $= 30''$ divided by 12 months in all $= 2.5''$ monthly mean

2. $6 \times 90 = 540$
   $\underline{4 \times 70 = 280}$
   Total $= 820$ divided by 10 students $= 82\%$

78   BASIC SKILLS REVIEW

Median

- The *median* of a set of numbers arranged in ascending or descending order is the middle number (if there is an odd number of items in the set). If there is an even number of items in the set, their median is the arithmetic mean of the middle two numbers. The median is easy to calculate and is not influenced by extreme measurements. *For example:*

  1. Find the median of 3, 4, 6, 9, 21, 24, 56.
     9 is the median.

  2. Find the median of 4, 5, 6, 10.
     5½ is the median.

Practice: Median Problems

Find the median of each group of numbers.

1. 9, 3, 5
2. 18, 16, 0, 7, 12

3. 100, 101, 102, 20
4. 71, −5, −3, −100

Answers: Median Problems

1. 5—3, ⑤, 9

2. 12—0, 7, ⑫ 16, 18

3. 100.5—20, 100, 101, 102
   $\overset{100.5}{\frown}$

4. −4—−100, −5, −3, 71
   $\overset{-4}{\frown}$

Mode

- The set, class, or classes that appear most, or whose frequency is the greatest is the *mode* or modal class. (Mode is not greatly influenced by extreme cases but is probably the least important or least used of the three types.) *For example:*

Find the mode of 3, 4, 8, 9, 9, 2, 6, 11

The mode is 9 because it appears more often than any other number.

Practice: Mode Problems

Find the mode of each group of numbers.

1. 2, 2, 3
2. 8, 4, 3, 5, 4, 6

3. 7, 8, 4, −3, 2, −3
4. 100, 101, 100, 102, 100, 101

Answers: Mode Problems

1. 2   2. 4   3. −3   4. 100

Range

- For a set of numbers, the *range* is the difference between the largest and the smallest number. The range depends solely on the extreme values. *For example:*

    Find the range of the following numbers. 3, 5, 7, 3, 2
    $7 - 2 = 5$ The range is 5.

Practice: Range Problems

1. Find the range of 2, 45, 106, 99
2. Find the range of 6, 101, 152, −5

Answers: Range Problems

1. $106 - 2 = 104$ 2. $152 - (-5) = 157$

Practice: Measures of Central Tendencies Problems

Find the mean, mode, median, and range of each of the following sets.

1. 7, 8, 8, 14, 18   2. 9, 10, 106, 120, 120   3. −3, −1, 0, 2, 2, 3

Answers: Measure of Central Tendencies Problems

1. Mean = 11
   $55 ÷ 5 = 11$
   Mode = 8
   Median = 8
   Range = 11
   $18 - 7 = 11$

2. Mean = 73
   $365 ÷ 5 = 73$
   Mode = 120
   Median = 106
   Range = 111
   $120 - 9 = 111$

3. Mean = .5
   $3 ÷ 6 = .5$
   Mode = 2
   Median = 1
   average of 0 and 2
   Range = 6
   $3 - (-3) = 6$

Number Series

- *Series or progressions of numbers* are sequences with some patterns. Unless the series has a simple repeat pattern (1, 2, 4, 1, 2, 4, . . . or 1, 1, 2, 2, 2, 3, 3, 3, 3, . . .) , you should first look for a *common difference between the numbers* to solve the problem. *For example:*

- If this does not give the pattern, you may wish to take a closer look at the difference between the numbers to see if a *pattern* arises there. *For example:*

- If this does not give the pattern, you may wish to check to see if the numbers themselves are being added, multiplied, or squared (subtracted or divided is also possible but not as common) to get the following number. *For example:*

1.

$$
\begin{array}{ccccccc}
(2 + 3 = 5) & & (5 + 8 = 13) & & & \\
2, & 3, & 5, & 8, & 13, & 21, \ldots \\
& (3 + 5 = 8) & & & &
\end{array}
$$

2.

$$
\begin{array}{cccc}
(2 \times 4 = 8) & & & \\
2, & 8, & 32, & 128, \ldots \\
& (8 \times 4 = 32) & &
\end{array}
$$

- Finally if using the actual numbers or the relationships between adjacent numbers doesn't solve the pattern, you should try to find a pattern between adjacent numbers or possibly even the use of more than one operation between adjacent numbers. *For example:*

1.
$$
\begin{array}{cccccc}
 & +2 & +2 & +2 & +2 & \\
1, & 5, & 3, & 7, & 5, & 9
\end{array}
$$

$(0 \times 1) + 1 = 1 \qquad (1 \times 2) + 1 = 3$

2. 0,   1,   1,   2,   3,   7,   22, ...

$(1 \times 1) + 1 = 2 \qquad (2 \times 3) + 1 = 7$

Multiply adjacent numbers and add 1.

Practice: Number Series Problems

Find the next number in each series.

1. 37, 35, 32, 28, 23, _____
2. 31, 33, 29, 35, 27, 37, 25, _____
3. 2, 6, 18, 54, _____
4. 0, 10, 19, 27, 34, 40, _____
5. 49, 64, 81, 100, 121, _____
6. 3, 9, 4, 8, 5, 7, 6, _____
7. 1, 3, 2, 5, 9, 44, _____

Answers: Number Series Problems

1. 17 (-2, -3, -4, etc.)
2. 39 ($+2$, -4, $+6$, -8, etc., or alternate numbers -2 then $+2$)
3. 162 (multiplying by 3)
4. 45 ($+10$, $+9$, $+8$, $+7$, etc.)
5. 144 (consecutive perfect squares)
6. 6 (alternate numbers up 1, down 1)
7. 395 (multiply adjacent numbers and subtract 1) (very difficult)

Measures

Measurement Systems

CUSTOMARY SYSTEM, OR
ENGLISH SYSTEM
Length
   12 inches (in) = 1 foot (ft)
   3 feet = 1 yard (yd)
   36 inches = 1 yard
   1,760 yards = 1 mile (mi)
   5,280 feet = 1 mile

Area
   144 square inches (sq in) = 1 square foot (sq ft)
   9 square feet = 1 square yard (sq yd)

Weight
   16 ounces (oz) = 1 pound (lb)
   2000 pounds = 1 ton (T)

Capacity
   2 cups = 1 pint (pt)
   2 pints = 1 quart (qt)
   4 quarts = 1 gallon (gal)
   4 pecks = 1 bushel

Time
   365 days = 1 year
   52 weeks = 1 year
   10 years = 1 decade
   100 years = 1 century

METRIC SYSTEM

Length—meter
   Kilometer (km) = 1000 meters (m)
   Hectometer (hm) = 100 meters
   Dekameter (dam) = 10 meters

      Meter
   10 decimeters (dm) = 1 meter
   100 centimeters (cm) = 1 meter
   1000 millimeters (mm) = 1 meter

Volume—liter
   Common measures
   1000 milliliters (ml, or mL) = 1 liter (l, or L)
   1000 liters = 1 kiloliter (kl, or kL)

Mass—gram
  Common measures
    1000 milligrams (mg) = 1 gram (g)
    1000 grams = 1 kilogram (kg)
    1000 kilograms = 1 metric ton (t)

Some Approximations
  Meter is a little more than a yard
  Kilometer is about .6 mile
  Kilogram is about 2.2 pounds
  Liter is slightly more than a quart

Converting Units of Measure

Examples:

1. If 36 inches equals 1 yard, then 3 yards equals how many inches?

   Intuitively: $3 \times 36 = 108$ inches

   By proportion: $\dfrac{3}{x} = \dfrac{1}{36}$

   Remember to place the same units across from each other—inches across from inches, etc. Then solve.

   $$\frac{3}{x} = \frac{1}{36}$$

   $$108 = x$$

   $$x = 108 \text{ inches}$$

2. If 2.2 pounds equals 1 kilogram, then 10 pounds equals approximately how many kilograms?

   Intuitively: $10 \div 2.2 = 4.5$ kilograms

   By proportion: $\dfrac{x}{10} = \dfrac{1}{2.2}$

   $$2.2x = 10$$

$$\frac{2.2x}{2.2} = \frac{10}{2.2}$$

x = 4.5 kilograms

3. Change 3 decades into weeks.

Since 1 decade equals 10 years and 1 year equals 52 weeks, then 3 decades equal 30 years.

30 years × 52 weeks = 1,560 weeks in 30 years or 3 decades

Notice that this was converted step-by-step. It could have been done in one step.

3 × 10 × 52 = 1,560 weeks

Practice: Simple Conversion Problems

1. If 1,760 yards equal 1 mile, how many yards are in 5 miles?
2. If 1 kilometer equals approximately .6 mile, approximately how many kilometers are there in 3 miles?
3. How many cups are in 3 gallons?
4. How many ounces are in 6 pounds?
5. If 1 kilometer equals 1,000 meters and 1 dekameter equals 10 meters, how many dekameters are in
   a. 1 kilometer
   b. 3 kilometers

Answers: Simple Conversion Problems

1. 1,760 × 5 = 8,800 yards in 5 miles.

2. $\dfrac{1}{.6} = \dfrac{x}{3}$

   .6x = 3

   $\dfrac{.6x}{.6} = \dfrac{3}{.6}$

   x = 5 kilometers

3. 4 × 3 × 2 × 2 = 48 cups in 3 gallons.

4. $6 \times 16 = 96$ ounces in 6 pounds.

5. a. $\dfrac{1}{10} = \dfrac{x}{1,000}$

   $10x = 1,000$

   $\dfrac{\cancel{10}x}{\cancel{10}} = \dfrac{1,000}{10}$

   $x = 100$ dekameters

   b. $\dfrac{1}{10} = \dfrac{x}{3,000}$

   $10x = 3,000$

   $\dfrac{\cancel{10}x}{\cancel{10}} = \dfrac{3,000}{10}$

   $x = 300$ dekameters

ARITHMETIC REVIEW TEST

Questions

1. The numbers 1, 2, 3, 4, . . . are called _____.

2. The numbers 0, 1, 2, 3, . . . are called _____.

3. The numbers . . . $-2, -1, 0, 1, 2,$ . . . are called _____.

4. Fractions and integers fall into a category called _____.

5. $\sqrt{3}$ and π are examples of _____.

6. A prime number is a number that can be divided evenly by _____.

7. A composite number is divisible by _____.

8. The first four square numbers greater than zero are _____, _____, _____, _____.

9. The first four cube numbers greater than zero are _____, _____, _____, _____.

10. Give the symbol or symbols for each of the following.
    (a) is equal to _____
    (b) is not equal to _____
    (c) is greater than _____
    (d) is less than _____
    (e) is greater than or equal to_____
    (f) is less than or equal to _____
    (g) is parallel to _____

11. "5 times 4" can be written a number of ways. Show three of them. _____, _____, _____

12. List the properties that are represented by each of the following.
    (a) $3 + 0 = 3$
    (b) $4 \times 1 = 4$
    (c) $3 + 6 = 6 + 3$
    (d) $4 + (6 + 2) = (4 + 6) + 2$
    (e) $3 + (-3) = 0$
    (f) $4(3 + 5) = 4(3) + 4(5)$

(g) $7 \times \frac{1}{7} = 1$

(h) $6 \times 8 = 8 \times 6$

(i) $(2 \times 6) \times 3 = 2 \times (6 \times 3)$

13. In the number 543,216, which digit is in the ten thousands place?

14. Express 367 in expanded notation.

15. $(4 \times 10^2) + (3 \times 10^0) + (2 \times 10^{-2}) =$

16. Simplify $3[5 + 2(3 - 1)]$

17. Simplify $2 + 3\{2 + 4[6 + 4(2 + 1)]\}$

18. Simplify $8 + 2 \times 6 + 10^2 + (2 + 3) \times 5$

19. Round off 7.1779 to the nearest thousandth.

20. Complete the number line below

21. $-8 + 5 =$

22. $8 - 17 =$

23. $-6 - 5 =$

24. $12 - (-6) =$

25. $\begin{array}{r} -19 \\ - +24 \\ \hline \end{array}$

26. $12 - (4 - 7 + 6) =$

27. $(-18)(5) =$

28. $-15 \div -3 =$

29. $0 \div 5 =$

30. $\frac{8}{0} =$

31. The number 8,424 is divisible by which numbers between 1 and 10?

32. An improper fraction has _____.

33. Change $^{17}\!/_3$ to a mixed number.

34. Change $9\frac{1}{4}$ to an improper fraction.

35. Reduce $^{14}\!/_{35}$.

36. Change $\frac{1}{4}$ to twelfths.

37. List all the factors of 30.

38. Find the greatest common factor of 18 and 24.

39. List the first four multiples of 7.

40. Find the least common multiple of 6 and 8.

41. $^3\!/_7 + ^4\!/_5 =$

42. $-\dfrac{6}{7} + \dfrac{1}{4} =$

43. $^5\!/_8 - ^1\!/_3 =$

44. $^1\!/_4 - ^2\!/_3 =$

45. $3\frac{1}{5} + 4\frac{3}{8} =$

46. $-5\frac{1}{2} + 4\frac{1}{4} =$

47. $6\frac{1}{4} - 3\frac{3}{5} =$

48. $^3\!/_5 \times ^{25}\!/_{36} =$

49. $-\dfrac{1}{6} \times -\dfrac{2}{7} =$

50. $8 \times ^1\!/_6 =$

51. $-6\frac{1}{2} \times 2\frac{4}{13} =$

52. $^4\!/_9 \div ^5\!/_8 =$

53. $\dfrac{^3\!/_4}{^4\!/_5}$

54. $4\frac{1}{3} \div 3\frac{3}{4} =$

55. Simplify $\dfrac{1}{2 + \dfrac{1}{4 + \frac{1}{2}}}$

56. Change .35 to a fraction in lowest terms.

57. $4.6 + 3.924 + 1.88 =$

58. $6.009 - 4.11 =$

59. $8.9 \times .32 =$

60. $23.44 \div .4 =$

61. Change $\frac{5}{8}$ to a decimal.

62. Change .66 to a fraction in lowest terms.

63. Change .6 to a percent.

64. Change 57% to a decimal.

65. Change $\frac{7}{25}$ to a percent.

66. Change 78% to a fraction in lowest terms.

67. What is 45% of 30?

68. 15 is what percent of 120?

69. 21 is 30% of what number?

70. What is the percent increase from 120 to 150?

71. Express 360,000 in scientific notation.

72. Express .0002 in scientific notation.

73. $(3 \times 10^5)(2 \times 10^7) =$

74. $(7 \times 10^3)(5 \times 10^8) =$

75. $(1.5 \times 10^{-6})(3 \times 10^8) =$

76. $(9 \times 10^8) \div (3 \times 10^3) =$

77. $\dfrac{9 \times 10^2}{5 \times 10^8} =$

78. $(3 \times 10^7) \div (5 \times 10^{-4}) =$

79. $4^3 =$

80. $8^0 =$

81. $5^{-2} =$

82. $7^3 \times 7^5 =$ (with exponent)

83. $5^8 \div 5^3 =$ (with exponent)

84. $8^2 \times 3^2 =$

85. $2^6 - 5^2 =$

86. $(4^3)^2 =$ (with exponent)

87. $\sqrt{64} =$

88. $\sqrt[3]{27} =$

89. Approximate $\sqrt{50}$ to the nearest tenth.

90. Simplify $\sqrt{60}$.

91. Using the equally spaced spinner (right), what is the probability of spinning either an A or a B in one spin?

92. What is the probability that equally spaced spinner A will stop on 5 and equally spaced spinner B will stop on 2 if each spinner is given one spin?

A

B

93. What is the probability of rolling two dice on one toss so that they total 6?

94. What is the probability of tossing tails five consecutive times with a two-sided fair coin?

95. How many different ways are there to arrange four books in a row on a shelf?

96. If among five people, two game show contestants must be chosen, how many possible combinations of contestants are there?

97. Find the arithmetic mean, mode, median, and range of the following set of numbers. 7, 4, 3, 9, 6, 8, 9

98. Find the next number in the series. 4, 6, 9, 13, 18, _____

99. How many ounces in 12 pounds?

100. If 1 decimeter is 10 centimeters and 1 centimeter is 10 millimeters, then how many millimeters are there in a decimeter?

Answers

Page numbers following each answer refer to the review section applicable to this problem type.

1. natural or counting numbers (p. 13)

2. whole numbers (p. 13)

3. integers (p. 13)

4. rational numbers (p. 13)

5. irrational numbers (p. 13)

6. one and itself (p. 13)

7. more than just 1 and itself (p. 13)

8. 1, 4, 9, 16 (p. 13)

9. 1, 8, 27, 64 (p. 13)

10. (a) =, (b) ≠, (c) >, (d) <, (e) ≥, (f) ≤, (g) ∥ (p. 14)

11. 5 × 4, 5 · 4, 5(4) (p. 14)

12. (a) additive identity (p. 14)
    (b) multiplicative identity (p. 15)
    (c) commutative property of addition (p. 14)
    (d) associative property of addition (p. 14)
    (e) additive inverse (p. 14)
    (f) distributive property of multiplication and addition (p. 16)
    (g) multiplicative inverse (p. 15)
    (h) commutative property of multiplication (p. 15)
    (i) associative property of multiplication (p. 15)

13. 4 (p. 17)

14. $(3 \times 10^2) + (6 \times 10^1) + (7 \times 10^0)$ (p. 17)

15. 403.02 (p. 17)

16. 27 (p. 18)

17. 224 (p. 18)

18. 145 (p. 19)

19. 7.178 (p. 20)

20. A = -2, B = -1, C = ½, D = 1½ (p. 21)

21. -3 (p. 22)

22. -9 (p. 23)

23. -11 (p. 23)

24. $+18$ (p. 24)

25. -43 (p. 23)

26. 9 (p. 24)

27. -90 (p. 24)

28. 5 (p. 24)

29. 0 (p. 25)

30. undefined (p. 25)

31. 2, 3, 4, 6, 8, 9 (p. 25)

32. a numerator larger than the denominator (p. 28)

33. $5\frac{2}{3}$ (p. 28)

34. $\frac{37}{4}$ (p. 28)

35. $\frac{2}{5}$ (p. 29)

36. $\frac{3}{12}$ (p. 30)

37. 1, 2, 3, 5, 6, 10, 15, 30 (p. 30)

38. 6 (p. 32)

39. 7, 14, 21, 28 (p. 33)

40. 24 (p. 33)

41. $\frac{43}{35} = 1\frac{8}{35}$ (p. 34)

42. $-\dfrac{17}{28}$ (p. 35)

43. $\frac{7}{24}$ (p. 36)

44. $-\dfrac{5}{12}$ (p. 36)

45. $7\,\frac{23}{40}$ (p. 39)

46. $-1\frac{1}{4}$ (p. 39)

47. $2\frac{13}{20}$ (p. 41)

48. $\frac{5}{12}$ (p. 42)

49. $\frac{1}{21}$ (p. 42)

50. $\frac{4}{3} = 1\frac{1}{3}$ (p. 42)

51. -15 (p. 43)

52. $\frac{32}{45}$ (p. 44)

53. $\frac{15}{16}$ (p. 45)

54. $\frac{52}{45} = 1\frac{7}{45}$ (p. 46)

55. $\frac{9}{20}$ (p. 47)

56. $\frac{7}{20}$ (p. 48)

57. 10.404 (p. 49)

58. 1.899 (p. 49)

59. 2.848 (p. 50)

60. 58.6 (p. 51)

61. .625 (p. 51)

62. $^{33}/_{50}$ (p. 48)

63. 60% (p. 52)

64. .57 (p. 53)

65. 28% (p. 53)

66. $^{39}/_{50}$ (p. 54)

67. 13.5 or 13½ (p. 55)

68. 12.5% (p. 55)

69. 70 (p. 55)

70. 25% (p. 59)

71. 3.6×10^5 (p. 60)

72. 2×10^{-4} (p. 60)

73. 6×10^{12} (p. 61)

74. $35 \times 10^{11} = \underline{3.5 \times 10^{12}}$ (p. 61)

75. 4.5×10^2 (p. 61)

76. 3×10^5 (p. 62)

77. 1.8×10^{-6} (p. 62)

78. $.6 \times 10^{11} = \underline{6 \times 10^{10}}$ (p. 62)

79. 64 (p. 63)

80. 1 (p. 63)

81. ½₅ or $1/(5^2)$ (p. 63)

82. 7^8 (p. 65)

83. 5^5 (p. 65)

84. 576 (p. 65)

85. 39 (p. 65)

86. 4^6 (p. 65)

87. 8 (p. 66)

88. 3 (p. 67)

89. 7.1 (p. 67)

90. $2\sqrt{15}$ (p. 69)

91. $\frac{2}{8} = \frac{1}{4}$ (p. 70)

92. $\frac{1}{32}$ (p. 70)

93. $\frac{5}{36}$ (p. 70)

94. $\frac{1}{32}$ (p. 70)

95. 24 ways (p. 73)

96. 10 possible combinations (p. 73)

97. mean = $6\frac{4}{7}$, mode = 9, median = 7, range = 6 (p. 76)

98. 24 (p. 80)

99. 192 ounces (p. 83)

100. 100 millimeters (p. 83)

ARITHMETIC GLOSSARY OF TERMS

ADDITIVE INVERSE: The opposite (negative) of the number. Any number plus its additive inverse equals 0.

ASSOCIATIVE PROPERTY: Grouping of elements does not make any difference in the outcome. Only true for multiplication and addition.

BRACES: Grouping symbols used after the use of brackets. Also used to represent a set. { }

BRACKETS: Grouping symbols used after the use of parentheses. [ ]

CANCELING: In multiplication of fractions, dividing the same number into both a numerator and a denominator.

CLOSURE PROPERTY: When all answers fall into the original set.

COMBINATIONS: The total number of independent possible choices.

COMMON DENOMINATOR: A number that can be divided evenly by all denominators in the problem.

COMMON FACTORS: Factors which are the same for two or more numbers.

COMMON MULTIPLES: Multiples which are the same for two or more numbers.

COMMUTATIVE PROPERTY: Order of elements does not make any difference in the outcome. Only true for multiplication and addition.

COMPLEX FRACTION: A fraction having a fraction or fractions in the numerator and/or denominator.

COMPOSITE NUMBER: A number divisible by more than just 1 and itself. (4, 6, 9, . . .) 0 and 1 are *not* composite numbers.

CUBE: The result when a number is multiplied by itself twice.

CUBE ROOT: The number that when multiplied by itself twice gives you the original number. For example, 5 is the cube root of 125. Its symbol is $\sqrt[3]{}$. $\sqrt[3]{125} = 5$

DECIMAL FRACTION: Fraction with a denominator 10, 100, 1,000, etc., written using a decimal point. For example, .3, .275.

DECIMAL POINT: A point used to distinguish decimal fractions from whole numbers.

DENOMINATOR: The bottom symbol or number of a fraction.

DEPENDENT EVENTS: When the outcome of one event has a bearing or effect on the outcome of another event.

DIFFERENCE: The result of subtraction.

DISTRIBUTIVE PROPERTY: The process of distributing the number on the outside of the parentheses to each number on the inside. $a(b + c) = ab + ac$

EVEN NUMBER: An integer (positive whole numbers, zero, and negative whole numbers) divisible by 2 with no remainder.

EXPANDED NOTATION: Pointing out the place value of a digit by writing the number as the digit times its place value. $342 = (3 \times 10^2) + (4 \times 10^1) + (2 \times 10^0)$

EXPONENT: A positive or negative number placed above and to the right of a number. Expresses the power to which the quantity is to be raised or lowered.

FACTOR (noun): A number or symbol which divides evenly into a larger number. For example, 6 is a factor of 24.

FACTOR (verb): To find two or more quantities whose product equals the original quantity.

FRACTION: A symbol expressing part of a whole. Consists of a numerator and a denominator. For example, ⅗ or ¾.

GREATEST COMMON FACTOR: The largest factor common to two or more numbers.

HUNDREDTH: The second decimal place to the right of the decimal point. For example, .08 is eight hundredths.

IDENTITY ELEMENT FOR ADDITION: 0. Any number added to 0 gives the original number.

IDENTITY ELEMENT FOR MULTIPLICATION: 1. Any number multiplied by 1 gives the original number.

IMPROPER FRACTION: A fraction in which the numerator is greater than the denominator. For example, 3/2.

INDEPENDENT EVENTS: When the outcome of one event has no bearing or effect on the outcome of another event.

INTEGER: A whole number, either positive, negative, or zero.

INVERT: Turn upside down, as in "invert ⅔" = 3/2.

IRRATIONAL NUMBER: A number that is not rational (cannot be written as a fraction x/y, with x a natural number and y an integer). For example, $\sqrt{3}$ or π.

LEAST COMMON MULTIPLE: The smallest multiple that is common to two or more numbers.

LOWEST COMMON DENOMINATOR: The smallest number that can be divided evenly by all denominators in the problem.

MEAN (arithmetic): The average of a number of items in a group (total the items and divide by the number of items).

MEDIAN: The middle item in an ordered group. If the group has an even number of items, the median is the average of the two middle terms.

MIXED NUMBER: A number containing both a whole number and a fraction. For example, $5\frac{1}{2}$.

MODE: The number appearing most frequently in a group.

MULTIPLES: Numbers found by multiplying a number by 2, by 3, by 4, etc.

MULTIPLICATIVE INVERSE: The reciprocal of the number. Any number multiplied by its multiplicative inverse equals 1.

NATURAL NUMBER: A counting numbers. 1, 2, 3, 4, etc.

NEGATIVE NUMBER: A number less than zero.

NUMBER LINE: A visual representation of the positive and negative numbers and zero. The line may be thought of as an infinitely long ruler with negative numbers to the left of zero and positive numbers to the right of zero.

NUMBER SERIES: A sequence of numbers with some pattern. One number follows another in some defined manner.

NUMERATOR: The top symbol or number of a fraction.

ODD NUMBER: An integer (whole number) not divisible evenly by 2.

OPERATION: Multiplication, addition, subtraction, or division.

ORDER OF OPERATIONS: The priority given to an operation relative to other operations. For example, multiplication takes precedence (is performed before) addition.

PARENTHESES: Grouping symbols. ( )

PERCENTAGE: A common fraction with 100 as its denominator. For example, 37% is $\frac{37}{100}$.

PERMUTATIONS: The total number of dependent choices.

PLACE VALUE: The value given a digit by the position of a digit in the number.

POSITIVE NUMBER: A number greater than zero.

POWER: A product of equal factors. $4 \times 4 \times 4 = 4^3$, read "four to the third power" or "the third power of four." *Power* and *exponent* are sometimes used interchangeably.

PRIME NUMBER: A number that can be divided by only itself and one. For example, 2, 3, 5, 7, etc. 0 and 1 are *not* prime.

PROBABILITY: The numerical measure of the chance of an outcome or event occurring.

PRODUCT: The result of multiplication.

PROPER FRACTION: A fraction in which the numerator is less than the denominator. For example, ⅔.

PROPORTION: Written as two equal ratios. For example, 5 is to 4 as 10 is to 8, or $5/4 = 10/8$.

QUOTIENT: The result of division.

RANGE: The difference between the largest and the smallest number in a set of numbers.

RATIO: A comparison between two numbers or symbols. May be written x:y, x/y, or x is to y.

RATIONAL NUMBER: An integer or fraction such as ⁷/₇ or ⁹/₄ or ⁵/₁. Any number that can be written as a fraction x/y with x a natural number and y an integer.

REAL NUMBER: Any rational or irrational number.

RECIPROCAL: The multiplicative inverse of a number. For example, ⅔ is the reciprocal of 3/2.

REDUCING: Changing a fraction into its lowest terms. For example, ²/₄ is reduced to ½.

ROUNDING OFF: Changing a number to a nearest place value as specified. A method of approximating.

SCIENTIFIC NOTATION: A number between 1 and 10 and multiplied by a power of 10. Used for writing very large or very small numbers. For example, 2.5×10^4.

SQUARE: The result when a number is multiplied by itself.

SQUARE ROOT: The number which when multiplied by itself gives you the original number. For example, 5 is the square root of 25. Its symbol is $\sqrt{\ }$. $\sqrt{25} = 5$

SUM: The result of addition.

TENTH: The first decimal place to the right of the decimal point. For example, .7 is seven tenths.

WEIGHTED MEAN: The mean of a set of numbers which have been weighted (multiplied by their relative importance or times of occurrence).

WHOLE NUMBER: 0, 1, 2, 3, etc.

ALGEBRA

ALGEBRA DIAGNOSTIC TEST

Questions

1. $\{1, 3, 5\} \cap \{1, 2, 3\} =$

2. $\{2, 5\} \cup \{3, 4, 5\} =$

3. True or false: $\{3, 4, 6\} = \{4, 3, 6\}$

4. True or false: $\{8, 9, 10\} \sim \{a, b, c\}$

5. Express algebraically: five increased by three times x

6. Evaluate: $x^2 - 3x - 4$ if $x = 5$

7. Evaluate: $\dfrac{x}{3} - \dfrac{x + 2y}{y}$ if $x = 2$ and $y = 6$

8. Solve for x: $2x - 9 = 21$

9. Solve for y: $\dfrac{4}{7}y + 6 = 18$

10. Solve for x: $8x - 8 = 4x + 3$

11. Solve for x: $wx + r = t$

12. Solve for m: x is to y as a is to m

13. Solve for y: $\dfrac{8}{y} = \dfrac{3}{7}$

14. Solve this system for x and y:
    $8x + 2y = 7$
    $3x - 4y = 5$

15. $\quad 4xy^2z$
    $\underline{-7xy^2z}$

16. $12x + 4x - 23x - (-3x) =$

17. $6x^2y(4xy^2) =$

18. $(2x^3y^4)^3 =$

19. $\dfrac{a^7b^3}{a^2b} =$

20. $\dfrac{-5(a^3b^2)(2a^2b^5)}{a^4b^3} =$

21. $(4x - 7z) - (3x - 4z) =$

22. $(4x + 2y)(3x - y) =$

23. $\dfrac{16x^2y + 18xy^3}{2xy} =$

24. $(x^2 + 3x - 18) \div (x + 6) =$

25. Factor completely: $8x^3 - 12x^2$

26. Factor: $16a^2 - 81$

27. Factor: $x^2 - 2x - 63$

28. Factor: $3a^2 - 4a + 1$

29. Factor: $m^2 - 2mn - 3n^2$

30. Solve for r: $r^2 - 10r = -24$

31. Solve for x: $x^2 - 49 = 0$

32. Reduce: $\dfrac{x^2 - 3x + 2}{3x - 6}$

33. $\dfrac{x^3}{2y} \cdot \dfrac{5y^2}{6x} =$

34. $\dfrac{x - 5}{x} \cdot \dfrac{x + 2}{x^2 - 2x - 15} =$

35. $\dfrac{6x - 3}{2} \div \dfrac{2x - 1}{x} =$

36. $\dfrac{3x - 2}{x + 1} - \dfrac{2x - 1}{x + 1} =$

37. $\dfrac{5}{x} + \dfrac{7}{y} =$

38. $\dfrac{3}{a^3b^5} + \dfrac{2}{a^4b^2} =$

39. $\dfrac{2x}{x - 1} - \dfrac{x}{x + 2} =$

40. Solve for x: $2x + 3 < 11$

41. Solve for x: $3x + 4 \geq 5x - 8$

42. Graph: $\{x: 2 \leq x < 9\}$

43. Graph: $\{x: -1 < x \leq 6, x \text{ is an integer}\}$

44. $|-5 - 4| =$

45. Give the coordinates represented by points A and B.

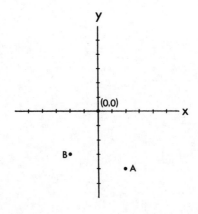

46. Is $x^2 + y = 4$ linear or nonlinear?

47. Graph: $y = x + 2$

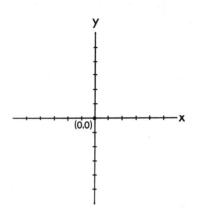

48. Simplify: $\sqrt{18} + 2$

49. $\sqrt{3} \cdot \sqrt{12} =$

50. $\dfrac{\sqrt{27}}{\sqrt{3}} =$

51. $\sqrt{18} + \sqrt{2} =$

In problems 52 through 55, each variable is nonnegative.

52. $\sqrt{36a^2b^8} =$

53. $\sqrt{50a^3b^7} =$

54. $\sqrt{5xy} \cdot \sqrt{8x^2yz} =$

55. $3\sqrt{2} \cdot 4\sqrt{5} =$

56. In the binary operation $*$ is defined for all integers x and y by

$$x * y = \frac{x^2 + y^2}{x^2} \text{ where } x \neq 0$$

What is the value of $3 * -2$?

Answers

Page numbers following each answer refer to the review section applicable to this problem type.

1. $\{1, 3\}$ (p. 107)

2. $\{2, 3, 4, 5\}$ (p. 107)

3. true (p. 107)

4. true (p. 107)

5. $5 + 3x$ (p. 108)

6. 6 (p. 110)

7. $\dfrac{-10}{6} = \dfrac{-5}{3} = -1\frac{2}{3}$ (p. 110)

8. $x = 15$ (p. 113)

9. $y = 21$ (p. 113)

10. $x = \dfrac{11}{4} = 2\frac{3}{4}$ (p. 113)

11. $x = \dfrac{t - r}{w}$ (p. 116)

12. $m = \dfrac{ay}{x}$ (p. 119)

13. $y = \dfrac{56}{3} = 18\frac{2}{3}$ (p. 120)

14. $x = 1, y = -\dfrac{1}{2}$ (p. 122)

15. $-3xy^2z$ (p. 128)

16. $-4x$ (p. 128)

17. $24x^3y^3$ (p. 129)

18. $8x^9y^{12}$ (p. 129)

19. a^5b^2 (p. 130)

20. $-10ab^4$ (p. 130)

21. $x - 3z$ (p. 131)

22. $12x^2 + 2xy - 2y^2$ (p. 133)

23. $8x + 9y^2$ (p. 135)

24. $(x - 3)$ (p. 136)

25. $4x^2(2x - 3)$ (p. 140)

26. $(4a - 9)(4a + 9)$ (p. 140)

27. $(x - 9)(x + 7)$ (p. 141)

28. $(3a - 1)(a - 1)$ (p. 141)

29. $(m + n)(m - 3n)$ (p. 141)

30. $\{6, 4\}$ (p. 146)

31. $\{7, -7\}$ (p. 146)

32. $\dfrac{x - 1}{3}$ (p. 150)

33. $\dfrac{5x^2y}{12}$ (p. 151)

34. $\dfrac{x + 2}{x(x + 3)}$ or $\dfrac{x + 2}{x^2 + 3x}$ (p. 151)

35. $\dfrac{3x}{2}$ (p. 153)

36. $\dfrac{x - 1}{x + 1}$ (p. 154)

37. $\dfrac{5y + 7x}{xy}$ (p. 154)

38. $\dfrac{3a + 2b^3}{a^4b^5}$ (p. 154)

39. $\dfrac{x^2 + 5x}{(x - 1)(x + 2)}$ (p. 154)

40. $\{x: x < 4\}$ (p. 159)

41. $\{x: x \le 6 \}$ (p. 159)

42.

43.

44. 9 (p. 163)

45. A. $(2, -4)$
    B. $(-2, -3)$ (p. 163)

46. nonlinear (p. 166)

47.

x	y
0	2
1	3
2	4

(p. 166)

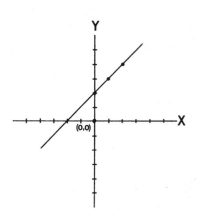

48. $\sqrt{20} = 2\sqrt{5}$ (p. 173)

49. $\sqrt{36} = 6$ (p. 171)

50. $\sqrt{9} = 3$ (p. 172)

51. $4\sqrt{2}$ (p. 173)

52. $6ab^4$ (p. 171)

53. $5ab^3\sqrt{2ab}$ (p. 171)

54. $\sqrt{40x^3y^2z} = 2xy\sqrt{10xz}$ (p. 175)

55. $12\sqrt{10}$ (p. 175)

56. $1\frac{3}{9}$ or $1\frac{4}{9}$ (p. 176)

ALGEBRA REVIEW

Algebra is essentially arithmetic with some of the numbers replaced by letters or variables. The letters or variables are merely substitutes for numbers. Initially, algebra referred to equation solving, but now it encompasses the language of algebra and the patterns of reasoning. The rules for algebra are basically the same as the rules for arithmetic.

Some Basic Language

Understood Multiplication

- When two or more letters, or a number and letter(s) are written next to each other, they are *understood to be multiplied*. Thus, 8x means 8 times x. (x8 is never written.) Or ab means a times b. Or 18ab means 18 times a times b.
- Parentheses also represent multiplication. Thus, 3(4) means 3 times 4. A raised dot also means multiplication. Thus, 6 · 5 means 6 times 5.

Letters to Be Aware of

- Although they may appear in some texts, we recommend that you never use o, e, or i as variables. (Technically, e and i stand for constants or predetermined numbers, and o is too easily confused with 0—zero.) When using z, you may wish to write it as $\bar{z}$ so it is not confused with 2.

Basic Terms in Set Theory

- A *set* is a group of objects, numbers, etc. {1, 2, 3}
- An *element* is a member of a set. $3 \in \{1, 2, 3\}$
  3 is an element of the set of 1, 2, 3.

Special Sets

- A *subset* is a set within a set. $\{2, 3\} \subset \{1, 2, 3\}$
  The set of 2, 3 is a subset of the set of 1, 2, 3.

- The *universal set* is the general category set, or the set of all those elements under consideration.
- The *empty set,* or *null set,* is a set with no members. $\emptyset$ or $\{\ \}$

Describing Sets

- *Rule* is a method of naming a set by describing its elements.

$$\{x \mid x > 3, x \text{ is a whole number}\}$$
$$\{\text{all students in the class with blue eyes}\}$$

- *Roster* is a method of naming a set by listing its members.

$$\{4, 5, 6 \ldots\}$$
$$\{\text{Fred, Tom, Bob}\}$$

- *Venn Diagrams* (and Euler Circles) are ways of pictorially describing sets.

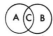

Types of Sets

- *Finite sets* are countable. They stop. $\{1, 2, 3, 4\}$
- *Infinite sets* are uncountable, they continue forever. $\{1, 2, 3, \ldots\}$

Comparing Sets

- *Equal sets* are those that have the exact same members.
  $\{1, 2, 3\} = \{3, 2, 1\}$
- *Equivalent sets* are sets that have the same number of members.
  $\{1, 2, 3\} \sim \{a, b, c\}$

Operations with Sets

- The *union* of two or more sets is all of the members in those sets.

$$\{1, 2, 3\} \cup \{3, 4, 5\} = \{1, 2, 3, 4, 5\}$$

The union of sets with members 1, 2, 3 and 3, 4, 5 is the set with members 1, 2, 3, 4, 5.

- The *intersection* of two or more sets is where they intersect, or overlap.

$$\{1, 2, 3\} \cap \{3, 4, 5\} = \{3\}$$

The intersection of a set with members 1, 2, 3 and a set with members 3, 4, 5 is a set with only member 3.

Practice: Set Theory Problems

1. True or false—$\{3\} \in \{$prime numbers$\}$
2. True or false—$\{2, 3, 5\} = \{3, 2, 5\}$
3. True or false—$\{1, 2, 3, 4\} \sim \{a, b, c, d\}$
4. True or false—$\{1, 5\} \subset \{2, 3, 4, 5\}$
5. $\{3, 4\} \cup \{1, 2, 3\} =$
6. $\{6, 7, 8\} \cap \{4, 5, 6\} =$
7. $\{1, 2, 3\} \cap \{4, 5\} =$

Answers: Set Theory Problems

1. True
2. True
3. True
4. False

5. $\{1, 2, 3, 4\}$
6. $\{6\}$
7. $\emptyset$ or $\{ \ \}$

Variables and Algebraic Expressions

- A *variable* is a symbol used to denote any element of a given set—often a letter used to stand for a number. Variables are used to change verbal expressions into *algebraic expressions*. *For example:*

VERBAL EXPRESSION	ALGEBRAIC EXPRESSION
the sum of a number and 7	$n + 7$ or $7 + n$
the number diminished by 10	$n - 10$
seven times a number	$7n$
x divided by 4	$x/4$

Key Words Denoting Addition

sum	larger than	enlarge
plus	gain	rise
more than	increase	grow
greater than		

Key Words Denoting Subtraction

difference	smaller than	lower
minus	fewer than	diminish
lose	decrease	reduced
less than	drop	

Key Words Denoting Multiplication

product	times	of
multiplied by	twice	

Key Words Denoting Division

quotient	ratio
divided by	half

Practice: Expressing Operations Algebraically Problems

Express each of the following algebraically.

1. a number increased by four
2. five less than a number
3. a number reduced by twelve
4. the product of a number and six
5. a number divided by three
6. one half of a number
7. a number multiplied by fourteen
8. the ratio of five to a number
9. twelve decreased by four times y
10. the product of five and the sum of x and y
11. five times c, decreased by one-third of b
12. the average of x, y, and z

Answers: Expressing Operations Algebraically Problems

1. n + 4 or 4 + n
2. n − 5
3. n − 12
4. 6n
5. n/3
6. (½)n or n/2

7. 14n
8. 5/n
9. 12 − 4y
10. 5(x + y) or (x + y)5
11. 5c − ⅓b or 5c − (⅓)b
12. (x + y + z)/3

Evaluating Expressions

● To *evaluate* an *expression,* just replace the unknowns with grouping symbols, insert the value for the unknowns and do the arithmetic.

Examples:

1. Evaluate: ab + c if a = 5, b = 4, and c = 3.

   (5)(4) + 3 =
   20 + 3 =
   23

2. Evaluate: $2x^2 + 3y + 6$ if x = 2 and y = 9.

   $2(2)^2 + 3(9) + 6 =$
   2(4) + 27 + 6 =
   8 + 27 + 6 =
   35 + 6 =
   41

3. Evaluate: $-4p^2 + 5q - 7$ if p = −3 and q = −8.

   $-4(-3)^2 + 5(-8) - 7 =$
   −4(9) + 5(−8) − 7 =
   −36 − 40 − 7 =
   −76 − 7 =
   −83

4. Evaluate: $\dfrac{a + c}{5} + \dfrac{a}{b + c}$ if a = 3, b = −2, and c = 7.

$$\frac{(3) + (7)}{5} + \frac{3}{(-2) + (7)} =$$

$$\frac{10}{5} + \frac{3}{5} =$$

$$\frac{13}{5} =$$

$2\frac{3}{5}$

5. Evaluate: $5x^3y^2$ if $x = -2$ and $y = 3$.

$5(-2)^3(3)^2 =$
$5(-8)(9) =$
$-40(9) =$
-360

Practice: Evaluating Expressions Problems

1. Evaluate: $x^2 + 4x - 7$ if $x = 3$.
2. Evaluate: $y^2 - y + 8$ if $y = 5$.
3. Evaluate: $7s - 2t^2$ if $s = 3$ and $t = 8$.
4. Evaluate: $10m^2 - 5n - 25$ if $m = -6$ and $n = -3$.

5. Evaluate: $\dfrac{x}{2} + \dfrac{x + y}{y}$ if $x = 1$ and $y = 4$

6. Evaluate: $3x^2y^3z$ if $x = 2$, $y = 3$, and $z = -1$.

Answers: Evaluating Expressions Problems

1. Evaluate: $x^2 + 4x - 7$ if $x = 3$.

$(3)^2 + 4(3) - 7 =$
$9 + 12 - 7 =$
$21 - 7 =$
14

2. Evaluate: $y^2 - y + 8$ if $y = 5$.

$(5)^2 - 5 + 8 =$
$25 - 5 + 8 =$
$20 + 8 =$
28

3. Evaluate: $7s - 2t^2$ if $s = 3$ and $t = 8$.

$7(3) - 2(8)^2 =$
$7(3) - 2(64) =$
$21 - 128 =$
-107

4. Evaluate: $10m^2 - 5n - 25$ if $m = -6$ and $n = -3$.

$10(-6)^2 - 5(-3) - 25 =$
$10(36) + 15 - 25 =$
$360 + 15 - 25 =$
$375 - 25 =$
350

5. Evaluate: $\dfrac{x}{2} + \dfrac{x + y}{y}$ if $x = 1$ and $y = 4$.

$\dfrac{1}{2} + \dfrac{1 + 4}{4} =$

$\dfrac{1}{2} + \dfrac{5}{4} =$ (finding common denominator)

$\dfrac{2}{4} + \dfrac{5}{4} =$

$\dfrac{7}{4} =$

$1\frac{3}{4}$

6. Evaluate: $3x^2y^3z$ if $x = 2$, $y = 3$, and $z = -1$.

$3(2)^2(3)^3(-1) =$
$3(4)(27)(-1) =$
$12(27)(-1) =$
$324(-1) =$
-324

Equations

Solving Equations

- An *equation* is a mathematical sentence, a relationship between numbers and/or symbols. Remember that an equation is like a balance scale, with the equal sign (=) being the fulcrum, or center. Thus, if you do the *same thing to both sides* of the equal sign (say, add 5 to each side), the equation will still be balanced.

Examples:

1. x − 5 = 23

To solve the equation x − 5 = 23, you must get x by itself on one side; therefore, add 5 to both sides:

$$
\begin{array}{rl}
x - 5 &= 23 \\
+\ 5 & +5 \\
\hline
x &= 28
\end{array}
$$

In the same manner, you may subtract, multiply, or divide *both* sides of an equation by the same (nonzero) number, and the equation will not change. Sometimes you may have to use more than one step to solve for an unknown.

2. 3x + 4 = 19

Subtract 4 from both sides to get the 3x by itself on one side:

$$
\begin{array}{rl}
3x + 4 &= 19 \\
-\ 4 & -4 \\
\hline
3x &= 15
\end{array}
$$

Then divide both sides by 3 to get x:

$$
\frac{3x}{3} = \frac{15}{3}
$$

$$
x = 5
$$

Remember: Solving an equation is using opposite operations, until the letter is on a side by itself (for addition, subtract; for multiplication, divide, etc.).

To check, substitute your answer into the original equation.

$$3x + 4 = 19$$
$$3(5) + 4 = 19$$
$$15 + 4 = 19$$
$$19 \stackrel{\checkmark}{=} 19$$

3. $\dfrac{x}{5} - 4 = 2$

Add 4 to both sides.

$$\dfrac{x}{5} - 4 = 2$$
$$\underline{\quad + 4 \mid +4 \quad}$$
$$\dfrac{x}{5} \qquad = 6$$

Multiply both sides by 5 to get x.

$$(5)\dfrac{x}{5} = (5)6$$

$$x = 30$$

4. $\dfrac{3}{5}x - 6 = 12$

Add 6 to each side.

$$\dfrac{3}{5}x - 6 = 12$$
$$\underline{\quad + 6 \quad +6 \quad}$$
$$\dfrac{3}{5}x \qquad = 18$$

Multiply each side by ⅝.

$$\left(\dfrac{5}{3}\right)\dfrac{3}{5}x = \left(\dfrac{5}{3}\right)18$$

$$x = \left(\dfrac{5}{\cancel{3}_1}\right)\dfrac{\cancel{18}^{6}}{1}$$

$$x = 30$$

5. $5x = 2x - 6$

Add $-2x$ to each side.

$$5x = 2x - 6$$
$$\underline{-2x -2x}$$
$$3x = - 6$$

Divide both sides by 3.

$$\frac{3x}{3} = \frac{-6}{3}$$

$$x = -2$$

6. $6x + 3 = 4x + 5$

Add -3 to each side.

$$6x + 3 = 4x + 5$$
$$\underline{ - 3 - 3}$$
$$6x = 4x + 2$$

Add $-4x$ to each side.

$$6x = 4x + 2$$
$$\underline{-4x -4x}$$
$$2x = 2$$

Divide each side by 2.

$$\frac{2x}{2} = \frac{2}{2}$$

$$x = 1$$

Practice: Solving Equations Problems

Solve each equation for y.

1. $y + 8 = 19$
2. $y - 9 = 21$
3. $4y + 8 = 32$
4. $-\frac{y}{5} = 8$

5. $\frac{2}{3}y + 1 = 13$

6. $4y = 52$
7. $7y = 4y - 12$
8. $5y - 4 = 3y + 4$

Answers: Solving Equations Problems

1. $y + 8 = 19$
   $\underline{\quad -8 \quad -8}$
   $y \qquad = 11$

2. $y - 9 = 21$
   $\underline{\quad +9 \quad +9}$
   $y \qquad = 30$

3. $4y + 8 = 32$
   $\underline{\quad -8 \quad -8}$
   $4y \qquad = 24$

   $\dfrac{4y}{4} = \dfrac{24}{4}$

   $y = 6$

4. $-\dfrac{y}{5} = 8$

   $\left(\dfrac{-\cancel{5}^{\,1}}{1}\right) - \dfrac{y}{\cancel{5}_{1}} = 8(-5)$

   $y = -40$

5. $\dfrac{2}{3}y + 1 = 13$

   $\underline{\qquad -1 \quad -1}$

   $\dfrac{2}{3}y \qquad = 12$

   $\left(\dfrac{3}{2}\right)\dfrac{2}{3}y = 12\left(\dfrac{3}{2}\right)$

   $y = 18$

6. $\dfrac{4y}{4} = \dfrac{52}{4}$

   $y = 13$

7. $7y = \quad 4y - 12$
   $\underline{-4y \quad -4y}$
   $3y = \qquad -12$

   $\dfrac{3y}{3} = \dfrac{-12}{3}$

   $y = -4$

8. $5y - 4 = 3y + 4$
   $\underline{\quad +4 \qquad +4}$
   $5y \qquad = 3y + 8$

   $5y = \quad 3y + 8$
   $\underline{-3y \quad -3y}$
   $2y = \qquad 8$

   $\dfrac{2y}{2} = \dfrac{8}{2}$

   $y = 4$

Literal Equations

● *Literal equations* have no numbers, only symbols (letters).

Examples:

1. Solve for Q: $QP - X = Y$

First add X to both sides.

$$
\begin{array}{rl}
QP - X &= Y \\
+ X &\quad + X \\
\hline
QP &= Y + X
\end{array}
$$

Then divide both sides by P.

$$\frac{QP}{P} = \frac{Y + X}{P}$$

$$Q = \frac{Y + X}{P}$$

Operations opposite to those in the original equation were used to isolate Q. (To remove the $-X$, we *added* a $+X$ to both sides of the equation; since we had Q times P, we *divided* both sides by P.)

2. Solve for y: $\dfrac{y}{x} = c$

Multiply both sides by x to get y alone.

$$(x)\frac{y}{x} = (x)c$$

$$y = xc$$

3. Solve for x: $\dfrac{b}{x} = \dfrac{p}{q}$

To solve this equation quickly, you cross multiply. To cross multiply:
   a. bring the denominators up next to the opposite side numerators and
   b. multiply

$$\frac{b}{x} = \frac{p}{q}$$

$$bq = px$$

Then divide both sides by p to get x alone.

$$\frac{bq}{p} = \frac{px}{p}$$

$$\frac{bq}{p} = x \text{ or } x = \frac{bq}{p}$$

Cross multiplying can be used only when the format is two fractions separated by an equal sign.

4. Solve for c: $\dfrac{g}{m} = \dfrac{k}{c}$

Cross multiply. $gc = mk$

Divide both sides by g. $\dfrac{gc}{g} = \dfrac{mk}{g}$

Thus, $c = \dfrac{mk}{g}$

Be aware that cross multiplying is most effective only when the letter you are solving for is on the *bottom* (the denominator) of a fraction. If it is on top (numerator), it is easier simply to clear the denominator under the unknown you're solving for.

4. Solve for x: $\dfrac{x}{k} = \dfrac{p}{q}$

Multiply both sides by k. $(k)\dfrac{x}{k} = (k)\dfrac{p}{q}$

$$x = \frac{kp}{q}$$

In this problem, there was no need to cross multiply.

Practice: Literal Equations Problems

1. Solve for z: $\dfrac{b}{z} = \dfrac{d}{e}$ 3. Solve for c: $\dfrac{a}{b} = \dfrac{c}{d}$

2. Solve for q: $\dfrac{m}{n} = \dfrac{r}{q}$ 4. Solve for c: $\dfrac{d}{x} = \dfrac{y}{c}$

Answers: Literal Equations Problems

1. $\dfrac{b}{z} = \dfrac{d}{e}$

$be = dz$

$\dfrac{be}{d} = \dfrac{dz}{d}$

$\dfrac{be}{d} = z$

2. $\dfrac{m}{n} = \dfrac{r}{q}$

$mq = nr$

$\dfrac{mq}{m} = \dfrac{nr}{m}$

$q = \dfrac{nr}{m}$

3. $\dfrac{a}{b} = \dfrac{c}{d}$

$(d)\dfrac{a}{b} = (d)\dfrac{c}{d}$

$\dfrac{ad}{b} = c$

4. $\dfrac{d}{x} = \dfrac{y}{c}$

$dc = yx$

$\dfrac{dc}{d} = \dfrac{yx}{d}$

$c = \dfrac{yx}{d}$

Ratios and Proportions

Ratios

● A *ratio* is a method of comparing two or more numbers or variables. Ratios are written as a:b or in working form as a fraction:

$$a/b \quad or \quad \dfrac{a}{b}$$

and are read "a is to b." Notice that whatever comes after the "to" goes second or at the bottom of the fraction.

Proportions

● *Proportions* are written as two ratios (fractions) equal to each other

Examples:

1. Solve this proportion for x: p is to q as x is to y

First the proportion may be rewritten.

$$\dfrac{p}{q} = \dfrac{x}{y}$$

Now simply multiply each side by y.

$$(y)\dfrac{p}{q} = (y)\dfrac{x}{y} \qquad\qquad \dfrac{yp}{q} = x$$

2. Solve this proportion for t: s is to t as r is to q

Rewrite.
$$\frac{s}{t} = \frac{r}{q}$$

Cross multiply. $sq = rt$

Divide both sides by r

$$\frac{sq}{r} = \frac{rt}{r}$$

$$\frac{sq}{r} = t$$

Practice: Proportion Problems

1. Solve for p: c is to p as g is to h
2. Solve for s: t is to q as z is to s
3. Solve for h: l is to k as h is to d
4. Solve for b: a is to b as c is to d

Answers: Proportion Problems

1. $\dfrac{c}{p} = \dfrac{g}{h}$

   $ch = pg$

   $\dfrac{ch}{g} = \dfrac{pg}{g}$

   $\dfrac{ch}{g} = p$

2. $\dfrac{t}{q} = \dfrac{z}{s}$

   $ts = qz$

   $\dfrac{ts}{t} = \dfrac{qz}{t}$

   $s = \dfrac{qz}{t}$

3. $\dfrac{l}{k} = \dfrac{h}{d}$

   $(d)\dfrac{l}{k} = (d)\dfrac{h}{d}$

   $\dfrac{dl}{k} = h$

4. $\dfrac{a}{b} = \dfrac{c}{d}$

   $ad = bc$

   $\dfrac{ad}{c} = \dfrac{bc}{c}$

   $\dfrac{ad}{c} = b$

Solving Proportions for Value

● Use the same rule (p. 119) to solve for the unknown. *For example:*

$$\frac{4}{x} = \frac{2}{5}$$

Cross multiply.

$$(4)(5) = 2x$$
$$20 = 2x$$

Divide both sides by 2.

$$\frac{20}{2} = \frac{2x}{2}$$

$$10 = x$$

Practice: Solving Proportions for Value Problems

Solve for the unknown.

1. $\dfrac{3}{k} = \dfrac{1}{11}$

2. $\dfrac{2}{5} = \dfrac{8}{R}$

3. $\dfrac{14}{5} = \dfrac{7}{t}$

4. $\dfrac{15}{2} = \dfrac{25}{t}$

Answers: Solving Proportions for Value Problems

1. $\dfrac{3}{k} = \dfrac{1}{11}$

$$33 = 1k \text{ or } 33 = k$$

2. $\dfrac{2}{5} = \dfrac{8}{R}$

$$2R = 40$$

$$\frac{2R}{2} = \frac{40}{2}$$

$$R = 20$$

Note that this problem could have been done intuitively if you noticed that the second ratio (fraction) is four times the first.

$$\frac{2 \times 4}{5 \times 4} = \frac{8}{\boxed{20}}$$

3. $\dfrac{14}{5} = \dfrac{7}{t}$

$$14t = 35$$

$$\frac{14t}{14} = \frac{35}{14}$$

$$t = \frac{35}{14} = 2\,^{7}/_{14} = 2\tfrac{1}{2}$$

Intuitively: $\dfrac{14 \div 2}{5 \div 2} = \dfrac{7}{\boxed{2\tfrac{1}{2}}}$

4. $\dfrac{15}{2} = \dfrac{25}{t}$

$$15t = 50$$

$$\frac{15t}{15} = \frac{50}{15}$$

$$t = \frac{50}{15} = 3\,^{5}/_{15} = 3\tfrac{1}{3}$$

Solving for Two Unknowns—Systems of Equations

- If you solve *two equations with the same two unknowns in each,* you can solve for both unknowns. One method is:
  a. Multiply one or both equations by some number to make the number in front of one of the letters (unknowns) the same in each equation.
  b. Add or subtract the two equations to eliminate one letter.
  c. Solve for the other unknown.
  d. Insert the value of the first unknown in one of the original equations to solve for the second unknown.

Examples:

1. Solve for x and y: $3x + 3y = 24$
$$2x + y = 13$$

First multiply the bottom equation by 3. Now the y is preceded by a 3 in each equation

$$3x + 3y = 24 \qquad\qquad 3x + 3y = 24$$
$$3(2x) + 3(y) = 3(13) \qquad 6x + 3y = 39$$

Now we can subtract equations, eliminating the y terms.

$$
\begin{array}{rcr}
3x + 3y &=& 24 \\
-6x + -3y &=& -39 \\
\hline
-3x &=& -15
\end{array}
$$

$$\frac{-3x}{-3} = \frac{-15}{-3}$$

$$x = 5$$

Now insert $x = 5$ in one of the original equations to solve for y

$$2x + y = 13$$
$$2(5) + y = 13$$

$$
\begin{array}{rcr}
10 + y &=& 13 \\
-10 & & -10 \\
\hline
y &=& 3
\end{array}
$$

Answer: $x = 5, y = 3$

Of course, if the number in front of a letter is already the same in each equation, you do not have to change either equation. Simply add or subtract.

2. Solve for x and y: x + y = 7
                      x − y = 3

$$x + y = 7$$
$$\underline{x - y = 3}$$
$$2x \qquad = 10$$

$$\frac{2x}{2} = \frac{10}{2}$$

$$x = 5$$

Now, inserting 5 for x in the first equation gives:

$$5 + y = \quad 7$$
$$\underline{-5 \qquad -5}$$
$$y = \quad 2$$

Answer: x = 5, y = 2

You should note that this method will not work when the two equations are, in fact, the same.

3. Solve for a and b: 3a + 4b = 2
                      6a + 8b = 4

The second equation is actually the first equation multiplied by 2. In this instance, the system is unsolvable.

4. Solve for p and q: 3p + 4q = 9
                      2p + 2q = 6

Multiply the second equation by 2.

$$(2)2p + (2)2q = (2)6$$
$$4p + 4q = 12$$

Now subtract the equations.

$$3p + 4q = \quad 9$$
$$\underline{(-)4p + 4q = \quad 12}$$
$$-p \qquad = -3$$
$$p \qquad = \quad 3$$

Now that you know p = 3, you may plug in 3 for p in either of the two original equations to find q.

$$3p + 4q = 9$$
$$3(3) + 4q = 9$$
$$9 + 4q = 9$$
$$4q = 0$$
$$q = 0$$

Answer: p = 3, q = 0

Sometimes a system is more easily solved by the substitution method.

5. Solve for x and y: x = y + 8
          x + 3y = 48

From the first equation, substitute (y + 8) for x in the second equation.

$$(y + 8) + 3y = 48$$

Now solve for y. Simplify by combining y's.

$$4y + 8 = 48$$
$$\underline{ - 8 \ -8}$$
$$4y = 40$$

$$\frac{4y}{4} = \frac{40}{4}$$

$$y = 10$$

Now insert y = 10 in one of the original equations.

$$x = y + 8$$
$$x = 10 + 8$$
$$x = 18$$

Answer: y = 10, x = 18

Practice: Systems of Equations Problems

Solve for both unknowns.

1. 6a − 2b = 32
    3a + 2b = 22

2. 3a + 3b = 24
    2a + b = 13

3. 3x + 2y = 10
    2x + 3y = 5

4. 6x + 2y = 24
    x = −y + 5

Answers: Systems of Equations Problems

1. $6a - 2b = 32$
    $3a + 2b = 22$

Add the two equations:

$$6a - 2b = 32$$
$$\underline{(+)\ 3a + 2b = 22}$$
$$9a \qquad = 54$$

$$\frac{9a}{9} = \frac{54}{9}$$

$$a = 6$$

Now plug in 6 for a in one of the original equations.

$$3a + 2b = 22$$
$$3(6) + 2b = 22$$

$$18 + 2b = 22$$
$$\underline{-18 \qquad\quad -18}$$
$$2b = 4$$

$$\frac{2b}{2} = \frac{4}{2}$$

$$b = 2$$

Answer: a = 6, b = 2

2. $3a + 3b = 24$
    $2a + b = 13$

Multiply the second equation by 3.

$$(3)2a + (3)b = (3)13$$
$$6a + 3b = 39$$

Subtract the first equation from the second.

$$6a + 3b = 39$$
$$\underline{(-)\ 3a + 3b = 24}$$
$$3a \qquad = 15$$

$$\frac{3a}{3} = \frac{15}{3}$$

$$a = 5$$

Now plug in 5 for a in one of the original equations:

$$2a + b = 13$$
$$2(5) + b = 13$$

$$\begin{array}{r} 10 + b = 13 \\ -10 \qquad -10 \\ \hline b = \ \ 3 \end{array}$$

Answer: a = 5, b = 3

3. 3x + 2y = 10
   2x + 3y = 5

Multiply the first equation by 2.

$$(2)3x + (2)2y = (2)10$$
$$6x + 4y = 20$$

Multiply the second equation by 3.

$$(3)2x + (3)3y = (3)5$$
$$6x + 9y = 15$$

Subtract the second equation from the first.

$$\begin{array}{r} 6x + 4y = 20 \\ (-)\ 6x + 9y = 15 \\ \hline -5y = \ \ 5 \end{array}$$

$$\frac{-5y}{-5} = \frac{5}{-5}$$

$$y = -1$$

Now plug in −1 for y in one of the original equations.

$$3x + 2y = 10$$
$$3x + 2(-1) = 10$$

$$\begin{array}{r} 3x - 2 = 10 \\ + 2 \ + 2 \\ \hline 3x \qquad = 12 \end{array}$$

$$\frac{3x}{3} = \frac{12}{3}$$

$$x = 4$$

Answer: $y = -1$, $x = 4$

4. $6x + 2y = 24$
   $x = -y + 5$

Substitute the value of x from the second equation into the first equation.

$$6x + 2y = 24$$
$$6(-y + 5) + 2y = 24$$
$$-6y + 30 + 2y = 24$$

$$\begin{array}{r} -4y + 30 = 24 \\ -30 \; -30 \\ \hline -4y \qquad = -6 \end{array}$$

$$\frac{-4y}{-4} = \frac{-6}{-4}$$

$$y = \frac{3}{2} \text{ or } 1\frac{1}{2}$$

Now plug in $1\frac{1}{2}$ for y in one of the original equations.

$$x = -y + 5$$
$$x = -(1\frac{1}{2}) + 5$$
$$x = 3\frac{1}{2}$$

Answer: $y = 1\frac{1}{2}$, $x = 3\frac{1}{2}$

Monomials and Polynomials

- A *monomial* is an algebraic expression that consists of only one term. (A term is a numerical or literal expression with its own sign.) For instance, $9x$, $4a^2$, and $3mpxz^2$ are all monomials
- A *polynomial* consists of two or more terms. For instance, $x + y$, $y^2 - x^2$, and $x^2 + 3x + 5y^2$ are all polynomials.
- A *binomial* is a polynomial that consists of exactly two terms. For

instance, x + y is a binomial.
- A *trinomial* is a polynomial that consists of exactly three terms. For instance, $y^2 + 9y + 8$ is a trinomial.
- The number in front of the variable is called the *coefficient*. In 9y, 9 is the coefficient.

   Polynomials are usually arranged in one of two ways.
- *Ascending order* is basically when the power of a term increases for each succeeding term. For example, $x + x^2 + x^3$ or $5x + 2x^2 - 3x^3 + x^5$ are arranged in ascending order.
- *Descending order* is basically when the power of a term decreases for each succeeding term. For example, $x^3 + x^2 + x$ or $2x^4 + 3x^2 + 7x$ are arranged in descending order. Descending order is more commonly used.

Adding and Subtracting Monomials

- To *add* or *subtract monomials,* follow the same rules as with signed numbers (p. 22), *provided that the terms are alike.* Notice that you add or subtract the coefficients only and leave the variables the same.

Examples:

1. $15x^2yz$
     $\underline{-18x^2yz}$
     $-3x^2yz$

2. $3x + 2x = 5x$

3. $9y$
     $\underline{-\ 3y}$
     $6y$

4. $17q + 8q - 3q - (-4q) =$
    $22q - (-4q) =$
    $22q + 4q = 26q$

Remember that the rules for signed numbers apply to monomials as well.

Practice: Adding and Subtracting Monomials Problems

Perform the indicated operation.

1. $-9m^2s + 5m^2s =$

2. $+7qt^2 - 3qt^2 + 20qt^2 =$

3. $18pc$
     $\underline{(-)\ 7pc}$

4. $-7x^2y$
     $\underline{(-)\ -3x^2y}$

Answers: Adding and Subtracting Monomials Problems

1. $-4m^2s$ 2. $24qt^2$ 3. $11pc$ 4. $-4x^2y$

Multiplying Monomials

- Reminder: The rules and definitions for powers and exponents introduced in arithmetic (pp. 63–65) also apply in algebra. For example, $5 \cdot 5 = 5^2$ and $x \cdot x = x^2$. Similarly, $a \cdot a \cdot a \cdot b \cdot b = a^3b^2$.

- To *multiply monomials,* add the exponents of the same bases.

Examples:

1. $(x^3)(x^4) = x^7$

2. $(x^2y)(x^3y^2) = x^5y^3$

3. $(6k^5)(5k^2) = 30k^7$ (multiply numbers)

4. $-4(m^2n)(-3m^4n^3) = 12m^6n^4$

5. $(c^2)(c^3)(c^4) = c^9$

6. $(3a^2b^3c)(b^2c^2d) = 3a^2b^5c^3d$

Note that in example 4 the product of -4 and -3 is $+12$, the product of m^2 and m^4 is m^6, and the product of n and n^3 is n^4, since any monomial having no exponent indicated is assumed to have an exponent of 1.

- When monomials are being *raised to a power,* the answer is obtained by multiplying the exponents of each part of the monomial by the power to which it is being raised.

Examples:

1. $(a^7)^3 = a^{21}$
2. $(x^3y^2)^4 = x^{12}y^8$
3. $(2x^2y^3)^3 = (2)^3x^6y^9 = 8x^6y^9$

Practice: Multiplying Monomials Problems

1. $(m^3)(m^{10}) =$
2. $(a^5b^6)(a^4b^2) =$
3. $(5k^2)(8k^4) =$
4. $-2(x^2y^3)(6xy^4) =$
5. $(2x^2)(-4x)(x^3y) =$
6. $(d^4)^5 =$
7. $(c^3d^2)^5 =$
8. $(3a^2bc^3)^2 =$

Answers: Multiplying Monomials Problems

1. m^{13}
2. a^9b^8
3. $40k^6$
4. $-12x^3y^7$
5. $-8x^6y$
6. d^{20}
7. $c^{15}d^{10}$
8. $9a^4b^2c^6$

Dividing Monomials

- To *divide monomials*, subtract the exponent of the divisor from the exponent of the dividend of the same base.

Examples:

1. $\dfrac{y^{15}}{y^4} = y^{11}$ or $y^{15} \div y^4 = y^{11}$

2. $\dfrac{x^5y^2}{x^3y} = x^2y$

3. $\dfrac{36a^4b^6}{-9ab} = -4a^3b^5$ (divide the numbers)

4. $\dfrac{fg^{15}}{g^3} = fg^{12}$

5. $\dfrac{x^5}{x^8} = \dfrac{1}{x^3}$ (may also be expressed x^{-3})

6. $\dfrac{-3\,(xy)(xy^2)}{xy}$

You can simplify the numerator first.

$$\frac{-3(xy)(xy^2)}{xy} = \frac{-3x^2y^3}{xy} = -3xy^2$$

Or, since the numerator is all multiplication, we can cancel.

$$\frac{-3(\cancel{xy})(xy^2)}{\cancel{xy}} = -3xy^2$$

Practice: Dividing Monomials Problems

1. $\dfrac{x^8}{x^3} =$

5. $\dfrac{x^8y^3}{x^5} =$

2. $a^9 \div a^6 =$

6. $3p^5q^3 \div 12p^4q^9 =$

3. $\dfrac{m^5n^4}{m^2n^3} =$

7. $\dfrac{s^4t^6}{s^7t^3} =$

4. $\dfrac{-10x^4z^9}{5x^3z^4} =$

8. $\dfrac{2(x^2y)(3x^2y^3)}{x^2y^2} =$

Answers: Dividing Monomials Problems

1. x^5

2. a^3

3. m^3n

4. $-2xz^5$

5. x^3y^3

6. $\dfrac{\cancel{3}p^{5^1}\cancel{q^3}}{_4\cancel{12}p^4q^{9^6}} = \dfrac{1p}{4q^6} = \dfrac{p}{4q^6}$ or $.25pq^{-6}$

7. $\dfrac{t^3}{s^3}$ or $s^{-3}t^3$

8. $\dfrac{2(x^2y)(3x^2y^3)}{x^2y^2} = \dfrac{6x^4y^4}{x^2y^2} = 6x^2y^2$ or $\dfrac{2(\cancel{x^2}y)(3x^2y^{3^1})}{\cancel{x^2}\cancel{y^2}} = 6x^2y^2$

Adding and Subtracting Polynomials

- To *add* or *subtract polynomials,* just arrange *like terms* in columns and then add or subtract. (Or simply add or subtract like terms when rearrangement is not necessary.)

Examples:

1. Add:
$$\begin{array}{r} a^2 + ab + b^2 \\ 3a^2 + 4ab - 2b^2 \\ \hline 4a^2 + 5ab - b^2 \end{array}$$

2. $(5y - 3x) + (9y + 4x) =$

    $(5y - 3x) + (9y + 4x) = 14y + x \text{ or } x + 14y$

3. Subtract:
$$\begin{array}{r} a^2 + b^2 \\ (-) \; 2a^2 - b^2 \\ \hline \end{array} \qquad \begin{array}{r} a^2 + b^2 \\ (+) \; -2a^2 + b^2 \\ \hline -a^2 + 2b^2 \end{array}$$

4. $(3cd - 6mt) - (2cd - 4mt) =$
   $(3cd - 6mt) + (-2cd + 4mt) =$

   $(3cd - 6mt) + (-2cd + 4mt) = cd - 2mt$

5. $3a^2bc + 2ab^2c + 4a^2bc + 5ab^2c =$

$$\begin{array}{r} 3a^2bc + 2ab^2c \\ + \; 4a^2bc + 5ab^2c \\ \hline 7a^2bc + 7ab^2c \end{array}$$

or

$3a^2bc + 2ab^2c + 4a^2bc + 5ab^2c = 7a^2bc + 7ab^2c$

Practice: Adding and Subtracting Polynomials Problems

Perform the indicated operations and simplify.

1.
$$\begin{array}{r} 5x^2y^2 - 4ab \\ -6x^2y^2 + 3ab \\ -2x^2y^2 - ab \\ \hline \end{array}$$

2. $(7gr - 3nt) + (5gr - 2nt) =$

3. $(9kb^2 + 6ht - 3ab) - (4kb^2 - 6ht + 2ab) =$

4. $7xyz^2 + 8x^2yz + 9xy^2z + 8xyz^2 + 3xy^2z - 3x^2yz =$

Answers: Adding and Subtracting Polynomials Problems

1. $-3x^2y^2 - 2ab$ 3. $5kb^2 + 12ht - 5ab$
2. $12gr - 5nt$ 4. $15xyz^2 + 5x^2yz + 12xy^2z$

Multiplying Polynomials

● To *multiply polynomials,* multiply each term in one polynomial by each term in the other polynomial. Then simplify if necessary.

Examples:

1.
$$
\begin{array}{r}
2x - 2a \\
\times \quad 3x + a \\
\hline
+2ax - 2a^2 \\
6x^2 - 6ax \\
\hline
6x^2 - 4ax - 2a^2
\end{array}
\qquad similar\ to \qquad
\begin{array}{r}
21 \\
\times 23 \\
\hline
63 \\
42 \\
\hline
483
\end{array}
$$

Or you may wish to use the "F.O.I.L." method with *binomials.* F.O.I.L. means First terms, Outside terms, Inside terms, Last terms. Then simplify if necessary.

2. $(3x + a)(2x - 2a) =$

Multiply *first* terms from each quantity.

$(3x + a)(2x - 2a) = 6x^2$ _____

Now *outside* terms.

$(3x + a)(2x - 2a) = 6x^2 - 6ax$ _____

Now *inside* terms.

$(3x + a)(2x - 2a) = 6x^2 - 6ax + 2ax$ ___

Finally *last* terms.

$(3x + a)(2x - 2a) = 6x^2 - 6ax + 2ax - 2a^2$

Now simplify.

$6x^2 - 6ax + 2ax - 2a^2 = 6x^2 - 4ax - 2a^2$

3. $(x + y)(x + y + z) =$

$$
\begin{array}{r}
x + y + z \\
\times \qquad\quad x + y \\
\hline
xy + y^2 + yz \\
x^2 + xz + \ xy \qquad\quad\ \\
\hline
x^2 + xz + 2xy + y^2 + yz
\end{array}
$$

Practice: Multiplying Polynomials Problems

1. $(2x + y)(3x + 5y) =$
2. $(7a + b)(2a - 3b) =$
3. $(9x + 5)(3x - 2) =$
4. $(-6y + z^2)(2y - 3z) =$

Answers: Multiplying Polynomials Problems

1.
$$
\begin{array}{r}
2x + y \\
\times \quad 3x + 5y \\
\hline
+10xy + 5y^2 \\
+6x^2 + \ 3xy \qquad\quad \\
\hline
6x^2 + 13xy + 5y^2
\end{array}
$$

2.
$$
\begin{array}{r}
7a \ + \ b \\
\times \ 2a \ - \ 3b \\
\hline
-21ab - 3b^2 \\
+14a^2 + \ 2ab \qquad\quad \\
\hline
14a^2 - 19ab - 3b^2
\end{array}
$$

3.
$$
\begin{array}{r}
9x + 5 \\
\times \ 3x - 2 \\
\hline
-18x - 10 \\
+27x^2 + 15x \qquad\quad \\
\hline
27x^2 - \ 3x - 10
\end{array}
$$

4.
$$
\begin{array}{r}
-6y \ + z^2 \\
\times \quad 2y \ - 3z \\
\hline
+ \ 18yz - 3z^2 \\
-12y^2 + 2yz^2 \qquad\qquad \\
\hline
-12y^2 + 2yx^2 + \ 18yz - 3z^3
\end{array}
$$

or $-12y^2 + 18yz + 2yz^2 - 3z^3$

Dividing Polynomials by Monomials

- To *divide a polynomial by a monomial,* just divide each term in the polynomial by the monomial.

Examples:

1. $(6x^2 + 2x) \div 2x =$

$$\frac{6x^2 + 2x}{2x} = \frac{6x^2}{2x} + \frac{2x}{2x} = 3x + 1$$

2. $(16a^7 - 12a^5) \div 4a^2 =$

$$\frac{16a^7 - 12a^5}{4a^2} = \frac{16a^7}{4a^2} - \frac{12a^5}{4a^2} = 4a^5 - 3a^3$$

Practice: Dividing Polynomials by Monomials Problems

1. $(3x - 9) \div 3 =$
2. $(16x^3 + 4x^2 + 8x) \div 2x =$
3. $(14a^2b - 8ab + 4a) \div 2a =$
4. $(84c^2d - 38cd + 18cd^3) \div 2cd =$

Answers: Dividing Polynomials by Monomials Problems

1. $(3x - 9) \div 3 =$

$$\frac{3x - 9}{3} = \frac{3x}{3} - \frac{9}{3} = x - 3$$

2. $(16x^3 + 4x^2 + 8x) \div 2x =$

$$\frac{16x^3 + 4x^2 + 8x}{2x} = \frac{16x^3}{2x} + \frac{4x^2}{2x} + \frac{8x}{2x} = 8x^2 + 2x + 4$$

3. $(14a^2b - 8ab + 4a) \div 2a =$

$$\frac{14a^2b - 8ab + 4a}{2a} = \frac{14a^2b}{2a} - \frac{8ab}{2a} + \frac{4a}{2a} = 7ab - 4b + 2$$

4. $(84c^2d - 38cd + 18cd^3) \div 2cd =$

$$\frac{84c^2d - 38cd + 18cd^3}{2cd} = \frac{84c^2d}{2cd} - \frac{38cd}{2cd} + \frac{18cd^3}{2cd}$$

$$= 42c - 19 + 9d^2$$

Dividing Polynomials by Polynomials

● To *divide a polynomial by a polynomial,* make sure both are in descending order; then use long division (Remember: Divide by the first term, multiply, subtract, bring down.)

Examples:

1. Divide $4a^2 + 18a + 8$ by $a + 4$

First divide a into $4a^2$.

$$a + 4 \overline{)\, 4a^2 + 18a + 8} \quad {}^{4a}$$

Now multiply 4a times $(a + 4)$.

$$\begin{array}{r} 4a \\ a + 4 \overline{)\, 4a^2 + 18a + 8} \\ 4a^2 + 16a \end{array}$$

Now subtract.

$$\begin{array}{r} 4a \\ a + 4 \overline{)\, 4a^2 + 18a + 8} \\ (-)\ \underline{4a^2 + 16a} \\ 2a \end{array}$$

Now bring down the $+8$.

$$\begin{array}{r} 4a \\ a + 4 \overline{)\, 4a^2 + 18a + 8} \\ (-)\ \underline{4a^2 + 16a} \\ 2a + 8 \end{array}$$

Now divide a into 2a.

$$\begin{array}{r} 4a + 2 \\ a + 4 \overline{)\, 4a^2 + 18a + 8} \\ (-)\ \underline{4a^2 + 16a + 8} \\ 2a + 8 \end{array}$$

Now multiply 2 times $(a + 4)$.

$$\begin{array}{r} 4a + 2 \\ a + 4 \overline{)\, 4a^2 + 18a + 8} \\ (-)\ \underline{4a^2 + 16a} \\ 2a + 8 \\ 2a + 8 \end{array}$$

Now subtract.

$$\begin{array}{r} 4a + 2 \\ a + 4\overline{)\,4a^2 + 18a + 8} \\ (-)\ \underline{4a^2 + 16a} \\ 2a + 8 \\ (-)\ \underline{2a + 8} \\ 0 \end{array}$$

$$\begin{array}{r} 4a + 2 \\ a + 4\overline{)\,4a^2 + 18a + 8} \\ (-)\ \underline{4a^2 + 16a} \\ 2a + 8 \\ (-)\ \underline{2a + 8} \\ 0 \end{array} \qquad similar\ to \qquad \begin{array}{r} 23 \\ 53\overline{)\,1219} \\ (-)\ \underline{106} \\ 159 \\ (-)\ \underline{159} \\ 0 \end{array}$$

2. $(3x^2 + 4x + 1) \div (x + 1) =$

$$\begin{array}{r} 3x + 1 \\ x + 1\overline{)\,3x^2 + 4x + 1} \\ (-)\ \underline{3x^2 + 3x} \\ x + 1 \\ (-)\ \underline{x + 1} \\ 0 \end{array}$$

3. $(2x + 1 + x^2) \div (x + 1) =$

First change to descending order: $x^2 + 2x + 1$
Then divide.

$$\begin{array}{r} x + 1 \\ x + 1\overline{)\,x^2 + 2x + 1} \\ (-)\ \underline{x^2 + 1x} \\ x + 1 \\ (-)\ \underline{x + 1} \\ 0 \end{array}$$

4. $(m^3 - m) \div (m + 1)$

Note: when terms are missing, be sure to leave proper room between terms.

$$\begin{array}{r} m^2 - m \\ m + 1\overline{)\,m^3 + 0m^2 - m} \\ (-)\ \underline{m^3 +\ \ m^2} \\ - m^2 - m \\ (-)\ \underline{- m^2 - m} \\ 0 \end{array}$$

5. $(10a^2 - 29a - 21) \div (2a - 7) =$

$$
\begin{array}{r}
5a + 3 \\
2a - 7\overline{)10a^2 - 29a - 21} \\
(-)\ \underline{10a^2 - 35a} \\
6a - 21 \\
(-)\ \underline{6a - 21} \\
0
\end{array}
$$

Note that remainders are possible.

6. $(x^2 + 2x + 4) \div (x + 1) =$

$$
\begin{array}{r}
x + 1\ \text{(with remainder 3)} \\
x + 1\overline{)x^2 + 2x + 4} \\
(-)\ \underline{x^2 + x} \\
x + 4 \\
(-)\ \underline{x + 1} \\
3
\end{array}
$$

This answer can be rewritten as $(x + 1) + \dfrac{3}{x + 1}$

Practice: Dividing Polynomials by Polynomials Problems

1. $(x^2 + 18x + 45) \div (x + 3) =$
2. $(21t + 5 + 4t^2) \div (t + 5) =$
3. $(z^3 - 1) \div (z - 1) =$
4. $(t^2 + 4t - 6) \div (t + 2) =$
5. $(14x^2 + 11x + 2) \div (2x + 1) =$

Answers: Dividing Polynomials by Polynomials Problems

1. $(x^2 + 18x + 45) \div (x + 3) =$

$$
\begin{array}{r}
x + 15 \\
x + 3\overline{)x^2 + 18x + 45} \\
(-)\ \underline{x^2 + 3x} \\
15x + 45 \\
(-)\ \underline{15x + 45} \\
0
\end{array}
$$

2. $(21t + 5 + 4t^2) \div (t + 5) =$
Reorder: $4t^2 + 21t + 5$

$$
\begin{array}{r}
4t + 1 \\
t + 5 \overline{)\, 4t^2 + 21t + 5} \\
(-)\ \underline{4t^2 + 20t} \\
t + 5 \\
(-)\ \underline{t + 5} \\
0
\end{array}
$$

3. $(z^3 - 1) \div (z - 1) =$

$$
\begin{array}{r}
z^2 + z + 1 \\
z - 1 \overline{)\, z^3 \ - 1} \\
(-)\ \underline{z^3 - z^2} \\
z^2 \\
(-)\ \underline{z^2 - z} \\
z - 1 \\
(-)\ \underline{z - 1} \\
0
\end{array}
$$

4. $(t^2 + 4t - 6) \div (t + 2) =$

$$
\begin{array}{r}
t + 2 \ (\text{with remainder} -10 \text{ or } (t + 2) - \dfrac{10}{t + 2} \\
t + 2 \overline{)\, t^2 + 4t - 6} \\
(-)\ \underline{t^2 + 2t} \\
2t - 6 \\
(-)\ \underline{2t + 4} \\
-10
\end{array}
$$

5. $(14x^2 + 11x + 2) \div (2x + 1) =$

$$
\begin{array}{r}
7x + 2 \\
2x + 1 \overline{)\, 14x^2 + 11x + 2} \\
(-)\ \underline{14x^2 + 7x} \\
4x + 2 \\
(-)\ \underline{4x + 2} \\
0
\end{array}
$$

Factoring

- To *factor* means to find two or more quantities whose product equals the original quantity.

Factoring out a Common Factor

- To *factor out a common factor*
  - (a) Find the largest common monomial factor of each term.
  - (b) Divide the original polynomial by this factor to obtain the second factor. The second factor will be a polynomial.

Examples:

1. $5x^2 + 4x = x(5x + 4)$
2. $2y^3 - 6y = 2y(y^2 - 3)$
3. $x^5 - 4x^3 + x^2 = x^2(x^3 - 4x + 1)$

Practice: Factoring out a Common Factor Problems

Factor the following completely.

1. $a^2 + 26a =$ 3. $3m^3 + 6m^2 + 9m =$
2. $t^2 - 35t =$ 4. $12p^3 + 24p^2 =$

Answers: Factoring out a Common Factor Problems

1. $a(a + 26)$ 3. $3m(m^2 + 2m + 3)$
2. $t(t - 35)$ 4. $12p^2(p + 2)$

Factoring the Difference Between Two Squares

- To *factor the difference between two squares*
  - (a) Find the square root of the first term and the square root of the second term.
  - (b) Express your answer as the product of: the sum of the quantities from step a, times the difference of those quantities.

Examples:

1. $x^2 - 144 = (x + 12)(x - 12)$
2. $a^2 - b^2 = (a + b)(a - b)$
3. $9y^2 - 1 = (3y + 1)(3y - 1)$

Note: $x^2 + 144$ is *not* factorable.

Practice: Factoring the Difference Between Two Squares Problems

Factor the following.

1. $x^2 - 25 =$ 4. $x^2y^2 - z^2 =$
2. $p^2 - q^2 =$ 5. $4a^2 - 9 =$
3. $144 - h^2 =$ 6. $2t^2 - 50 =$

Answers: Factoring the Difference Between Two Squares Problems

1. $(x + 5)(x - 5)$ 4. $(xy + z)(xy - z)$
2. $(p + q)(p - q)$ 5. $(2a + 3)(2a - 3)$
3. $(12 + h)(12 - h)$ 6. $2(t^2 - 25) = 2(t + 5)(t - 5)$

Factoring Polynomials Having Three Terms of the Form $Ax^2 + Bx + C$

- To *factor polynomials having three terms of the form* $Ax^2 + Bx + C$
  - (a) Check to see if you can monomial factor (factor out common terms). Then if $A = 1$ (that is, the first term is simply x^2) use double parentheses and factor the first term. Place these factors in the left sides of the parentheses. For example, $(x\quad)(x\quad)$.
  - (b) Factor the last term and place the factors in the right sides of the parentheses.

To decide on the signs of the numbers do the following.
If the sign of the last term is *negative*
  - (1) Find two numbers whose product is the last term and whose *difference* is the *coefficient* (number in front) of the middle term.
  - (2) Give the larger of these two numbers the sign of the middle term and the *opposite* sign to the other factor.

If the sign of the last term is *positive*
  - (1) Find two numbers whose product is the last term and whose *sum* is the coefficient of the middle term.
  - (2) Give both factors the sign of the middle term.

Examples:

1. Factor $x^2 - 3x - 10$

First check to see if you can monomial factor (factor out common terms). Since this is not possible, use double parentheses and factor the first term as follows: $(x\quad)(x\quad)$. Next, factor the last term, 10, into 2 times 5 (using step b above, 5 must take the negative sign and 2 must take the positive sign because they will then total the coefficient of the middle term, which is -3) and add the proper signs leaving

$$(x - 5)(x + 2)$$

Multiply *means* (inner terms) and *extremes* (outer terms) to check.

$$(x - 5)(x + 2)$$
$$-5x$$
$$\underline{+2x}$$
$$-3x \text{ (which is the middle term)}$$

To completely check, multiply the factors together.

$$
\begin{array}{r}
x - 5 \\
\times \quad x + 2 \\
\hline
+ 2x - 10 \\
x^2 - 5x \quad\;\; \\
\hline
x^2 - 3x + 10
\end{array}
$$

2. Factor $x^2 + 8x + 15$

$$(x + 3)(x + 5)$$

Notice that $3 \times 5 = 15$ and $3 + 5 = 8$, the coefficient of the middle term. Also note that the signs of both factors are $+$, the sign of the middle term. To check

$$(x + 3)(x + 5)$$
$$+3x$$
$$\underline{+5x}$$
$$+8x \text{ (the middle term)}$$

3. Factor $x^2 - 5x - 14$

   $(x - 7)(x + 2)$

Notice that $7 \times 2 = 14$ and $7 - 2 = 5$, the coefficient of the middle term. Also note that the sign of the larger factor, 7, is $-$, while the other factor, 2, has a $+$ sign. To check

$$(x - 7)(x + 2)$$
$$-7x$$
$$+2x$$
$$-5x \text{ (the middle term)}$$

If, however, $A \neq 1$ (that is, the first term has a coefficient—for example, $4x^2 + 5x + 1$—then additional trial and error will be necessary.

4. Factor $4x^2 + 5x + 1$

$(2x + \quad)(2x + \quad)$ might work for the first term. But when 1's are used as factors to get the last term—$(2x + 1)(2x + 1)$—the middle term comes out as *4x* instead of *5x*.

$$(2x + 1)(2x + 1)$$
$$+ 2x$$
$$+ 2x$$
$$+ 4x$$

Therefore, try $(4x + \quad)(x + \quad)$. Now using 1's as factors to get the last terms gives $(4x + 1)(x + 1)$. Checking for the middle term

$$(4x + 1)(x + 1)$$
$$+ 1x$$
$$+ 4x$$
$$+ 5x$$

Therefore, $4x^2 + 5x + 1 = (4x + 1)(x + 1)$.

5. Factor $4a^2 + 6a + 2$

Factoring out a 2 leaves $2(2a^2 + 3a + 1)$

Now factor as usual giving $2(2a + 1)(a + 1)$

To check

$(2a + 1)(a + 1)$
$\underbrace{\qquad}_{+1a}$
$+2a$
$+3a$

(the middle term after 2 was factored out)

6. Factor $5x^3 + 6x^2 + x$

Factoring out an x leaves $x(5x^2 + 6x + 1)$

Now factor as usual giving $x(5x + 1)(x + 1)$

To check

$(5x + 1)(x + 1)$
$+1x$
$+5x$
$+6x$

(the middle term after x was factored out)

7. Factor $5 + 7b + 2b^2$ (a slight twist)

$(5 + 2b)(1 + b)$

To check $(5 + 2b)(1 + b)$
$+2b$
$+5b$
$+7b$ (the middle term)

Note that $(5 + b)(1 + 2b)$ is incorrect because it gives the wrong middle term.

8. Factor $x^2 + 2xy + y^2$

   $(x + y)(x + y)$

To check

$$+xy$$
$$\underline{+xy}$$
$$+2xy \qquad \text{(the middle term)}$$

Note: there are polynomials that are not factorable.

Practice: Factoring Polynomials Problems

Factor each of the following.

1. $x^2 + 8x + 15 =$
2. $x^2 + 2x - 24 =$
3. $r^3 + 14r^2 + 45r =$
4. $x^2 - 16x + 48 =$
5. $1 + 2x + x^2 =$
6. $c^2 - 2cd + d^2 =$
7. $3y^2 + 4yz + z^2 =$
8. $7a^2 - 20a - 3 =$

Answers: Factoring Polynomials Problems

1. $(x + 3)(x + 5)$
2. $(x + 6)(x - 4)$
3. $r(r + 9)(r + 5)$
4. $(x - 4)(x - 12)$
5. $(1 + x)(1 + x)$
6. $(c - d)(c - d)$
7. $(3y + z)(y + z)$
8. $(7a + 1)(a - 3)$

Solving Quadratic Equations

- A *quadratic equation* is an equation that could be written as $Ax^2 + Bx + C = 0$. To solve a quadratic equation
  - (a) Put all terms on one side of the equal sign, leaving zero on the other side.
  - (b) Factor.
  - (c) Set each factor equal to zero.
  - (d) Solve each of these equations.
  - (e) Check by inserting your answer in the original equation.

Examples:

1. Solve: $x^2 - 6x = 16$

Now, following the steps, $x^2 - 6x = 16$ becomes $x^2 - 6x - 16 = 0$.

Factor.

$$(x - 8)(x + 2) = 0$$

$x - 8 = 0$ *or*	$x + 2 = 0$
$x = 8$	$x = -2$

Then to check

$8^2 - 6(8) = 16$ *or*	$(-2)^2 - 6(-2) = 16$
$64 - 48 = 16$	$4 + 12 = 16$
$16 = 16$	$16 = 16$

Both values 8 and -2 are solutions to the original equation.

2. Solve: $y^2 = -6y - 5$

Setting all terms equal to zero

$$y^2 + 6y + 5 = 0$$

Factoring $(y + 5)(y + 1) = 0$

Setting each factor to 0

$y + 5 = 0$ *or*	$y + 1 = 0$
$y = -5$	$y = -1$

To check $(-5)^2 = -6(-5) - 5$ *or* $(-1)^2 = -6(-1) - 5$
$\qquad 25 = 30 - 5$ $\qquad 1 = 6 - 5$
$\qquad 25 = 25$ $\qquad 1 = 1$

A quadratic with a term missing is called an *incomplete quadratic*.

3. Solve: $x^2 - 16 = 0$

Factor. $(x + 4)(x - 4) = 0$
$\qquad x + 4 = 0$ *or* $x - 4 = 0$
$\qquad x = -4$ $\qquad x = 4$

To check $(-4)^2 - 16 = 0$ *or* $(4)^2 - 16 = 0$
$\qquad 16 - 16 = 0$ $\qquad 16 - 16 = 0$
$\qquad 0 = 0$ $\qquad 0 = 0$

4. Solve: $x^2 + 6x = 0$

Factor. $x(x + 6) = 0$
$\qquad x = 0$ *or* $x + 6 = 0$
$\qquad x = 0$ $\qquad x = -6$

To check $(0)^2 + 6(0) = 0$ or $(-6)^2 + 6(-6) = 0$
$\qquad 0 + 0 = 0$ $\qquad 36 + (-36) = 0$
$\qquad 0 = 0$ $\qquad 0 = 0$

5. Solve: $2x^2 + 2x - 1 = x^2 + 6x - 5$

First, simplify by putting all terms on one side and combining like terms.

$$
\begin{aligned}
2x^2 + 2x - 1 &= x^2 + 6x - 5 \\
-x^2 - 6x + 5 \quad &\quad -x^2 - 6x + 5 \\
\hline
x^2 - 4x + 4 &= 0
\end{aligned}
$$

Now factor. $\qquad$ $(x - 2)(x - 2) = 0$
$$x - 2 = 0$$
$$x = 2$$

To check $\qquad$ $2(2)^2 + 2(2) - 1 = (2)^2 + 6(2) - 5$
$$8 + 4 - 1 = 4 + 12 - 5$$
$$11 = 11$$

Practice: Solving Quadratic Equations Problems

Solve each of the following.

1. $x^2 + 7x = -10$
2. $y^2 - 18y = -45$
3. $x^2 - 25 = 0$

4. $3t^2 + 4t + 1 = 0$
5. $2b^2 - b = 0$
6. $3n^2 - 2n = -1 + 2n^2$

Answers: Solving Quadratic Equations Problems

1. $x^2 + 7x = -10$
$x^2 + 7x + 10 = 0$
$(x + 2)(x + 5) = 0$

$x + 2 = 0$ $\quad$ *or* $\quad$ $x + 5 = 0$
$x = -2$ $\qquad\qquad$ $x = -5$

2. $y^2 - 18y = -45$
$y^2 - 18y + 45 = 0$
$(y - 15)(y - 3) = 0$

$y - 15 = 0$ $\quad$ *or* $\quad$ $y - 3 = 0$
$y = 15$ $\qquad\qquad$ $y = 3$

3. $x^2 - 25 = 0$
$(x + 5)(x - 5) = 0$

$x + 5 = 0$ $\quad$ *or* $\quad$ $x - 5 = 0$
$x = -5$ $\qquad\qquad$ $x = 5$

4. $3t^2 + 4t + 1 = 0$
$(3t + 1)(t + 1) = 0$

$$3t + 1 = 0 \quad or \quad t + 1 = 0$$
$$3t = -1 \qquad\qquad t = -1$$
$$t = -\frac{1}{3} \qquad\qquad t = -1$$

5. $2b^2 - b = 0$
   $b(2b - 1) = 0$

   $b = 0 \quad or \quad 2b - 1 = 0$
   $b = 0 \qquad\qquad 2b = 1$
   $b = 0 \qquad\qquad b = \frac{1}{2}$

6. $\quad 3n^2 - 2n = -1 + 2n^2$
   $\quad \underline{-2n^2 \qquad\qquad -2n^2}$
   $\qquad n^2 - 2n = -1$

   $n^2 - 2n + 1 = 0$
   $(n - 1)(n - 1) = 0$
   $n - 1 = 0$
   $n = 1$

Algebraic Fractions

- *Algebraic fractions* are fractions using a variable in the numerator or denominator, such as $3/x$. Since division by 0 is impossible, variables in the denominator have certain restrictions. The denominator can *never* equal 0. Therefore in the fractions

$$\frac{5}{x} \quad \text{x cannot equal 0 } (x \neq 0)$$

$$\frac{2}{x - 3} \quad \text{x cannot equal 3 } (x \neq 3)$$

$$\frac{3}{a - b} \quad \begin{array}{l} a - b \text{ cannot equal 0 } (a - b \neq 0) \\ \text{so a cannot equal b } (a \neq b) \end{array}$$

$$\frac{4}{a^2b} \quad \begin{array}{l} a \text{ cannot equal 0 and b cannot equal 0} \\ (a \neq 0 \text{ and } b \neq 0) \end{array}$$

Be aware of these types of restrictions.

Operations with Algebraic Fractions

Reducing Algebraic Fractions

- To *reduce an algebraic fraction* to lowest terms, first factor the numerator and the denominator; then cancel (or divide out) common factors.

Examples:

1. Reduce $\dfrac{4x^3}{8x^2}$

$$\frac{\overset{1}{\cancel{4}}x^{\overset{1}{\cancel{3}}}}{\underset{2}{\cancel{8}}\cancel{x^2}} = \frac{1}{2}x$$

2. Reduce $\dfrac{3x - 3}{4x - 4}$

$$\frac{3x - 3}{4x - 4} = \frac{3(x - 1)}{4(x - 1)} = \frac{3(\cancel{x - 1})}{4(\cancel{x - 1})} = \frac{3}{4}$$

3. Reduce $\dfrac{x^2 + 2x + 1}{3x + 3}$

$$\frac{x^2 + 2x + 1}{3x + 3} = \frac{(x + 1)(x + 1)}{3(x + 1)} = \frac{(\cancel{x + 1})(x + 1)}{3(\cancel{x + 1})}$$

$$= \frac{x + 1}{3}$$

WARNING: Do *not* cancel through an addition or subtraction sign. For example:

$$\frac{x + 1}{x + 2} \neq \frac{\cancel{x} + 1}{\cancel{x} + 2} \neq \frac{1}{2}$$

or

$$\frac{x + 6}{6} \neq \frac{x + \cancel{6}}{\cancel{6}} \neq x$$

Practice: Reducing Algebraic Fractions Problems

Reduce each of the following.

1. $\dfrac{8a^2b}{12a^3b}$

2. $\dfrac{5xy^3}{10x^3y}$

3. $\dfrac{10x + 5}{8x + 4}$

4. $\dfrac{x^2 - y^2}{x + y}$

5. $\dfrac{a^2 + a}{2a^2 + 4a + 2}$

Answers: Reducing Algebraic Fractions Problems

1. $\dfrac{8a^2b}{12a^3b} = \dfrac{2\,\cancel{8}\cancel{a}^2\cancel{b}}{3\,\cancel{12}a^3\cancel{b}} = \dfrac{2}{3a}$

2. $\dfrac{5xy^3}{10x^3y} = \dfrac{1\,\cancel{5}\cancel{x}y^2}{2\,\cancel{10}x^2\cancel{y}} = \dfrac{1y^2}{2x^2}$ or $\dfrac{y^2}{2x^2}$

3. $\dfrac{10x + 5}{8x + 4} = \dfrac{5(2x + 1)}{4(2x + 1)} = \dfrac{5\cancel{(2x+1)}}{4\cancel{(2x+1)}} = \dfrac{5}{4}$ or $1\frac{1}{4}$

4. $\dfrac{x^2 - y^2}{x + y} = \dfrac{(x - y)(x + y)}{x + y} = \dfrac{(x - y)\cancel{(x+y)}}{\cancel{x+y}} = \dfrac{x - y}{1} = x - y$

5. $\dfrac{a^2 + a}{2a^2 + 4a + 2} = \dfrac{a(a + 1)}{2(a^2 + 2a + 1)} = \dfrac{a(a + 1)}{2(a + 1)(a + 1)} =$

$\dfrac{a\cancel{(a+1)}}{2(a + 1)\cancel{(a+1)}} = \dfrac{a}{2(a + 1)}$

Multiplying Algebraic Fractions

● To *multiply algebraic fractions,* first factor the numerator and denominators that are polynomials; then cancel where possible. Multiply the remaining numerators together and denominators together. (If you've canceled properly, your answer will be in reduced form.)

Examples:

1. $\dfrac{2x}{3} \cdot \dfrac{y}{5} = \dfrac{2x}{3} \cdot \dfrac{y}{5} = \dfrac{2xy}{15}$

2. $\dfrac{x^2}{3y} \cdot \dfrac{2y}{3x} = \dfrac{x^2}{3\cancel{y}} \cdot \dfrac{2\cancel{y}}{3\cancel{x}} = \dfrac{2x}{9}$

3. $\dfrac{x+1}{5y+10} \cdot \dfrac{y+2}{x^2+2x+1} = \dfrac{x+1}{5(y+2)} \cdot \dfrac{y+2}{(x+1)(x+1)} =$

$\dfrac{\cancel{x+1}}{5\cancel{(y+2)}} \cdot \dfrac{\cancel{y+2}}{\cancel{(x+1)}(x+1)} = \dfrac{1}{5(x+1)}$

Practice: Multiplying Algebraic Fractions Problems

1. $\dfrac{6x}{11} \cdot \dfrac{2}{5y} =$

2. $\dfrac{3a^2}{5b} \cdot \dfrac{2b}{9a} =$

3. $\dfrac{5}{x+1} \cdot \dfrac{3x+3}{6} =$

4. $\dfrac{x^2-4}{6} \cdot \dfrac{3y}{2x+4} =$

5. $\dfrac{x^2+4x+4}{x-3} \cdot \dfrac{5}{3x+6} =$

Answers: Multiplying Algebraic Fractions Problems

1. $\dfrac{6x}{11} \cdot \dfrac{2}{5y} = \dfrac{12x}{55y}$

2. $\dfrac{3a^2}{5b} \cdot \dfrac{2b}{9a} = \dfrac{\overset{1}{\cancel{3}}a^2}{5\cancel{b}} \cdot \dfrac{2\cancel{b}}{\underset{3}{\cancel{9}\cancel{a}}} = \dfrac{2a}{15}$

3. $\dfrac{5}{x+1} \cdot \dfrac{3x+3}{6} = \dfrac{5}{x+1} \cdot \dfrac{3(x+1)}{6} = \dfrac{5}{\cancel{x+1}} \cdot \dfrac{\overset{1}{\cancel{3}}\cancel{(x+1)}}{\underset{2}{\cancel{6}}}$

$= \dfrac{5}{2} = 2\tfrac{1}{2}$

4. $\dfrac{x^2 - 4}{6} \cdot \dfrac{3y}{2x + 4} = \dfrac{(x + 2)(x - 2)}{6} \cdot \dfrac{3y}{2(x + 2)} =$

$\dfrac{(\cancel{x + 2})(x - 2)}{\cancel{6}_2} \cdot \dfrac{\cancel{3}^1 y}{2(\cancel{x + 2})} = \dfrac{(x - 2)y}{4}$

5. $\dfrac{x^2 + 4x + 4}{x - 3} \cdot \dfrac{5}{3x + 6} = \dfrac{(x + 2)(x + 2)}{x - 3} \cdot \dfrac{5}{3(x + 2)} =$

$\dfrac{(x + 2)(\cancel{x + 2})}{x - 3} \cdot \dfrac{5}{3(\cancel{x + 2})} = \dfrac{5(x + 2)}{3(x - 3)}$

Dividing Algebraic Fractions

● To *divide algebraic fractions,* invert the fraction and multiply. Remember, you can cancel only after you invert.

Examples:

1. $\dfrac{3x^2}{5} \div \dfrac{2x}{y} = \dfrac{3x^2}{5} \cdot \dfrac{y}{2x} = \dfrac{3x\cancel{x}^1}{5} \cdot \dfrac{y}{2\cancel{x}} = \dfrac{3xy}{10}$

2. $\dfrac{4x - 8}{6} \div \dfrac{x - 2}{3} = \dfrac{4x - 8}{6} \cdot \dfrac{3}{x - 2} = \dfrac{4(x - 2)}{6} \cdot \dfrac{3}{x - 2} =$

$\dfrac{4(\cancel{x - 2})^1}{\cancel{6}_2} \cdot \dfrac{\cancel{3}^1}{\cancel{x - 2}_1} = \dfrac{4}{2} = 2$

Practice: Dividing Algebraic Fractions Problems

1. $\dfrac{8x^3}{15} \div \dfrac{6x^2}{3} =$ 3. $\dfrac{2x + 6}{5} \div \dfrac{x + 3}{10} =$

2. $\dfrac{y^2}{5} \div y^2 =$ 4. $\dfrac{x^2}{x^2 + 5x + 6} \div \dfrac{x}{x + 3} =$

Answers: Dividing Algebraic Fractions Problems

1. $\dfrac{8x^3}{15} \div \dfrac{6x^2}{3} = \dfrac{8x^3}{15} \cdot \dfrac{3}{6x^2} = \dfrac{\cancel{8}^4 x^{\cancel{3}1}}{\cancel{15}_5} \cdot \dfrac{\cancel{3}^1}{\cancel{6x^2}_3} = \dfrac{4x}{15}$

2. $\dfrac{y^2}{5} \div y^2 = \dfrac{y^2}{5} \div \dfrac{y^2}{1} = \dfrac{y^2}{5} \cdot \dfrac{1}{y^2} = \dfrac{\cancel{y^2}}{5} \cdot \dfrac{1}{\cancel{y^2}} = \dfrac{1}{5}$

3. $\dfrac{2x + 6}{5} \div \dfrac{x + 3}{10} = \dfrac{2x + 6}{5} \cdot \dfrac{10}{x + 3} = \dfrac{2(x + 3)}{5} \cdot \dfrac{10}{x + 3} =$

$\dfrac{2(\cancel{x + 3})}{\cancel{5}_1} \cdot \dfrac{\cancel{10}^2}{\cancel{x + 3}} = \dfrac{4}{1} = 4$

4. $\dfrac{x^2}{x^2 + 5x + 6} \div \dfrac{x}{x + 3} = \dfrac{x^2}{x^2 + 5x + 6} \cdot \dfrac{x + 3}{x} =$

$\dfrac{x^2}{(x + 3)(x + 2)} \cdot \dfrac{x + 3}{x} = \dfrac{x^{\cancel{2}^1}}{(\cancel{x + 3})(x + 2)} \cdot \dfrac{\cancel{x + 3}}{\cancel{x}} = \dfrac{x}{x + 2}$

Adding or Subtracting Algebraic Fractions

● To *add or subtract albegraic fractions having a common denomi-nator,* simply keep the denominator and combine (add or subtract) the numerators. Reduce if necessary.

Examples:

1. $\dfrac{4}{x} + \dfrac{5}{x} = \dfrac{4 + 5}{x} = \dfrac{9}{x}$

2. $\dfrac{x - 4}{x + 1} + \dfrac{3}{x + 1} = \dfrac{x - 4 + 3}{x + 1} = \dfrac{x - 1}{x + 1}$

3. $\dfrac{3x}{y} - \dfrac{2x - 1}{y} = \dfrac{3x - (2x - 1)}{y} = \dfrac{3x - 2x + 1}{y} = \dfrac{x + 1}{y}$

Practice: Adding or Subtracting Algebraic Fractions Problems

1. $\dfrac{3}{x} + \dfrac{2}{x} =$ 3. $\dfrac{4x - 3}{x} - \dfrac{3x - 3}{x} =$

2. $\dfrac{x - 1}{y} + \dfrac{3x + 2}{y} =$ 4. $\dfrac{6x - 3}{x - 4} - \dfrac{x + 2}{x - 4} =$

Answers: Adding or Subtracting Algebraic Fractions Problems

1. $\dfrac{3}{x} + \dfrac{2}{x} = \dfrac{3 + 2}{x} = \dfrac{5}{x}$

2. $\dfrac{x - 1}{y} + \dfrac{3x + 2}{y} = \dfrac{x - 1 + 3x + 2}{y} = \dfrac{4x + 1}{y}$

3. $\dfrac{4x - 3}{x} - \dfrac{3x - 3}{x} = \dfrac{4x - 3 - (3x - 3)}{x} = \dfrac{4x - 3 - 3x + 3}{x} =$

   $\dfrac{x}{x} = 1$

4. $\dfrac{6x - 3}{x - 4} - \dfrac{x + 2}{x - 4} = \dfrac{6x - 3 - (x + 2)}{x - 4} = \dfrac{6x - 3 - x - 2}{x - 4} =$

   $\dfrac{5x - 5}{x - 4}$ or $\dfrac{5(x - 1)}{x - 4}$

- To *add or subtract algebraic fractions having different denominators,* first find a lowest common denominator (LCD), change each fraction to an equivalent fraction with the common denominator, then combine each numerator. Reduce if necessary.

Examples:

1. $\dfrac{2}{x} + \dfrac{3}{y} =$

   LCD = xy

   $\dfrac{2}{x} \cdot \dfrac{y}{y} + \dfrac{3}{y} \cdot \dfrac{x}{x} = \dfrac{2y}{xy} + \dfrac{3x}{xy} = \dfrac{2y + 3x}{xy}$

2. $\dfrac{x + 2}{3x} + \dfrac{x - 3}{6x} =$

   LCD = 6x

   $\dfrac{x + 2}{3x} \cdot \dfrac{2}{2} + \dfrac{x - 3}{6x} = \dfrac{2x + 4}{6x} + \dfrac{x - 3}{6x} = \dfrac{2x + 4 + x - 3}{6x} = \dfrac{3x + 1}{6x}$

If there is a common variable factor with more than one exponent, use its greatest exponent.

3. $\dfrac{2}{y^2} - \dfrac{3}{y} =$

LCD $= y^2$

$$\dfrac{2}{y^2} - \dfrac{3}{y} \cdot \dfrac{y}{y} = \dfrac{2}{y^2} - \dfrac{3y}{y^2} = \dfrac{2 - 3y}{y^2}$$

4. $\dfrac{4}{x^3y} + \dfrac{3}{xy^2} =$

LCD $= x^3y^2$

$$\dfrac{4}{x^3y} \cdot \dfrac{y}{y} + \dfrac{3}{xy^2} \cdot \dfrac{x^2}{x^2} = \dfrac{4y}{x^3y^2} + \dfrac{3x^2}{x^3y^2} = \dfrac{4y + 3x^2}{x^3y^2}$$

5. $\dfrac{x}{x + 1} - \dfrac{2x}{x + 2} =$

LCD $= (x + 1)(x + 2)$

$$\dfrac{x}{x + 1} \cdot \dfrac{(x + 2)}{(x + 2)} - \dfrac{2x}{x + 2} \cdot \dfrac{(x + 1)}{(x + 1)} =$$

$$\dfrac{x^2 + 2x}{(x + 1)(x + 2)} - \dfrac{2x^2 + 2x}{(x + 1)(x + 2)} =$$

$$\dfrac{x^2 + 2x - 2x^2 - 2x}{(x + 1)(x + 2)} = \dfrac{-x^2}{(x + 1)(x + 2)}$$

To find the lowest common denominator, it is often necessary to factor the denominators and proceed as follows.

6. $\dfrac{2x}{x^2 - 9} - \dfrac{5}{x^2 + 4x + 3} = \dfrac{2x}{(x + 3)(x - 3)} - \dfrac{5}{(x + 3)(x + 1)} =$

LCD $= (x + 3)(x - 3)(x + 1)$

$$\dfrac{2x}{(x + 3)(x - 3)} \cdot \dfrac{(x + 1)}{(x + 1)} - \dfrac{5}{(x + 3)(x + 1)} \cdot \dfrac{(x - 3)}{(x - 3)} =$$

$$\frac{2x^2 + 2x}{(x + 3)(x - 3)(x + 1)} - \frac{5x - 15}{(x + 3)(x - 3)(x + 1)} =$$

$$\frac{2x^2 + 2x - (5x - 15)}{(x + 3)(x - 3)(x + 1)} = \frac{2x^2 + 2x - 5x + 15}{(x + 3)(x - 3)(x + 1)} =$$

$$\frac{2x^2 - 3x + 15}{(x + 3)(x - 3)(x + 1)}$$

Practice: Adding or Subtracting Algebraic Fractions Problems

1. $\dfrac{5}{x} + \dfrac{2}{y} =$

2. $\dfrac{x}{4} - \dfrac{y}{3} =$

3. $\dfrac{y + 5}{2y} + \dfrac{y - 2}{8y} =$

4. $\dfrac{7}{x} + \dfrac{3}{x^3} =$

5. $\dfrac{3x}{x^2y} + \dfrac{2x}{xy^2} =$

6. $\dfrac{x}{3x + 3} + \dfrac{2x}{x + 1} =$

7. $\dfrac{3}{x^2 - 4} - \dfrac{2x}{x^2 + 4x + 4} =$

8. $\dfrac{1}{x} + \dfrac{1}{y} + \dfrac{1}{z} =$

Answers: Adding or Subtracting Algebraic Fractions Problems

1. $\dfrac{5}{x} + \dfrac{2}{y} =$

LCD = xy

$$\frac{5}{x} \cdot \frac{y}{y} + \frac{2}{y} \cdot \frac{x}{x} = \frac{5y}{xy} + \frac{2x}{xy} = \frac{5y + 2x}{xy}$$

2. $\dfrac{x}{4} - \dfrac{y}{3} =$

LCD = 12

$$\frac{x}{4} \cdot \frac{3}{3} - \frac{y}{3} \cdot \frac{4}{4} = \frac{3x}{12} - \frac{4y}{12} = \frac{3x - 4y}{12}$$

3. $\dfrac{y + 5}{2y} + \dfrac{y - 2}{8y} =$

LCD = 8y

$\dfrac{y + 5}{2y} \cdot \dfrac{4}{4} + \dfrac{y - 2}{8y} = \dfrac{4y + 20}{8y} + \dfrac{y - 2}{8y} =$

$\dfrac{4y + 20 + y - 2}{8y} = \dfrac{5y + 18}{8y}$

4. $\dfrac{7}{x} + \dfrac{3}{x^3} =$

LCD = x^3

$\dfrac{7}{x} \cdot \dfrac{x^2}{x^2} + \dfrac{3}{x^3} = \dfrac{7x^2}{x^3} + \dfrac{3}{x^3} = \dfrac{7x^2 + 3}{x^3}$

5. $\dfrac{3x}{x^2y} + \dfrac{2x}{xy^2} =$

LCD = x^2y^2

$\dfrac{3x}{x^2y} \cdot \dfrac{y}{y} + \dfrac{2x}{xy^2} \cdot \dfrac{x}{x} = \dfrac{3xy}{x^2y^2} + \dfrac{2x^2}{x^2y^2} = \dfrac{3xy + 2x^2}{x^2y^2}$

6. $\dfrac{x}{3x + 3} + \dfrac{2x}{x + 1} = \dfrac{x}{3(x + 1)} + \dfrac{2x}{x + 1}$

LCD = 3(x + 1)

$\dfrac{x}{3(x + 1)} + \dfrac{2x}{x + 1} \cdot \dfrac{3}{3} = \dfrac{x}{3(x + 1)} + \dfrac{6x}{3(x + 1)} =$

$\dfrac{x + 6x}{3(x + 1)} = \dfrac{7x}{3(x + 1)}$

7. $\dfrac{3}{x^2 - 4} - \dfrac{2x}{x^2 + 4x + 4} = \dfrac{3}{(x + 2)(x - 2)} - \dfrac{2x}{(x + 2)(x + 2)}$

LCD = (x + 2)(x - 2)(x + 2)

$$\frac{3}{(x + 2)(x - 2)} \cdot \frac{(x + 2)}{(x + 2)} - \frac{2x}{(x + 2)(x + 2)} \cdot \frac{(x - 2)}{(x - 2)} =$$

$$\frac{3x + 6}{(x + 2)(x - 2)(x + 2)} - \frac{2x^2 - 4x}{(x + 2)(x + 2)(x - 2)} =$$

$$\frac{3x + 6 - (2x^2 - 4x)}{(x + 2)(x - 2)(x + 2)} = \frac{3x + 6 - 2x^2 + 4x}{(x + 2)(x - 2)(x + 2)} =$$

$$\frac{-2x^2 + 7x + 6}{(x + 2)(x - 2)(x + 2)}$$

8. $\dfrac{1}{x} + \dfrac{1}{y} + \dfrac{1}{z} =$

LCD = xyz

$$\frac{1}{x} \cdot \frac{yz}{yz} + \frac{1}{y} \cdot \frac{xz}{xz} + \frac{1}{z} \cdot \frac{xy}{xy} = \frac{yz}{xyz} + \frac{xz}{xyz} + \frac{xy}{xyz} = \frac{yz + xz + xy}{xyz}$$

Inequalities

● An *inequality* is a statement in which the relationships are not equal. Instead of using an equal sign (=) as in an equation, we use > (greater than) and < (less than), or ≥ (greater than or equal to) and ≤ (less than or equal to).

Solving Inequalities

● When working with inequalities, treat them exactly like equations (*except,* if you multiply or divide both sides by a negative number, you must *reverse* the direction of the sign).

Examples:

1. Solve for x: $2x + 4 > 6$

$$
\begin{array}{r}
2x + 4 > 6 \\
-4 - 4 \\
\hline
2x \quad\ \ > 2
\end{array}
$$

$$\frac{2x}{2} > \frac{2}{2} \qquad x > 1$$

Answers are sometimes written in set builder notation $\{x: x > 1\}$ which is read "all x such that x is greater than 1."

2. Solve for x: $-7x > 14$ (divide by -7 and reverse the sign)

$$\frac{-7x}{-7} < \frac{14}{-7}$$

$x < -2$

3. Solve for x: $3x + 2 \geq 5x - 10$

$$\begin{array}{r} 3x + 2 \geq \quad 5x - 10 \\ - 2 \qquad\quad - 2 \\ \hline 3x \quad\ \geq \quad 5x - 12 \end{array}$$

$$\begin{array}{r} 3x \quad \geq \quad 5x - 12 \\ -5x \qquad\quad -5x \\ \hline -2x \quad \geq \qquad -12 \end{array}$$

Notice opposite operations are used. Divide both sides by -2 and reverse the sign.

$$\frac{-2x}{-2} \leq \frac{-12}{-2} \qquad\qquad x \leq 6$$

In set builder notation: $\{x: x \leq 6\}$

Practice: Solving Inequalities Problems

Solve each of the following for x.

1. $7x + 4 > 32$ 3. $3 - 2x > 7$
                                    4. $5x + 6 > 2x + 21$
2. $\frac{2}{3}x + 5 \leq 17$

Answers: Solving Inequalities Problems

1. $$\begin{array}{r} 7x + 4 > 3\,2 \\ - 4 \quad -4 \\ \hline 7x \quad\ > 2\,8 \end{array}$$

$$\frac{7x}{7} > \frac{28}{7}$$

$x > 4$ or $\{x: x > 4\}$

2. $$\begin{array}{r} \frac{2}{3}x + 5 \leq 17 \\ - 5 - 5 \\ \hline \frac{2}{3}x \quad\ \leq 12 \end{array}$$

$$\frac{3}{2} \cdot \frac{2}{3}x \leq \frac{\cancel{12}^{6}}{1} \cdot \frac{3}{\cancel{2}}$$

$x \leq 18$ or $\{x: x \leq 18\}$

3. $3 - 2x > 7$

$$\frac{\begin{array}{r} -3 \qquad -3 \\ \hline -2x > 4 \end{array}}{}$$

$$\frac{-2x}{-2} < \frac{4}{-2}$$

$x < -2$ or $\{x: x < -2\}$

4. $5x + 6 > 2x + 21$

$$\frac{\begin{array}{r} -2x - 6 \quad -2x - 6 \\ \hline 3x \quad > \qquad 15 \end{array}}{}$$

$$\frac{3x}{3} > \frac{15}{3}$$

$x > 5$ or $\{x: x > 5\}$

Graphing on a Number Line

- Integers and real numbers can be represented on a *number line*. The point on this line associated with each number is called the graph of the number. Notice that number lines are spaced equally or proportionately.

Graphing Inequalities

Examples:

When graphing inequalities involving only integers, dots are used.
1. Graph the set of x such that $1 \le x \le 4$ and x is an integer.
   $\{x: 1 \le x \le 4, x \text{ is an integer}\}$

When graphing inequalities involving real numbers, lines, rays, and dots are used. A *dot* is used if the number is included. A *hollow dot* is used if the number is not included.

2. Graph the set of x such that $x \ge 1$. $\{x: x \ge 1\}$

3. Graph the set of x such that $x > 1$. $\{x: x > 1\}$

4. Graph the set of x such that x < 4.   {x: x < 4}

This ray is often called an *open ray* or a *half line*. The hollow dot distinguishes an open ray from a ray.

Intervals

● An *interval* consists of all the numbers that lie within two certain boundaries. If the two boundaries, or fixed numbers, are included, then the interval is called a *closed interval*. If the fixed numbers are not included, then the interval is called an *open interval*.

Closed interval   {x: $-1 \le x \le 2$}

Open interval   {x: $-1 < x < 2$}

If the interval includes only one of the boundaries, then it is called a *half-open interval*.

Half-open interval   {x: $-1 < x \le 2$}

Practice: Graphing Inequalities Problems

Graph each of the following.

1. {x: $2 \le x \le 6$, x is an integer}   4. {x: $x < 3$}
2. {x: $-3 < x < 5$, x is an integer}   5. {x: $x \le -1$}
3. {x: $x \ge -2$}

Answers: Graphing Inequalities Problems

1.

2.

3.

4.

5.

Absolute Value

- The numerical value when direction or sign is not considered is called the *absolute value*. The absolute value of x is written |x|. The absolute value of a number is always positive except when the number is 0.

$$|0| = 0 \qquad |x| > 0 \qquad |-x| > 0$$

Examples:

1. $|4| = 4$
2. $|-6| = 6$
3. $|7 - 9| = |-2| = 2$
4. $3 - |-6| = 3 - 6 = -3$ (note that absolute value is taken first)

Practice: Absolute Value Problems

1. $|-9| =$
2. $|6| =$
3. $|-3 + 2| =$
4. $|-6 - 6| =$

5. $|4 - 8| =$
6. $|-5| + 3 =$
7. $9 + |-5| =$
8. $6 - |-8| =$

Answers: Absolute Value Problems

1. 9
2. 6
3. $|-3 + 2| = |-1| = 1$
4. $|-6 - 6| = |-12| = 12$

5. $|4 - 8| = |-4| = 4$
6. $|-5| + 3 = 5 + 3 = 8$
7. $9 + |-5| = 9 + 5 = 14$
8. $6 - |-8| = 6 - 8 = -2$

Analytic Geometry

Coordinate Graphs

- Each point on a number line is assigned a number. In the same way, each point in a plane is assigned a pair of numbers. These numbers represent the placement of the point relative to two intersecting lines. In *coordinate graphs,* two perpendicular number lines are used and are called *coordinate axes.* One axis is horizontal and is called the *x axis.* The other is vertical and is called the *y axis.* The point of intersection of the two number lines is called the *origin* and is represented by the coordinates (0, 0).

Each point on a plane is located by a unique ordered pair of numbers called the coordinates. Some coordinates are noted below.

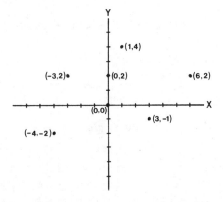

Notice that on the x-axis, numbers to the right of 0 are positive and to the left of 0 are negative. On the y-axis, numbers above 0 are positive and below 0 are negative. Also, note that the first number in the ordered pair is called the *x-coordinate,* or *abscissa,* while the second number is the *y-coordinate,* or *ordinate.* The x-coordinate shows the right or left direction, and the y coordinate shows the up or down direction.

The coordinate graph is divided into four quarters called *quadrants*. These quadrants are labeled below.

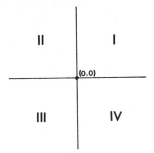

Notice that
In quadrant I, x is always positive and y is always positive.
In quadrant II, x is always negative and y is always positive.
In quadrant III, x and y are both always negative.
In quadrant IV, x is always positive and y is always negative.

Practice: Coordinate Graph Problems

Identify the points (A, B, C, D, E, and F) on the coordinate graph below.

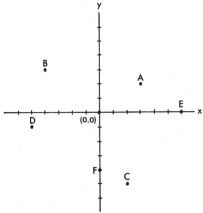

Answers: Coordinate Graph Problems

A. (3, 2)   D. (−5, −1)
B. (−4, 3)   E. (6, 0)
C. (2, −5)   F. (0, −4)

Graphing Equations on the Coordinate Plane

● To *graph an equation on the coordinate plane,* find the solutions by giving a value to one variable and solving the resulting equation for the other value. Repeat this process to find other solutions. (When giving a value for one variable, start with 0, then try 1, etc.) Then graph the solutions.

Examples:

1. Graph the equation $x + y = 6$.

If x is 0, then y is 6.

$$(0) + y = 6$$
$$y = 6$$

If x is 1, then y is 5.

$$\begin{array}{r} (1) + y = 6 \\ -1 \qquad -1 \\ \hline y = 5 \end{array}$$

If x is 2, then y is 4.

$$\begin{array}{r} (2) + y = 6 \\ -2 \qquad -2 \\ \hline y = 4 \end{array}$$

Using a simple chart is helpful.

x	y
0	6
1	5
2	4

Now plot these coordinates.

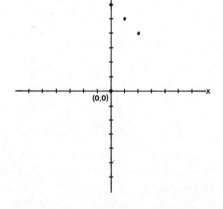

Notice that these solutions, when plotted, form a straight line. Equations whose solution sets form a straight line are called *linear equations*. Equations that have a variable raised to a power, show division by a variable, involve variables with square roots, or have variables multiplied together will not form a straight line when their solutions are graphed. These are called *nonlinear equations*.

2. Graph the equation $y = x^2 + 4$.

If x is 0, then y is 4.

$$y = (0)^2 + 4$$
$$y = 0 + 4$$
$$y = 4$$

If x is 1, then y is 5.

$$y = (1)^2 + 4$$
$$y = 1 + 4$$
$$y = 5$$

If x is 2, then y is 8.

$$y = (2)^2 + 4$$
$$y = 4 + 4$$
$$y = 8$$

Use a simple chart.

x	y
0	4
1	5
2	8

Now plot these coordinates.

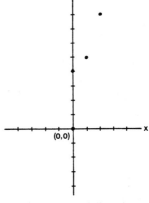

Notice that these solutions, when plotted, give a curved line (nonlinear). The more points plotted, the easier it is to see and describe the solution set.

Practice: Graphing Equations on the Coordinate Plane Problems

State whether the equations are linear or nonlinear in problems 1–6.

1. $x - 5 = 5$
2. $x + 5 = y$
3. $x^2 + y = 3$
4. $xy = 0$
5. $x + \frac{5}{y} = 0$
6. $y = x + 7$

Graph each of the equations in problems 7–14.

7. $x - y = 3$
8. $y = x + 2$
9. $y = x^2 + 1$
10. $3x + y = 12$
11. $x + 4 = y + 2x - 3$
12. $y = 4$

Answers: Graphing Equations on the Coordinate Plane Problems

1. linear
2. linear
3. nonlinear
4. nonlinear
5. nonlinear
6. linear

7. $x - y = 3$

x	y
3	0
4	1
5	2

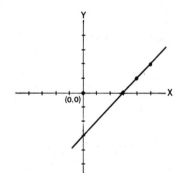

8. $y = x + 2$

x	y
0	2
1	3
2	4

9. $y = x^2 + 1$

$x = 0$	$x = 1$	$x = 2$
$y = (0)^2 + 1$	$y = (1)^2 + 1$	$y = (2)^2 + 1$
$y = 0 + 1$	$y = 1 + 1$	$y = 4 + 1$
$y = 1$	$y = 2$	$y = 5$

$x = -1$	$x = -2$
$y = (-1)^2 + 1$	$y = (-2)^2 + 1$
$y = 1 + 1$	$y = 4 + 1$
$y = 2$	$y = 5$

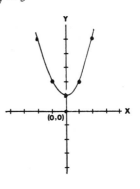

x	y
0	1
1	2
2	5
−1	2
−2	5

10. $3x + y = 12$

$x = 0$	$x = 1$
$3(0) + y = 12$	$3(1) + y = 12$
$0 + y = 12$	$3 + y = 12$
$y = 12$	$\underline{-3 \qquad -3}$
	$y = \quad 9$

$x = 2$
$3(2) + y = 12$
$6 + y = 12$
$\underline{-6 \qquad -6}$
$y = \quad 6$

x	y
0	12
1	9
2	6

11. $x + 4 = y + 2x - 3$

First simplify by combining like terms.

$$
\begin{array}{rcl}
x + 4 &=& y + 2x - 3 \\
-2x & & \quad\quad -2x \\
\hline
-x + 4 &=& y \quad\quad -3 \\
+3 & & \quad\quad +3 \\
\hline
-x + 7 &=& y
\end{array}
$$
or $7 = x + y$

x	y
0	7
1	6
2	5

12. $y = 4$

x	y
0	4
1	4
2	4

Roots and Radicals

Note: This subject is introduced in the Arithmetic Review.

- The symbol $\sqrt{}$ is called a *radical sign* and is used to designate *square root*. To designate *cube root*, a small three is placed above the radical sign, $\sqrt[3]{}$. When two radical signs are next to each other, they automatically mean that the two are multiplied. The multiplication sign may be omitted. Note that the square root of a negative number is not possible within the real number system. A completely different system of imaginary numbers is used. The typical standardized exams use only the real number system as general practice. The (so-called) imaginary numbers are multiples of the imaginary unit i. $\sqrt{-1} = i$, $\sqrt{-4} = 2i$, $\sqrt{-9} = 3i$, etc. The ACT and some college placement exams do deal with simple imaginary numbers and their operations.

Simplifying Square Roots

Examples:

1. $\sqrt{9} = 3$ ⎱ Reminder: this notation is used on most standardized exams and will

2. $-\sqrt{9} = -3$ ⎰ be adhered to in this book.

3. $\sqrt{18} = \sqrt{9 \cdot 2} = \sqrt{9} \cdot \sqrt{2} = 3\sqrt{2}$

4. If each variable is nonnegative (not a negative number), $\sqrt{x^2} = x$

5. If each variable is nonnegative, $\sqrt{x^4} = x^2$

6. If each variable is nonnegative, $\sqrt{x^6 y^8} = \sqrt{x^6} \sqrt{y^8} = x^3 y^4$

7. If each variable is nonnegative, $\sqrt{25a^4 b^6} = \sqrt{25} \sqrt{a^4} \sqrt{b^6} = 5a^2 b^3$

8. If each variable is nonnegative, $\sqrt{x^7} = \sqrt{x^6(x)} = \sqrt{x^6} \sqrt{x} = x^3 \sqrt{x}$

9. If each variable is nonnegative, $\sqrt{x^9 y^8} = \sqrt{x^9} \sqrt{y^8} = \sqrt{x^8(x)} \sqrt{y^8} = x^4 \sqrt{x} \cdot y^4 = x^4 y^4 \sqrt{x}$

10. If each variable is nonnegative, $\sqrt{16x^5} = \sqrt{16} \sqrt{x^5} = \sqrt{16} \sqrt{x^4(x)} = 4x^2 \sqrt{x}$

Practice: Simplifying Square Root Problems

Simplify each of the following. All variables are nonnegative.

1. $\sqrt{36} =$

2. $-\sqrt{49} =$

3. $\sqrt{121} =$

4. $\sqrt{50} =$

5. $\sqrt{72} =$

6. $\sqrt{y^6} =$

7. $\sqrt{x^6 y^{10}} =$

8. $\sqrt{36a^2 b^8} =$

9. $\sqrt{a^9} =$

10. $\sqrt{49a^5 b^4} =$

Answers: Simplifying Square Root Problems

1. 6

2. -7

3. 11

4. $\sqrt{50} = \sqrt{25 \cdot 2} = \sqrt{25} \cdot \sqrt{2} = 5\sqrt{2}$

5. $\sqrt{72} = \sqrt{36 \cdot 2} = \sqrt{36}\,\sqrt{2} = 6\sqrt{2}$

6. y^3

7. $\sqrt{x^6 y^{10}} = \sqrt{x^6}\,\sqrt{y^{10}} = x^3 y^5$

8. $\sqrt{36a^2 b^8} = \sqrt{36}\,\sqrt{a^2}\,\sqrt{b^8} = 6ab^4$

9. $\sqrt{a^9} = \sqrt{a^8(a)} = a^4\sqrt{a}$

10. $\sqrt{49a^5 b^4} = \sqrt{49}\,\sqrt{a^5}\,\sqrt{b^4} = \sqrt{49}\,\sqrt{a^4(a)}\,\sqrt{b^4} = 7a^2\sqrt{a}\,(b^2) = 7a^2 b^2 \sqrt{a}$

Operations with Square Roots

- You may perform *operations under a single radical sign.*

Examples:

1. $\sqrt{(5)(20)} = \sqrt{100} = 10$

2. $\sqrt{30 + 6} = \sqrt{36} = 6$

3. $\sqrt{\dfrac{32}{2}} = \sqrt{16} = 4 \left(\text{Note: } \sqrt{\dfrac{32}{2}} = \dfrac{\sqrt{32}}{\sqrt{2}} \right)$

4. $\sqrt{30 - 5} = \sqrt{25} = 5$

5. $\sqrt{2 + 5} = \sqrt{7}$

- You can *add or subtract square roots themselves only if the values under the radical sign are equal.* Then simply add or subtract the coefficients (numbers in front of the radical sign) and keep the original number in the radical sign.

Examples:

1. $2\sqrt{3} + 3\sqrt{3} = (2 + 3)\sqrt{3} = 5\sqrt{3}$

2. $4\sqrt{6} - 2\sqrt{6} = (4 - 2)\sqrt{6} = 2\sqrt{6}$

3. $5\sqrt{2} + \sqrt{2} = 5\sqrt{2} + 1\sqrt{2} = (5 + 1)\sqrt{2} = 6\sqrt{2}$

Note that 1 is understood in $\sqrt{2}$. $(1\sqrt{2})$

● You *may not add or subtract different square roots.*

Examples:

1. $\sqrt{28} - \sqrt{3} \neq \sqrt{25}$
2. $\sqrt{16} + \sqrt{9} \neq \sqrt{25}$

Practice: Operations under the Radical and Adding and Subtracting Square Roots Problems

1. $\sqrt{(18)(2)} =$

2. $\sqrt{\dfrac{200}{8}} =$

3. $\sqrt{17 + 32} =$

4. $\sqrt{31 - 16} =$

5. $4\sqrt{3} + 2\sqrt{3} =$

6. $12\sqrt{7} - 6\sqrt{7} =$

7. $8\sqrt{11} - \sqrt{11} =$

8. $3\sqrt{5} - 7\sqrt{5} =$

Answers: Operations under the Radical and Adding and Subtracting Square Roots Problems

1. $\sqrt{(18)(2)} = \sqrt{36} = 6$

2. $\sqrt{\dfrac{200}{8}} = \sqrt{25} = 5$

3. $\sqrt{17 + 32} = \sqrt{49} = 7$

4. $\sqrt{31 - 16} = \sqrt{15}$

5. $6\sqrt{3}$

6. $6\sqrt{7}$

7. $7\sqrt{11}$ derived from $8\sqrt{11} - 1\sqrt{11}$

8. $-4\sqrt{5}$ derived from $3\sqrt{5} - 7\sqrt{5} = (3 - 7)\sqrt{5} = -4\sqrt{5}$

Addition and Subtraction of Square Roots after Simplifying

● Sometimes after *simplifying the square root(s), addition or subtraction becomes possible.* Always simplify if possible.

Examples:

1. $\sqrt{50} + 3\sqrt{2} =$

These cannot be added until $\sqrt{50}$ is simplified.

$$\sqrt{50} = \sqrt{25 \cdot 2} = \sqrt{25} \cdot \sqrt{2} = 5\sqrt{2}$$

Now, since both are alike under the radical sign

$$5\sqrt{2} + 3\sqrt{2} = (5 + 3)\sqrt{2} = 8\sqrt{2}$$

2. $\sqrt{300} + \sqrt{12} =$

Try to simplify each one.

$$\sqrt{300} = \sqrt{100 \cdot 3} = \sqrt{100} \cdot \sqrt{3} = 10\sqrt{3}$$
$$\sqrt{12} = \sqrt{4 \cdot 3} = \sqrt{4} \cdot \sqrt{3} = 2\sqrt{3}$$

Now, since both are alike under the radical sign

$$10\sqrt{3} + 2\sqrt{3} = (10 + 2)\sqrt{3} = 12\sqrt{3}$$

Practice: Addition and Subtraction of Square Roots after Simplifying Problems

1. $4\sqrt{5} - \sqrt{20} =$ 3. $9\sqrt{7} - \sqrt{28} =$

2. $\sqrt{18} + \sqrt{32} =$ 4. $\sqrt{40} + \sqrt{27} =$

Answers: Addition and Subtraction of Square Roots after Simplifying Problems

1. $4\sqrt{5} - \sqrt{20} =$

   $(\sqrt{20} = \sqrt{4 \cdot 5} = \sqrt{4} \cdot \sqrt{5} = \underline{2\sqrt{5}})$

   $4\sqrt{5} - 2\sqrt{5} = 2\sqrt{5}$

2. $\sqrt{18} + \sqrt{32} =$

   $(\sqrt{18} = \sqrt{9 \cdot 2} = \sqrt{9} \cdot \sqrt{2} = \underline{3\sqrt{2}})$

   $(\sqrt{32} = \sqrt{16 \cdot 2} = \sqrt{16} \cdot \sqrt{2} = \underline{4\sqrt{2}})$

   $3\sqrt{2} + 4\sqrt{2} = 7\sqrt{2}$

3. $9\sqrt{7} - \sqrt{28} =$

$(\sqrt{28} = \sqrt{4 \cdot 7} = \sqrt{4} \cdot \sqrt{7} = \underline{2\sqrt{7}})$

$9\sqrt{7} - 2\sqrt{7} = 7\sqrt{7}$

4. $\sqrt{40} + \sqrt{27} =$

$(\sqrt{40} = \sqrt{4 \cdot 10} = \sqrt{4} \cdot \sqrt{10} = \underline{2\sqrt{10}})$

$(\sqrt{27} = \sqrt{9 \cdot 3} = \sqrt{9} \cdot \sqrt{3} = \underline{3\sqrt{3}})$

$2\sqrt{10} + 3\sqrt{3}$ cannot be added

Products of Nonnegative Roots

Remember that in multiplication of roots, the multiplication sign may be omitted. Always simplify the answer when possible.

Examples:

1. $\sqrt{2} \cdot \sqrt{8} = \sqrt{16} = 4$

2. If each variable is nonnegative,

$\sqrt{x^3} \cdot \sqrt{x^5} = \sqrt{x^8} = x^4$

3. If each variable is nonnegative.

$\sqrt{ab} \cdot \sqrt{ab^3c} = \sqrt{a^2b^4c} = \sqrt{a^2}\sqrt{b^4}\sqrt{c} = ab^2\sqrt{c}$

4. If each variable is nonnegative,

$\sqrt{3x} \cdot \sqrt{6xy^2} \cdot \sqrt{2xy} = \sqrt{36x^3y^3} = \sqrt{36}\sqrt{x^3}\sqrt{y^3} =$
$\sqrt{36}\sqrt{x^2(x)}\sqrt{y^2(y)} = 6xy\sqrt{xy}$

5. $2\sqrt{5} \cdot 7\sqrt{3} = (2 \cdot 7)\sqrt{5 \cdot 3} = 14\sqrt{15}$

Practice: Products of Nonnegative Roots Problems

In the following, all variables are nonnegative.

1. $\sqrt{12} \cdot \sqrt{3} =$

2. $\sqrt{6} \cdot \sqrt{8} =$

3. $\sqrt{y^5} \cdot \sqrt{y^7} =$

4. $\sqrt{x^2y} \cdot \sqrt{xy^2} =$

5. $\sqrt{abc} \cdot \sqrt{bc} \cdot \sqrt{ac^2} =$

6. $\sqrt{5a^2} \cdot \sqrt{2ab} \cdot \sqrt{10b^2} =$

7. $3\sqrt{2} \cdot 2\sqrt{5} =$

8. $4\sqrt{2} \cdot 5\sqrt{8} =$

Answers: Products of Nonnegative Roots Problems

1. $\sqrt{12} \cdot \sqrt{3} = \sqrt{36} = 6$

2. $\sqrt{6} \cdot \sqrt{8} = \sqrt{48} = \sqrt{16 \cdot 3} = \sqrt{16} \cdot \sqrt{3} = 4\sqrt{3}$

3. $\sqrt{y^5} \cdot \sqrt{y^7} = \sqrt{y^{12}} = y^6$

4. $\sqrt{x^2 y} \cdot \sqrt{xy^2} = \sqrt{x^3 y^3} = \sqrt{x^2(x)y^2(y)} = xy\sqrt{xy}$

or

$\sqrt{x^2 y} \cdot \sqrt{xy^2} = x\sqrt{y} \cdot y\sqrt{x} = xy\sqrt{xy}$

5. $\sqrt{abc} \cdot \sqrt{bc} \cdot \sqrt{ac^2} = \sqrt{a^2 b^2 c^4} = abc^2$

6. $\sqrt{5a^2} \cdot \sqrt{2ab} \cdot \sqrt{10b^2} = \sqrt{100a^3 b^3} = \sqrt{100}\sqrt{a^3}\sqrt{b^3} =$
$\sqrt{100}\sqrt{a^2(a)}\sqrt{b^2(b)} = 10ab\sqrt{ab}$

7. $3\sqrt{2} \cdot 2\sqrt{5} = (3 \cdot 2)\sqrt{2 \cdot 5} = 6\sqrt{10}$

8. $4\sqrt{2} \cdot 5\sqrt{8} = (4 \cdot 5)\sqrt{2 \cdot 8} = 20\sqrt{16} = 20(4) = 80$

"False" Operations

- Many standardized exams include a question or two using operations created uniquely *for that particular problem*. The operation may be represented by unusual symbols (such as @ or * or #) and are then defined with standard operations of +, −, ×, ÷, etc. Don't let these new or different symbols alarm you.

1. If $x \odot y = \dfrac{x}{y}$ and $y \neq 0$, then what is $4 \odot 2$?

This operation shows that the first value is divided by the second value. Therefore,

$$4 \odot 2 = \frac{4}{2} = 2$$

The key to understanding these types of problems is simply understanding the definition of the operation—how to replace, or plug in, values. Notice that the definitions are given in terms of standard operations with which you are familiar.

2. If $x \$ y = x^2 + y^2$, then $2 \$ 5 = ?$

$2 \$ 5 = (2)^2 + (5)^2$
$\quad\;\;\; = 4 + 25$
$\quad\;\;\; = 29$

3. If $a \# b = \dfrac{a + b}{2}$, $3 \# 5 = ?$

$3 \# 5 = \dfrac{3 + 5}{2}$

$\quad\;\;\; = \dfrac{8}{2}$

$\quad\;\;\; = 4$

Practice: "False" Operations Problems

1. For all integers a and b, the binary operation $\#$ is defined by $a \# b = ab + b$. What is the value of $5 \# 7$?

2. $x \circ y = \dfrac{x^2 + y^2}{xy}$ for all real numbers x and y such that $xy \neq 0$.

   What is the value of $2 \circ 6$?

3. The operation ϕ is defined for all nonzero numbers x and y by the equation $x \phi y = (x - y)(x + y)(x)$. What is the value of $5 \phi 6$?

4. If $a * b$ means that a^2 is greater than b^2, then which of the following relationships must be true?

$$\text{I. } a = 0$$
$$\text{II. } a > b$$
$$\text{III. } a \neq 0$$

5. $\boxed{x|y|z} = x^2 + yz$ for all real numbers x, y, and z. What is the value of $\boxed{3|4|5}$?

6. The operation $\$$ is defined on ordered pairs of numbers as follows: $(x,y) \$ (w,z) = (xw, yz)$. What is the value of $(3,5) \$ (4,6)$?

7. If $x @ y = x^y$, for all positive integers x and y, what is the value of a if $b @ a = b$?

8. If $x \star y = \dfrac{x + y}{5}$, then which of the following must always be true?

$$\text{I. } a \star b = b \star a$$
$$\text{II. } a \star b = a \star a$$
$$\text{III. } a \star b = b \star b$$

Answers: "False" Operations Problems

1. $a \# b = ab + b$
   $5 \# 7 = (5)(7) + 7$
   $\qquad = 35 + 7$
   $\qquad = 42$

Note that *binary operation* simply means an operation between two values or variables.

2. $x \, o \, y = \dfrac{x^2 + y^2}{xy}$

   $2 \, o \, 6 = \dfrac{(2)^2 + (6)^2}{(2)(6)}$

   $\qquad = \dfrac{4 + 36}{12}$

   $\qquad = \dfrac{40}{12} = \dfrac{10}{3}$

3. $x \, \text{¢} \, y = (x - y)(x + y)x$
   $5 \, \text{¢} \, 6 = (5 - 6)(5 + 6)(5)$
   $\qquad = (-1)(11)(5)$
   $\qquad = -55$

4. Note that for a^2 to be greater than b^2, a^2 must be a positive number, as the smallest value for b^2 is 0. Therefore, statement I is false. Statement II is not necessarily true, since a could be -3 and b could be $+2$, yet $a^2 > b^2$. Statement III is true because if $a \neq 0$, a^2 will always be positive.

5. $\overline{x|y|z} = x^2 + yz$

   $\overline{3|4|5} = (3)^2 + (4)(5)$
   $\qquad = 9 + 20$
   $\qquad = 29$

6. $(x,y) \, \$ \, (w,z) = (zw, yz)$
   $(3,5) \, \$ \, (4,6) = (3 \cdot 4, 5 \cdot 6)$
   $\qquad\qquad = (12,30)$

7. $x @ y = x^y$
   $b @ a = b$

   Since b is the same as b^1, the above may be rewritten as $b @ a = b^1$. Therefore, the value of a is 1.

8. Only I is always true. The sum of $x + y$ equals the sum of $y + x$. Therefore, the original placement of a and b is irrelevant since

$$\frac{a + b}{5} = \frac{b + a}{5}$$

Statements II and III are not always true. They are true only if $a = b$.

ALGEBRA REVIEW TEST

Questions

1. A set within a set is called a _____ .

2. A set with no members is called the _____ or _____ .

3. Naming a set by describing its elements is called the _____ method.

4. A method of naming a set by listing its members is called _____ .

5. Sets that are countable or stop are called _____ .

6. Sets that continue forever are uncountable and are called _____ .

7. True or false: $\{1, 2, 3, 4\} = \{a, b, c, d\}$

8. True or false: $\{2, 4, 6\} \sim \{1, 3, 5\}$

9. $\{2, 7, 8\} \cap \{1, 3, 8\} =$

10. $\{4, 5, 6\} \cup \{1, 3, 5\} =$

11. Express each of the following algebraically.
    a. four more than twice a number
    b. a number decreased by six
    c. a number increased by ten
    d. a number x decreased by four times y

12. Evaluate: $p^2 + 7p - 5$ if $p = 6$

13. Evaluate: $4x^2y^3z^2$ if $x = 2$, $y = 3$, and $z = 4$

14. Evaluate: $\dfrac{xy}{4} - \dfrac{x + yz}{z}$ if $x = 3$, $y = 4$, and $z = 6$

15. Solve for x: $x + 18 = 64$

16. Solve for x: $4x - 8 = 32$

17. Solve for y: $\dfrac{y}{8} - 3 = 9$

18. Solve for z: $\frac{2}{5}z + 4 = 13$

19. Solve for x: $7x = 4x - 9$

20. Solve for n: $5n + 7 = 3n - 9$

21. Solve for y: $\frac{-y}{6} = 14$

22. Solve for y: $my - n = x$

23. Solve for m: $\frac{m}{n} = a$

24. Solve for x: $\frac{r}{x} = \frac{s}{t}$

25. Solve for x: x is to y as z is to a

26. Solve for x: $\frac{x}{6} = \frac{1}{2}$

27. Solve for c: $\frac{7}{2} = \frac{12}{c}$

28. Solve this system for x and y:
    $x - 2y = 8$
    $3x + 2y = 4$

29. Solve this system for a and b:
    $3a + 2b = 1$
    $2a - 3b = -8$

30. Solve this system for x and y:
    $y = x + 3$
    $2x + y = 8$

31. $12xy$
     $\underline{- 15xy}$

32. $6qt^2 - 2qt^2 + 6qt^2 =$

33. Simplify: $a \cdot a \cdot a \cdot x \cdot x \cdot y$

34. Simplify: $3(x)(y)(2)(z)$

35. $(y^3)(y^5) =$

36. $(a^2b)(a^3b^4) =$

37. $(-2x^2y)(3x^3y^4) =$

38. $-3(m^3n^3)(-2m^4n^2) =$

39. $(4a^2b^3c^3)(b^3c^2d) =$

40. $(x^7)^4 =$

41. $(a^2b^3)^3 =$

42. $(3x^3y^5)^2 =$

43. $x^5 \div x^2 =$

44. $\dfrac{a^6b^2}{a^4b} =$

45. $\dfrac{14\,x^6y^4}{2xy} =$

46. $3p^6q^4 \div 15p^4q^8 =$

47. $\quad \begin{aligned} x^2 + \ xy + 2y^2 \\ +\ 3x^2 + 5xy + 3y^2 \end{aligned}$

48. $(3x + 7y) + (6x - 2y) =$

49. $(3s^2 + 4st + 13t^2) - (2s^2 + 2st + 3t^2) =$

50. $2a^2b + 3ab^2 + 7a^2b - 5ab^2 =$

51. $(2x + 4)(3x - 1) =$

52. $(a + 3ab + 4)(2a + b) =$

53. $(12a^8 - 8a^7) \div 2a^3 =$

54. $\dfrac{-3(x^2y^3)(-4xy^4)}{2xy^2} =$

55. $(x^2 + 2x + 1) \div (x + 1) =$

56. $(5x^2 + 6x + 1) \div (x + 1) =$

57. $(a^3 - 27) \div (a - 3) =$

58. Factor: $9a - 6$

59. Factor completely: $5x^3 + 10x^2$

60. Factor: $n^2 - 9$

61. Factor: $36a^2 - b^2$

62. Factor completely: $2a^2 - 32$

63. Factor: $x^2 + 3x + 2$

64. Factor: $x^2 - 5x - 6$

65. Factor: $3x^2 - 20x - 7$

66. Factor completely: $x^3 - 4x^2 + 3x$

67. Factor: $24 - 10r + r^2$

68. Factor: $x^2 - 2xy + y^2$

69. Solve for y: $y^2 = 5y - 4$

70. Solve for x: $x^2 - 25 = 0$

71. Solve for x: $x^2 - 5x = 0$

72. Solve for t: $3t^2 + 21t = 2t^2 - 3t + 81$

73. Reduce: $\dfrac{9x^5}{12x^3}$

74. Reduce: $\dfrac{5x - 15}{4x - 12}$

75. Reduce: $\dfrac{x^2 - 9x + 20}{x^2 - x - 12}$

76. $\dfrac{8x^5}{9y^2} \cdot \dfrac{3y^4}{2x^3} =$

77. $\dfrac{x-1}{x} \cdot \dfrac{x + 3}{x^2 - 7x + 6} =$

78. $\dfrac{4x^3}{7} \div \dfrac{2x}{9} =$

79. $\dfrac{10y + 5}{4} \div \dfrac{2y + 1}{2} =$

80. $\dfrac{y + 3}{y} + \dfrac{2y + 5}{y} =$

81. $\dfrac{4x - 5}{x - 1} - \dfrac{3x + 6}{x - 1} =$

82. $\dfrac{7}{x} - \dfrac{6}{y} =$

83. $\dfrac{x - 3}{2x} + \dfrac{x + 1}{4x} =$

84. $\dfrac{7x}{x^4 y^7} + \dfrac{3}{x^6 y^2} =$

85. $\dfrac{3x}{x - 3} - \dfrac{2x}{x + 1} =$

86. $\dfrac{x}{x^2 - 16} + \dfrac{4x}{x^2 + 5x + 4} =$

87. Solve for x: $5x + 2 > 17$

88. Solve for y: $-4y - 8 \le 12$

89. Solve for x: $5x + 6 \ge 2x + 2$

90. Graph: $\{x: 5 \ge x \ge 3\}$

91. Graph: $\{x: -2 \le x < 8, x \text{ is an integer}\}$

92. Graph: $\{x: x > 1\}$

93. Graph: $\{x: x \le -2\}$

94. $|-6| =$

95. $|3 - 7| =$

96. $5 - |-3| =$

97. Give the coordinates represented by points
   A.
   B.
   C.
   D.

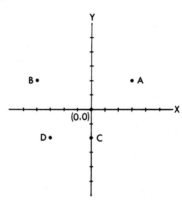

98. Is $x + \dfrac{3}{y} = 5$ linear or nonlinear?

99. Graph: $x + y = 9$

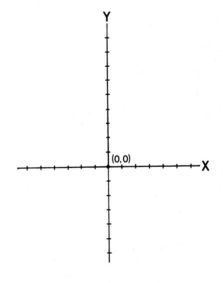

100. Graph: $y = x^2 + 3$

101. $- \sqrt{64} =$

102. $\sqrt{144} =$

103. Simplify: $\sqrt{75}$

In problems 104 through 118, each variable is nonnegative.

104. $\sqrt{x^8} =$

105. $\sqrt{x^2 y^8} =$

106. $\sqrt{9x^6 y^{10}} =$

107. $\sqrt{y^9} =$

108. $\sqrt{a^3 b^3} =$

109. $\sqrt{27 a^3 b^6} =$

110. $\sqrt{(18)(2)} =$

111. $\sqrt{25 + 4} =$

112. $7\sqrt{5} + 3\sqrt{5} =$

113. $\sqrt{60} + 2\sqrt{15} =$

114. $\sqrt{27} + \sqrt{48} =$

115. $\sqrt{6} \cdot \sqrt{10} =$

116. $\sqrt{x^3 y} \cdot \sqrt{x^2 yz} =$

117. $\sqrt{2xy} \cdot \sqrt{32x^3 y^2} =$

118. $6\sqrt{6} \cdot 2\sqrt{3} =$

119. a θ b = $(a + b)^2$, for all real numbers a and b. What is the value of 5 θ 4?

Answers

Page numbers following each answer refer to the review section applicable to this problem type.

1. subset (p. 106)

2. empty or null set (p. 106)

3. rule (p. 107)

4. roster (p. 107)

5. finite (p. 107)

6. infinite (p. 107)

7. false (p. 107)

8. true (p. 107)

9. {8} (p. 107)

10. {1, 3, 4, 5, 6} (p. 107)

11. a. 2x + 4 (p. 108)
     b. x − 6 (p. 108)
     c. x + 10 (p. 108)
     d. x − 4y (p. 108)

12. 73 (p. 110)

13. 6,912 (p. 110)

14. $-\dfrac{3}{2}$ or $-1\frac{1}{2}$ (p. 110)

15. x = 46 (p. 113)

16. x = 10 (p. 113)

17. y = 96 (p. 113)

18. $z = \dfrac{45}{2}$ or $22\frac{1}{2}$ (p. 113)

19. $x = -3$ (p. 113)

20. $n = -8$ (p. 113)

21. $y = -84$ (p. 113)

22. $y = \dfrac{x + n}{m}$ (p. 116)

23. $m = an$ (p. 116)

24. $x = \dfrac{rt}{s}$ (p. 116)

25. $x = \dfrac{zy}{a}$ (p. 119)

26. $x = 3$ (p. 120)

27. $c = \dfrac{24}{7}$ or $3\frac{3}{7}$ (p. 120)

28. $x = 3,\ y = \dfrac{-5}{2}$ or $-2\frac{1}{2}$ (p. 122)

29. $a = -1,\ b = 2$ (p. 122)

30. $x = \dfrac{5}{3}$ or $1\frac{2}{3}$, $y = \dfrac{14}{3}$ or $4\frac{2}{3}$ (p. 122)

31. $-3xy$ (p. 128)

32. $10qt^2$ (p. 128)

33. a^3x^2y (p. 129)

34. $6xyz$ (p. 129)

35. y^8 (p. 129)

36. a^5b^5 (p. 129)

37. $-6x^5y^5$ (p. 129)

38. $6m^7n^5$ (p. 129)

39. $4a^2b^6c^5d$ (p. 129)

40. x^{28} (p. 129)

41. a^6b^9 (p. 129)

42. $9x^6y^{10}$ (p. 129)

43. x^3 (p. 130)

44. a^2b (p. 130)

45. $7x^5y^3$ (p. 130)

46. $\dfrac{p^2}{5q^4}$ or $.2p^2q^{-4}$ (p. 130)

47. $4x^2 + 6xy + 5y^2$ (p. 131)

48. $9x + 5y$ (p. 131)

49. $s^2 + 2st + 10t^2$ (p. 131)

50. $9a^2b - 2ab^2$ (p. 131)

51. $6x^2 + 10x - 4$ (p. 133)

52. $2a^2 + 6a^2b + 8a + ab + 3ab^2 + 4b$ (p. 133)

53. $6a^5 - 4a^4$ (p. 135)

54. $6x^2y^5$ (p. 135)

55. $(x + 1)$ (p. 136)

56. $(5x + 1)$ (p. 136)

57. $(a^2 + 3a + 9)$ (p. 136)

58. $3(3a - 2)$ (p. 140)

59. $5x^2(x + 2)$ (p. 140)

60. $(n - 3)(n + 3)$ (p. 140)

61. $(6a - b)(6a + b)$ (p. 140)

62. $2(a - 4)(a + 4)$ (p. 140)

63. $(x + 1)(x + 2)$ (p. 141)

64. $(x - 6)(x + 1)$ (p. 141)

65. $(3x + 1)(x - 7)$ (p. 141)

66. $x(x - 3)(x - 1)$ (p. 141)

67. $(6 - r)(4 - r)$ (p. 141)

68. $(x - y)(x - y)$ (p. 141)

69. $y = 1, 4$ (p. 146)

70. $x = 5, -5$ (p. 146)

71. $x = 0, 5$ (p. 146)

72. $t = 3, -27$ (p. 146)

73. $\dfrac{3x^2}{4}$ (p. 150)

74. $\dfrac{5}{4}$ or $1\frac{1}{4}$ (p. 150)

75. $\dfrac{x - 5}{x + 3}$ (p. 150)

76. $\dfrac{4x^2y^2}{3}$ (p. 151)

77. $\dfrac{x + 3}{x(x - 6)}$ or $\dfrac{x + 3}{x^2 - 6x}$ (p. 151)

78. $\dfrac{18x^2}{7}$ (p. 153)

79. $\dfrac{5}{2}$ or $2\frac{1}{2}$ (p. 153)

80. $\dfrac{3y + 8}{y}$ (p. 154)

81. $\dfrac{x - 11}{x - 1}$ (p. 154)

82. $\dfrac{7y - 6x}{xy}$ (p. 154)

83. $\dfrac{3x - 5}{4x}$ (p. 154)

84. $\dfrac{7x^3 + 3y^5}{x^6y^7}$ (p. 154)

85. $\dfrac{x^2 + 9x}{(x - 3)(x + 1)}$ (p. 154)

86. $\dfrac{5x^2 - 15x}{(x + 4)(x - 4)(x + 1)}$ (p. 154)

87. $\{x: x > 3\}$ (p. 159)

88. $\{y: y \geq -5\}$ (p. 159)

89. $\left\{x: x \geq \dfrac{-4}{3}\right\}$ (p. 159)

90. (p. 161)

91. (p. 161)

92. (p. 161)

93. (p. 161)

94. 6 (p. 163)

95. 4 (p. 163)

96. 2 (p. 163)

97. A. (3,2) (p. 163)
    B. (−4,2) (p. 163)
    C. (0,−2) (p. 163)
    D. (−3,−2) (p. 163)

98. nonlinear (p. 166)

99.

x	y
0	9
1	8
2	7

(p. 166)

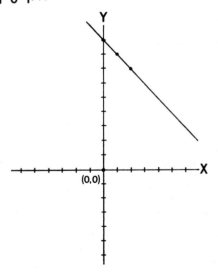

100.

x	y
0	3
1	4
2	7
−1	4
−2	7

(p. 166)

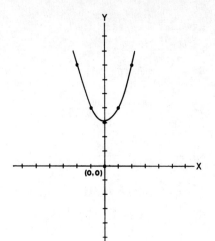

(0,0)

101. −8 (p. 171)

102. 12 (p. 171)

103. $5\sqrt{3}$ (p. 171)

104. x^4 (p. 171)

105. xy^4 (p. 171)

106. $3x^3y^5$ (p. 171)

107. $y^4\sqrt{y}$ (p. 171)

108. $ab\sqrt{ab}$ (p. 171)

109. $3ab^3\sqrt{3a}$ (p. 171)

110. 6 (p. 171)

111. $\sqrt{29}$ (p. 172)

112. $10\sqrt{5}$ (p. 172)

113. $4\sqrt{15}$ (p. 173)

114. $7\sqrt{3}$ (p. 173)

115. $2\sqrt{15}$ (p. 175)

116. $x^2y\sqrt{xz}$ (p. 175)

117. $8x^2y\sqrt{y}$ (p. 175)

118. $12\sqrt{18} = 36\sqrt{2}$ (p. 175)

119. 81 (p. 176)

ALGEBRA GLOSSARY OF TERMS

ABSCISSA: The distance along the horizontal axis in a coordinate graph.

ABSOLUTE VALUE: The numerical value when direction or sign is not considered.

ALGEBRA: Arithmetic operations using letters and/or symbols in place of numbers.

ALGEBRAIC FRACTIONS: Fractions using a variable in the numerator and/or denominator.

ASCENDING ORDER: Basically, when the power of a term increases for each succeeding term.

BINOMIAL: An algebraic expression consisting of two terms.

CARTESIAN COORDINATES: A system of assigning ordered number pairs to points on a plane.

CLOSED INTERVAL: An interval which includes both endpoints or fixed boundaries.

COEFFICIENT: The number in front of a variable. For example, in 9x, 9 is the coefficient.

COORDINATE AXES: Two perpendicular number lines used in a coordinate graph.

COORDINATE GRAPH: Two perpendicular number lines, the x axis and the y axis, creating a plane on which each point is assigned a pair of numbers.

CUBE: The result when a number is multiplied by itself twice. Designated by the exponent 3. (x^3)

CUBE ROOT: The number that when multiplied by itself twice gives you the original number. For example, 5 is the cube root of 125. Its symbol is $\sqrt[3]{}$. $\sqrt[3]{125} = 5$

DENOMINATOR: Everything below the fraction bar in a fraction.

DESCENDING ORDER: Basically, when the power of a term decreases for each succeeding term.

ELEMENT: A member of a set.

EMPTY SET: A set with no members. Null set.

EQUAL SETS: Sets that have exactly the same members.

EQUATION: A balanced relationship between numbers and/or symbols. A mathematical sentence.

EQUIVALENT SETS: Sets that have the same number of members.

EVALUATE: To determine the value, or numerical amount.

EXPONENT: A numeral used to indicate the power of a number.

EXTREMES: Outer terms.

FACTOR: To find two or more quantities whose product equals the original quantity.

FINITE: Countable. Having a definite ending.

F.O.I.L. METHOD: A method of multiplying binomials in which first terms, outside terms, inside terms, and last terms are multiplied.

HALF-OPEN INTERVAL: An interval that includes one endpoint, or one boundary.

IMAGINARY NUMBERS: Square roots of negative numbers. The imaginary unit is i.

INCOMPLETE QUADRATIC EQUATION: A quadratic equation with a term missing.

INEQUALITY: A statement in which the relationships are not equal. The opposite of an equation.

INFINITE: Uncountable. Continues forever.

INTERSECTION OF SETS: The members that overlap (are in both sets).

INTERVAL: All the numbers that lie within two certain boundaries.

LINEAR EQUATION: An equation whose solution set forms a straight line when plotted on a coordinate graph.

LITERAL EQUATION: An equation having mostly variables.

MEANS: Inner terms.

MONOMIAL: An algebraic expression consisting of only one term.

NONLINEAR EQUATION: An equation whose solution set does not form a straight line when plotted on a coordinate graph.

NULL SET: A set with no members. Empty set.

NUMBER LINE: A graphic representation of integers and real numbers. The point on this line associated with each number is called the graph of the number.

NUMERATOR: Everything above the fraction bar in a fraction.

OPEN INTERVAL: An interval that does not include endpoints or fixed boundaries.

OPEN RAY: A ray that does include its endpoint (half line).

ORDERED PAIR: Any pair of elements (x, y) having a first element x and a second element y. Used to identify or plot points on a coordinate grid.

ORDINATE: The distance along the vertical axis on a coordinate graph.

ORIGIN: The point of intersection of the two number lines on a coordinate graph. Represented by the coordinates (0,0).

POLYNOMIAL: An algebraic expression consisting of two or more terms.

PROPORTION: Two ratios equal to each other. For example, a is to c as b is to d.

QUADRANTS: Four quarters or divisions of a coordinate graph.

QUADRATIC EQUATION: An equation that could be written $Ax^2 + Bx + C = 0$.

RADICAL SIGN: The symbol used to designate square root.

RATIO: A method of comparing two or more numbers. For example, a:b. Often written as a fraction.

REAL NUMBERS: The set consisting of all rational and irrational numbers.

ROSTER: A method of naming a set by listing its members.

RULE: A method of naming a set by describing its elements.

SET: A group of objects, numbers, etc.

SET BUILDER NOTATION: A formal method of describing a set. Often used for inequalities. For example, $\{x: x > 1\}$, which is read "x such that all x is greater than 1."

SIMPLIFY: To combine several or many terms into fewer terms.

SOLUTION SET or SOLUTION: All the answers that satisfy the equation.

SQUARE: The result when a number is multiplied by itself. Designated by the exponent 2. (x^2)

SQUARE ROOT: The number that when multiplied by itself gives you the original number. For example, 5 is the square root of 25. Its symbol is $\sqrt{}$. $\sqrt{25} = 5$

SUBSET: A set within a set.

SYSTEM OF EQUATIONS: Simultaneous equations.

TERM: A numerical or literal expression with its own sign.

TRINOMIAL: An algebraic expression consisting of three terms.

UNION OF SETS: All the numbers in those sets.

UNIVERSAL SET: The general category set, or the set of all those elements under consideration.

UNKNOWN: A letter or symbol whose value is not known.

VALUE: Numerical amount.

VARIABLE: A symbol used to stand for a number.

VENN DIAGRAM: A pictorial description of sets.

X-AXIS: The horizontal axis in a coordinate graph.

X-COORDINATE: The first number in the ordered pair. Refers to the distance on the x-axis. Abscissa.

Y-AXIS: The vertical axis in a coordinate graph.

Y-COORDINATE: The second number in the ordered pair. Refers to the distance on the y-axis. Ordinate.

GEOMETRY

GEOMETRY DIAGNOSTIC TEST

Questions

1. Name any angle of this triangle three different ways.

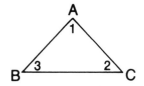

2. A(n) _____ angle measures less than 90 degrees.

3. A(n) _____ angle measures 90 degrees.

4. A(n) _____ angle measures more than 90 degrees but less than 180 degrees.

5. A(n) _____ angle measures 180 degrees.

6. Two angles are complementary when the sum of their measures is _____.

7. Two angles are supplementary when the sum of their measures is _____.

8. In the diagram, find the measure of ∠a, ∠b, and ∠c.

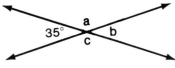

9. In the diagram, find the measure of all remaining angles. $\ell \parallel m$

10. Lines that stay the same distance apart and never meet are called _____ lines.

11. Lines that meet to form right angles are called _____ lines.

12. A(n) _____ triangle has three equal sides. Therefore, each interior angle measures _____.

13. In the diagram, △ABC is isosceles: AB = AC. Find ∠A and ∠C.

14. In the triangle, AC must be less than _____ inches.

15. In the triangle, which angle is smaller, ∠A or ∠C?

Questions 14 and 15

16. What is the measure of ∠ACD?

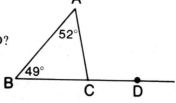

17. What is the length of AC?

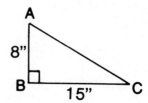

18. What is the length of BC?

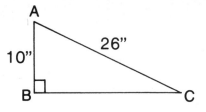

19. What is the value of x?

20. What is the value of a?

21. Name each of the following polygons.

    (A) AB = BC = AC   (B) AB = BC = CD = AD
        ∠A = ∠B = ∠C = 60°   ∠A = ∠B = ∠C = ∠D = 90°

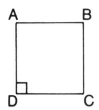

(C) AB ∥ DC
     AB = DC
     AD ∥ BC
     AD = BC

(D) AB = DC
     AD = BC
     ∠A = ∠B = ∠C = ∠D = 90°

(E) AB ∥ DC

22. Fill in the blanks for
    circle R.
    (A) RS is called the _____.
    (B) AB is called the _____.
    (C) CD is called a _____.

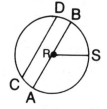

23. In the circle, if $\widehat{BS}$ = 62°,
    what is the measure of ∠BRS?

24. In this circle, if $\widehat{BS}$ = 62°,
    what is the measure of
    ∠BCS?

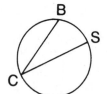

25. Find the area and circumference
    for the circle O ($\pi \simeq$ $^{22}/_7$).
    (A) area = _____
    (B) circumference = _____

26. Find the area and perimeter
of the trapezoid.
(A) area = _____
(B) perimeter = _____

27. Find the area and perimeter
of the figure (ABCD is a
parallelogram).
(A) area = _____
(B) perimeter = _____

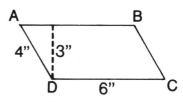

28. Find the volume of the
right circular cylinder
(use 3.14 for π).

29. What is the surface area
and volume of the cube?
(A) surface area = _____
(B) volume = _____

Answers

Page numbers following each answer refer to the review section applicable to this problem type.

1. ∠3, ∠CBA, ∠ABC, ∠B (p. 205)
   ∠1, ∠BAC, ∠CAB, ∠A (p. 205)
   ∠2, ∠ACB, ∠BCA, ∠C (p. 205)

2. acute (p. 206)

3. right (p. 206)

4. obtuse (p. 206)

202   BASIC SKILLS REVIEW

5. straight (p. 206)

6. 90° (p. 208)

7. 180° (p. 208)

8. a = 145°
   b = 35°
   c = 145° (p. 208)

9. ∠a, ∠c, ∠d, ∠f = 76°
   ∠b, ∠e, ∠g = 104° (p. 212)

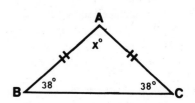

10. parallel (p. 212)

11. perpendicular (p. 212)

12. equilateral, 60° (p. 217)

13. 38° + 38° + x° = 180°
        76° + x° = 180°
              x° = 104°
           ∠A = 104°
           ∠C = 38°
           (p. 218)

14. 40 inches. Since AB + BC = 40 inches
             then AC < AB + BC
             and AC < 40 inches (p. 220)

15. ∠C must be the smaller angle, since it is opposite the shorter side AB. (p. 220)

16. ∠ACD = 101° (p. 221)

17. AC = 17 inches (p. 223)

18. BC = 24 inches. Since 5, 12, 13 is a Pythagorean triple, doubled is 10, <u>24</u>, 26. (p. 223)

19. x = $9\sqrt{2}$. Since this is an isosceles right triangle, the ratio of the sides is x, x, $x\sqrt{2}$. (p. 225)

20. a = 8. Since this is a 30-60-90 right triangle, the ratio of the sides is x, 2x, $x\sqrt{3}$. (p. 226)

21. (A) equilateral triangle or   (D) rectangle (p. 229)
        equilangular triangle (p. 217)   (E) trapezoid (p. 230)
    (B) square (p. 229)
    (C) parallelogram (p. 229)

22. (A) radius (p. 235)
    (B) diameter (p. 236)
    (C) chord (p. 236)

23. 62° (p. 238)

24. 31° (p. 239)

25. (A) area = πr^2
             = $\pi(7^2)$
             = $^{22}\!/_7 (7)(7)$
             = 154 square inches (p. 237)
    (B) circumference = πd
                       = $\pi(14)$ d = 14", since r = 7"
                       = $^{22}\!/_7 (14)$
                       = 22(2)
                       = 44 inches (p. 237)

26. (A) area = ½(a + b)h
             = ½(16 + 30)12
             = ½(46)12
             = 23(12)
             = 276 square inches (p. 232)
    (B) perimeter = 16 + 13 + 30 + 15 = 74 inches (p. 232)

27. (A) area = bh
             = 6(3)
             = 18 square inches (p. 232)
    (B) perimeter = 6 + 4 + 6 + 4 = 20 inches (p. 232)

28. Volume = (area of base)(height)
    $= (\pi r^2)h$
    $= (\pi \cdot 10^2)(12)$
    $= 3.14(100)(12)$
    $= 314(12)$
    = 3,768 cubic inches (p. 242)

29. (A) All six surfaces have an area of 4×4, or 16 square inches, since each surface is a square. Therefore, $16(6) = 96$ square inches in the surface area. (p. 243)

    (B) Volume = side $\times$ side $\times$ side, or $4^3 = 64$ cubic inches. (p. 242)

GEOMETRY REVIEW

- PLANE GEOMETRY is the study of shapes and figures in two dimensions (the plane). Plane figures have only length and width.
- SOLID GEOMETRY is the study of shapes and figures in three dimensions. Solid figures have length, width, and thickness.
- A POINT is the most fundamental idea in geometry. It is represented by a dot and named by a capital letter.

Angles

- An *angle* is formed by two rays that have the same endpoint. That point is called the *vertex;* the rays are called the *sides* of the angle. An angle is measured in degrees from 0 to 360. The number of degrees indicates the size of the angle or the difference in direction of the two rays.

In the diagram, the angle is formed by rays $\overrightarrow{AB}$ and $\overrightarrow{AC}$. A is the vertex. $\overrightarrow{AB}$ and $\overrightarrow{AC}$ are the sides of the angle.

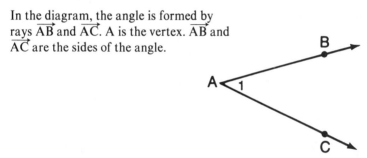

The symbol ∠ is used to denote an angle.
The symbol m ∠ is sometimes used to denote the measure of an angle.

- An angle can be named in various ways:

  1. By the letter of the vertex—therefore, the angle above could be named ∠A.
  2. By the number (or small letter) in its interior—therefore, the angle above could be named ∠1.
  3. By the letters of the three points that formed it—therefore, the angle above could be named ∠BAC or ∠CAB. The center letter is always the letter of the vertex.

Types of Angles

Right Angle

- A *right angle* has a measure of 90°. The symbol ⌐ in the interior of an angle designates the fact that a right angle is formed.

In the diagram, ∠ABC is
a right angle.

Acute Angle

- Any angle whose measure is less than 90° is called an *acute angle*.

In the diagram, ∠b is acute.

Obtuse Angle

- Any angle whose measure is larger than 90° but smaller than 180° is called an *obtuse angle*.

In the diagram,
∠4 is an obtuse angle.

Straight Angle

- A *straight angle* has a measure of 180°.

In the diagram, ∠BAC is a
straight angle (often called a line).

Practice: Angle Problems

Name the angles.

1.

2.

3.

4.

What kind of angle is formed between the hands of a clock (measured clockwise) when it is

5. 6 o'clock   6. 2 o'clock   7. 3 o'clock   8. 8 o'clock

Answers: Angle Problems

1. an acute angle
2. an obtuse angle
3. an acute angle
4. an obtuse angle

5. a straight angle
6. an acute angle
7. a right angle
8. an obtuse angle

Pairs of Angles

Adjacent Angles

● *Adjacent angles* are any angles that share a common side and a common vertex.

In the diagram, ∠1 and ∠2 are adjacent angles.

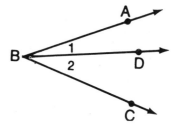

Vertical Angles

- If two straight lines intersect, they do so at a point. Four angles are formed. Those angles opposite each other are called *vertical angles*. Those angles sharing a common side and a common vertex are, again, *adjacent angles*. Vertical angles are always equal in measure.

In the diagram, line *l* and line *m* intersect at point Q. ∠1, ∠2, ∠3, and ∠4 are formed.

$$\left.\begin{array}{l}\angle 1 \text{ and } \angle 3 \\ \angle 2 \text{ and } \angle 4\end{array}\right\} \text{ are vertical angles}$$

$$\left.\begin{array}{l}\angle 1 \text{ and } \angle 2 \\ \angle 2 \text{ and } \angle 3 \\ \angle 3 \text{ and } \angle 4 \\ \angle 1 \text{ and } \angle 4\end{array}\right\} \text{ are adjacent angles}$$

Therefore,

$$\angle 1 = \angle 3$$
$$\angle 2 = \angle 4$$

Complementary Angles

- Two angles whose sum is 90° are called *complementary angles*.

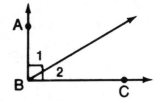

In the diagram, since ∠ABC is a right triangle, ∠1 + ∠2 = 90°.

Therefore, ∠1 and ∠2 are complementary angles. If ∠1 = 55°, its complement, ∠2, would be: 90° − 55° = 35°.

Supplementary Angles

- Two angles whose sum is 180° are called *supplementary angles*. Two adjacent angles that form a straight line are supplementary.

In the diagram, since ∠ABC is a straight angle, ∠3 + ∠4 = 180°.

Therefore, ∠3 and ∠4 are supplementary angles. If ∠3 = 122°, its supplement, ∠4, would have a measure of: 180° − 122° = 58°.

Angle Bisector

- A ray from the vertex of an angle that divides the angle into two angles of equal measure is called an *angle bisector*.

In the diagram, $\overrightarrow{AB}$ is the angle bisector of ∠CAD.

Therefore, ∠1 = ∠2.

Practice: Angle Problems

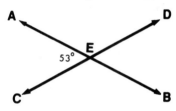

1. In the figure above, if lines AB and CD intersect at E, and if ∠AEC measures 53°, how many degrees are there in ∠BED?

2. Find the complement of the following angles.
   (a) 17°   (b) t°

3. Find the supplement of the following angles.
   (a) 124°   (b) (x + 9)°

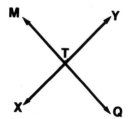

4. In the figure above, ∠XTM and ∠_____ are *vertical* angles.

5. Find the complement of an angle whose measure is
   (a) 74½°   (b) (q − 5)°

6. Find the supplement of an angle whose measure is
   (a) 180°   (b) (m − 30)°

Answers: Angle Problems

1. Since ∠AEC and ∠BED are vertical angles, ∠BED contains 53°.

2. (a) 90° − 17° = 73°
   (b) (90 − t)°

3. (a) 180° − 124° = 56°
   (b) 180° − (x + 9)° = 180° − x° − 9° = (171 − x)°

4. YTQ

5. (a) 90° − 74½° = 15½°
   (b) 90° − (q − 5)° = 90° − q° + 5° = (95 − q)°

6. (a) 180° − 180° = 0°
   (b) 180° − (m − 30)° = 180° − m° + 30° = (210 − m)°

Lines

Straight Lines

- A *straight line* is often described as the shortest distance between two points. It continues forever in both directions. A line consists of an infinite number of points and is named by any two points on the line. (*Line* means *straight line*) The symbol ↔ written on top of the two letters is used to denote that line.

This is line AB.
It is written $\overleftrightarrow{AB}$.

A line may also be named by one small letter.

This is line *l*.

Line Segments

- A *line segment* is a piece of a line. It has two endpoints and is named by its two endpoints. Sometimes the symbol — written on top of the two letters is used to denote that line segment.

This is line segment CD.
It is written $\overline{CD}$ or CD.
(Although there is a technical
difference, most standardized
exams use one form consistently
in context.)
Note that it is a piece of $\overleftrightarrow{AB}$.

- A midpoint of a line segment is the halfway point, or the point equidistant from the endpoints.

Rays

- A *ray* has only one endpoint (or origin) and continues forever in one direction. A ray could be thought of as a half-line with an endpoint. It is named by the letter of its endpoint and any other point on the ray. The symbol → written on top of the two letters is used to denote that ray.

This is ray AB.
It is written $\overrightarrow{AB}$.

This is ray BC.
It is written $\overrightarrow{BC}$ or $\overleftarrow{CB}$.

Note that the direction of the symbol is the direction of the ray.

Types of Lines

Intersecting Lines

- Two or more lines that meet at a point are called *intersecting lines*. That point would be on each of those lines.

In the diagram, lines *l* and *m*
intersect at Q.

Perpendicular Lines

- Two lines that meet to form right angles (90°) are called *perpendicular lines*. The symbol ⊥ is used to denote perpendicular lines.

In the diagram, line *l* ⊥ line *m*.

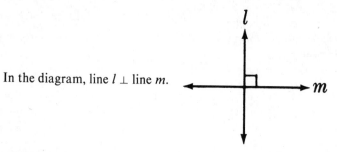

Parallel Lines

- Two or more lines that remain the same distance apart at all times are called *parallel lines*. Parallel lines never meet. The symbol ∥ is used to denote parallel lines.

In the diagram, *l* ∥ *m*.

Parallel Lines Cut by Transversal

- When two parallel lines are both intersected by a third line, it is termed *parallel lines cut by a transversal*. In the diagram below, line *n* is the transversal, and lines *m* and *l* are parallel. Eight angles are formed. There are many facts and relationships about these angles.

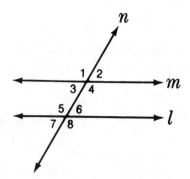

1. *Adjacent angles.* Angles 1 and 2 are adjacent and they form a straight line; therefore, they are supplementary. $\angle 1 + \angle 2 = 180°$.

Likewise:

$\angle 2 + \angle 4 = 180°$	$\angle 7 + \angle 8 = 180°$
$\angle 3 + \angle 4 = 180°$	$\angle 5 + \angle 7 = 180°$
$\angle 1 + \angle 3 = 180°$	$\angle 6 + \angle 8 = 180°$
$\angle 5 + \angle 6 = 180°$	

2. *Vertical angles.* Angles 1 and 4 are vertical angles; therefore, they are equal. $\angle 1 = \angle 4$.

Likewise: $\angle 2 = \angle 3$
$\angle 5 = \angle 8$
$\angle 7 = \angle 6$

3. *Corresponding angles.* If we could physically pick up line *l* and place it on line *m*, the angles that would coincide with each other would be equal in measure. They are called corresponding angles.

Therefore:

$\angle 1 = \angle 5$	$\angle 3 = \angle 7$
$\angle 2 = \angle 6$	$\angle 4 = \angle 8$

4. *Alternate interior and exterior angles.* Alternate angles are on the opposite sides of the transversal. Interior angles are those contained within the parallel lines. Exterior angles are those on the outsides of the parallel lines.

Therefore: $\angle 3$ and $\angle 6$ are alternate interior angles.
$\angle 3 = \angle 6$

$\angle 4$ and $\angle 5$ are alternate interior angles.
$\angle 4 = \angle 5$

$\angle 2$ and $\angle 7$ are alternate exterior angles.
$\angle 2 = \angle 7$

$\angle 1$ and $\angle 8$ are alternate exterior angles.
$\angle 1 = \angle 8$

5. *Consecutive interior angles.* Consecutive interior angles are on the same side of the transversal.

Therefore: ∠3 and ∠5 are consecutive interior angles.
∠3 + ∠5 = 180°
∠4 and ∠6 are consecutive interior angles.
∠4 + ∠6 = 180°

The sum of the measures of each pair of consecutive angles = 180°.

Using all of these facts, if we are given the measure of one of the eight angles, the other angle measures can all be determined. *For example:*

∠a + 83° = 180°

$\left. \begin{array}{l} ∠a = 97° \\ ∠b = 97° \end{array} \right\}$ vertical angles

$\left. \begin{array}{l} ∠c = 83° \\ ∠d = 83° \end{array} \right\}$ alternate interior angles

$\left. \begin{array}{l} ∠e = 97° \\ ∠f = 97° \end{array} \right\}$ vertical angles

$\left. \begin{array}{l} ∠g = 83° \end{array} \right\}$ alternate exterior angles

Note that since the lines are parallel, you can *see* which angles are equal, even if you cannot remember the rules.

Practice: Parallel Lines Cut by Transversal Problems

RS ∥ HJ

1. In the figure on the previous page, name all the pairs of the following types of angles.
   (a) vertical angles
   (c) corresponding angles
   (b) consecutive interior angles
   (d) alternate interior angles

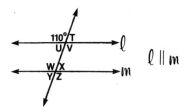

$\ell \parallel m$

2. In the figure above, find the measure of the angles T, U, V, W, X, Y, and Z.

Answers: Parallel Lines Cut by Transversal Problems

1. (a) Vertical angles are a and d, b and c, e and h, f and g.
   (b) Consecutive interior angles are c and e, d and f.
   (c) Corresponding angles are a and e, c and g, b and f, d and h.
   (d) Alternate interior angles are c and f, d and e.

2. Angles V, W, and Z each have a measure of 110°.
   Angles T, U, X, and Y each have a measure of 70°.

Polygons

• Closed shapes, or figures in a plane, with three or more sides are called *polygons*. (*Poly* means *many*, and *gon* means *sides*. Thus, *polygon* means *many sides*. A plane is often described as a flat surface.) Examples of polygons are:

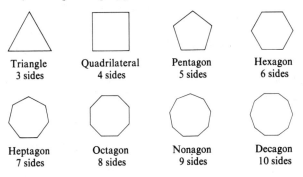

| Triangle | Quadrilateral | Pentagon | Hexagon |
| 3 sides | 4 sides | 5 sides | 6 sides |

| Heptagon | Octagon | Nonagon | Decagon |
| 7 sides | 8 sides | 9 sides | 10 sides |

Regular Polygons

- *Regular* means all sides have the same length and all angles have the same measure. A regular three-sided polygon is the equilateral triangle. A regular four-sided polygon is the square. There are no other special names. Other polygons will just be described as regular, if they are. For example, a regular five-sided polygon is called a regular pentagon. A regular six-sided polygon is called a regular hexagon.

Diagonals of Polygons

- A *diagonal of a polygon* is a line segment that connects one vertex with another vertex and is not itself a side. (AD and BC are both diagonals.)

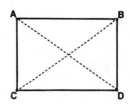

Convex Polygons

- A convex polygon has all diagonals within the figure.

Concave Polygons

- A concave polygon (caves in) has at least one diagonal outside the figure. (AB is the diagonal.)

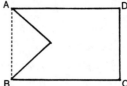

Triangles

- This section deals with those polygons having the fewest number of sides. A *triangle* is a three-sided polygon. It has three angles in its interior. The sum of the measure of these angles is *always* 180°. The symbol for triangle is △. A triangle is named by the three letters of its vertices.

This is △ABC.

Types of Triangles by Sides

Equilateral Triangles

- A triangle having all three
  sides equal in measure
  is called an
  equilateral triangle.
  Note: by angles, this would
  be called an *equiangular
  triangle*—all angles are equal.

Equilateral Triangle
(or Equiangular Triangle)

Isosceles Triangles

- A triangle having two equal sides
  is called an
  isosceles triangle.

Isosceles Triangle

Scalene Triangles

- A triangle having no equal
  sides is called
  a *scalene triangle.*

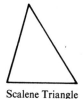

Scalene Triangle

Types of Triangles by Angles

Right Triangles

- A triangle having a right (90°)
  angle in its interior is
  called a *right triangle.*

Right Triangle

Obtuse Triangles

● A triangle having an obtuse angle
  (greater than 90° but less than
  180°) in its interior is called
  an *obtuse triangle*.

Obtuse Triangle

Acute Triangles

● A triangle having all acute
  angles (less than 90°) in
  its interior is called an
  acute triangle.

Acute Triangle

Examples: Triangle Problems

1. Two angles of a triangle measure 45° and 85°. How many degrees
   are there in the third angle?

Answer: The angles of a triangle add up to 180°. The sum of 45° and
85° is 130°. Therefore, the remaining angle must be 180° − 130° =
50°.

2. In △ABC above, ∠C is three times ∠A and ∠B is five times ∠A.
   Find the number of degrees in each angle of the triangle.

Answer: Let y equal the number of degrees in ∠A. Then 3y equals the
number of degrees in ∠C, and 5y equals the number of degrees in ∠B.
Since the sum of the angles of the triangle is 180°, we can say

$$y + 3y + 5y = 180$$

$$\frac{9y}{9} = \frac{180}{9}$$

$$y = 20° (\angle A)$$
$$3y = 60° (\angle C)$$
$$5y = 100° (\angle B)$$

Notice that 20° + 60° + 100° = 180°.

Facts about Triangles

Base and Height

● Every triangle has three *bases* (bottom side) and three *heights* (altitude). Every height is the *perpendicular* (forms right angles) distance from a vertex to its opposite side (the base).

In this diagram of △ABC, BC is the base and AE is the height. AE ⊥ BC.

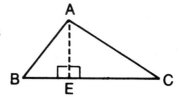

Median

● Every triangle has three medians. The median is the line segment drawn from a vertex to the midpoint of the opposite side.

In this diagram of △ABC, E is the midpoint of BC. Therefore, BE = EC. AE is the median of △ ABC.

Angles Opposite Equal Sides

● *Angles* that are *opposite from equal sides* are also equal.

In the diagram of △ABC:
∠A is opposite from side BC.
∠B is opposite from side AC.
∠C is opposite from side AB.
Therefore, if side AB = side AC, then ∠C = ∠B.

Angles of an Isosceles Triangle

● In an isosceles triangle, since two of the sides are equal, the angles opposite those sides are equal. There are always two equal sides in an isosceles triangle.

Angles of an Equilateral Triangle

● In an equilateral triangle, since all three sides are equal, all three angles will be equal; they are opposite equal sides. If all three angles are equal and their sum is 180°, the following must be true.

$$x + x + x = 180°$$
$$3x = 180°$$
$$x = 60°$$

Every angle of an equilateral triangle always has a measure of 60°.

Unequal Angles

● In any triangle, the longest side is always opposite from the largest angle. Likewise, the shortest side is always opposite from the smallest angle. In a right triangle, the longest side will always be opposite from the right angle, as the right angle will be the largest angle in the triangle.

AC is the longest side of right △ABC.

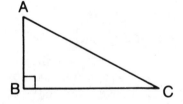

Adding Sides of a Triangle

● The sum of the lengths of any two sides of a triangle must be larger than the length of the third side.

In the diagram of △ABC:
AB + BC > AC
AB + AC > BC
AC + BC > AB

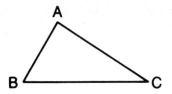

Exterior Angles

● If one side of a triangle is extended, the exterior angle formed by that extension is equal to the sum of the other two interior angles.

In the diagram of △ABC, side BC is extended to D. ∠ACD is the exterior angle formed.

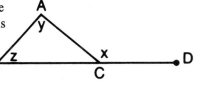

$\angle x = \angle y + \angle z$
$x = 82° + 41°$
$x = 123°$

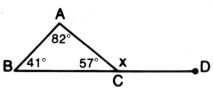

Practice: Triangle Problems

1. Two angles of a triangle measure 50° and 60°. How many degrees are there in the third angle?

2. One of the angles in a right triangle measures 35°. What is the measure of the other acute angle?

3. In an isosceles triangle, one of the angles opposite an equal side is 20°. What is the measure of each of the other two angles?

4. In △ABC, the measure of ∠A is twice the measure of ∠B. The measure of ∠C is three times the measure of ∠B. What is the measure of each of the three angles?

5. In the figure on the right, which side is the largest?

(Note: figure not drawn to scale.)

6. Which of the following measures could be the sides of a triangle?

2, 3, 4   2, 2, 5   4, 3, 7

3, 4, 5   3, 3, 6   1, 2, 3

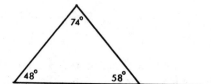

7. What is the measure of the exterior angle of the triangle above?

Answers: Triangle Problems

1. Since the measure of the three angles of a triangle must total 180°, there are 70° in the third angle.

2. Since in a right triangle one of the angles equals 90° and the total of the three angles equals 180°, there are 90° and 55° in the other two angles.

3. Since equal sides of a triangle have their opposite angles equal, the other two angles measure 20° and 140°.

4. Let the smallest angle equal x. Therefore, the larger angle equals 2x, and the largest angle equals 3x. Their total is 6x, which equals 180°.

$$6x = 180°$$
$$x = 30° \ (\angle B)$$
$$2x = 60° \ (\angle A)$$
$$3x = 90° \ (\angle C)$$

5. Side AC is largest, since in any triangle, the largest side is opposite the largest angle.

6. Since the sum of any two sides of a triangle must be greater than its third side, 2, 2, 5; 3, 3, 6; 1, 2, 3; and 4, 3, 7 cannot be sides of a triangle. The two other sets can.

7. Since an exterior angle of a triangle always equals the sum of the other two interior angles, the exterior angle measures 122°.

Pythagorean Theorem

- In any right triangle, the relationship between the lengths of the sides is stated by the *Pythagorean theorem*. The parts of a right triangle are:

∠C is the right angle.

The side opposite the right angle is called the *hypotenuse* (side c). (The hypotenuse will always be the longest side.)

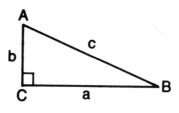

The other two sides are called the *legs* (sides a and b).

The three lengths a, b, and c will always be numbers such that

$$a^2 + b^2 = c^2$$

For example: If a = 3, b = 4, and c = 5,

$a^2 + b^2 = c^2$
$3^2 + 4^2 = 5^2$
$9 + 16 = 25$
$\quad 25 = 25$

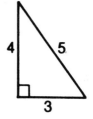

Therefore, 3-4-5 is called a *Pythagorean triple*. There are other values for a, b, and c that will always work. Some are: 5-12-13, and 8-15-17. Any multiple of one of these triples will also work. For example, using the 3-4-5: 6-8-10, 9-12-15, and 15-20-25 will also be Pythagorean triples.

- If perfect squares are known, the lengths of these sides can be determined easily. A knowledge of the use of algebraic equations can also be used to determine the lengths of the sides.

Examples: Pythagorean Theorem Problems

1. Find x in this right triangle.

Answer: $a^2 + b^2 = c^2$
$5^2 + 7^2 = x^2$
$25 + 49 = x^2$
$74 = x^2$
$\sqrt{74} = x$

2. Find x in this right triangle.

Answer: $a^2 + b^2 = c^2$
$x^2 + 10^2 = 15^2$
$x^2 + 100 = 225$
$x^2 = 125$
$x = \sqrt{125}$
$= \sqrt{25} \times \sqrt{5}$
$= 5\sqrt{5}$

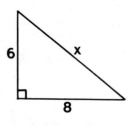

Practice: Pythagorean Theorem Problems

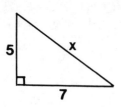

1. Find x in this right triangle.

2. Find y in this right triangle.

3. If the two legs of a right triangle measure 5 and 9, what is the length of the hypotenuse?

Answers: Pythagorean Theorem Problems

1. $6^2 + 8^2 = x^2$
   $36 + 64 = x^2$
   $100 = x^2$
   $10 = x$

2. $y^2 + 7^2 = 12^2$
   $y^2 + 49 = 144$
   $y^2 = 95$
   $y = \sqrt{95}$

3. $5^2 + 9^2 = x^2$
   $25 + 81 = x^2$
   $106 = x^2$
   $\sqrt{106} = x$

Special Triangles

Isosceles Right Triangles

● An *isosceles right triangle* has the characteristics of both the isosceles and the right triangles. It will have two equal sides, two equal angles, and one right angle. (The right angle cannot be one of the equal angles or the sum will be more than 180°.)

Therefore, in the diagram, $\triangle ABC$ is an isosceles right triangle. And the following must always be true:

$x + x + 90° = 180°$
$2x = 90°$
$x = 45°$

$\triangle ABC$ is isosceles
$AB = BC$
$\angle A = \angle C$
$\angle B = 90°$

The ratio of the sides of an isosceles right triangle is always 1, 1, $\sqrt{2}$ or x, x, x $\sqrt{2}$.

Example: Isosceles Right Triangle Problem

If one of the equal sides of an isosceles right triangle is 3, what is the measure of the other two sides?

Answer: Using the ratio x, x, x $\sqrt{2}$, the measure of the sides must be 3, 3, 3 $\sqrt{2}$.

Practice: Isosceles Right Triangle Problems

1. If one of the equal sides of an isosceles right triangle is 4, what is the measure of the other two sides?

2. If the longest side of an isosceles right triangle is 6 $\sqrt{2}$, what is the measure of each of the two equal sides?

3. What is the measure of sides x and y in the triangle above?

Answers: Isosceles Right Triangle Problems

1. The sides of an isosceles right triangle are always in the ratio x, x, x $\sqrt{2}$. Therefore, the other two sides are 4 and 4 $\sqrt{2}$.

2. The two equal sides each equal 6.

3. Since one angle measures 90° and another measures 45°, the third angle must also measure 45°. 180 − (90 + 45) = 45. Therefore, we have an isosceles right triangle with the ratio of sides x, x, x $\sqrt{2}$. Since one equal side is 6, the other must be 6, and the longest side is then 6 $\sqrt{2}$.

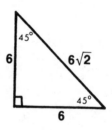

30°-60°-90° Right Triangles

● A *30°-60°-90° right triangle* has a unique ratio of its sides. It is a commonly referred to triangle. The ratio of the sides of a 30°-

60°-90° right triangle are 1, 2, $\sqrt{3}$, or x, 2x, x$\sqrt{3}$, placed as follows.

The side opposite 30° is 1 or x.
The side opposite 60° is 3 or x $\sqrt{3}$.
The side opposite 90° is the
longest side (hypotenuse), 2 or 2x.

Examples: 30°-60°-90° Right Triangle Problems

1. If the shortest side of a 30°-60°-90° right triangle is 4, what is the measure of the other sides?

Answer: Using the ratio x, 2x, x $\sqrt{3}$, the measure is 4, 8, 4 $\sqrt{3}$.

2. In the triangle above, find the remaining sides.

Answer: x is half of the hypotenuse, or 5. The side opposite 60° is x $\sqrt{3}$, or 5 $\sqrt{3}$.

Practice: 30°-60°-90° Right Triangle Problems

1. If the longest side of a 30°-60°-90° right triangle is 12, what are the measures of the other sides?

2. If one angle of a right triangle is 30° and the measure of the shortest side is 7, what is the measure of the remaining two sides?

Answers: 30°-60°-90° Right Triangle Problems

1. Since the ratio of the sides of a 30°-60°-90° right triangle are x, 2x, x $\sqrt{3}$ and the longest side, 2x, is 12, then the shortest side, x, is 6, and the third side is 6 $\sqrt{3}$.

2. If one angle of a right triangle is 30°, then the other angle must be 60°. Hence we have a 30°-60°-90° right triangle. Using the ratio x, 2x, x $\sqrt{3}$, with x equaling 7, 2x = 14 and the third side is 7 $\sqrt{3}$.

Quadrilaterals

● A polygon having four sides is called a *quadrilateral*. There are four angles in its interior. The sum of the measures of these interior angles will always be 360°. A quadrilateral is named by using the four letters of its vertices.

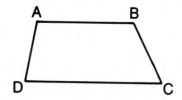

This is quadrilateral ABCD.

Types of Quadrilaterals

Square

- The *square* has four equal sides and four right angles.
- Its opposite sides are parallel.
- Diagonals of a square are equal and bisect each other.

Rectangle

- The *rectangle* has opposite sides equal and parallel and four right angles.
- Diagonals of a rectangle are equal and bisect each other.

Parallelogram

- The *parallelogram* has opposite sides equal and parallel, opposite angles equal, and consecutive angles supplementary. Every parallelogram has a height.
- Diagonals of a parallelogram are not necessarily equal but do bisect each other.

$\angle A = \angle C$
$\angle B = \angle D$
$\angle A + \angle B = 180°$
$\angle A + \angle D = 180°$
$\angle B + \angle C = 180°$
$\angle C + \angle D = 180°$

AE is the height of the parallelogram, AB ∥ DC, and AD ∥ BC.

Rhombus

- The *rhombus* is a parallelogram with four equal sides. A rhombus has a height. BE is the height.
- Diagonals of a rhombus are not necessarily equal but do bisect each other.

Trapezoid

- The *trapezoid* has only one pair of parallel sides. A trapezoid has a height. AE is the height. AB ∥ DC.
- The parallel sides are called the *bases*. AB and DC are bases. The nonparallel sides are called the *legs*. AD and BC are legs.
- The *median* of a trapezoid is a line segment that is parallel to the bases and bisects the legs (connects the midpoints of the legs). FG is the median.

Comparing Quadrilaterals

- A *parallelogram* is a quadrilateral with opposite sides and angles equal.
- A *rectangle* is a parallelogram with right angles.
- A *rhombus* is a parallelogram with equal sides.
- A *square* is a rhombus with right angles.
- A *trapezoid* is a quadrilateral with only one pair of parallel sides.

Practice: Polygon Problems

Identify the following figures.

7.   8. 9.

AB = BC = CD = DA

10.   All sides and angles
    are equal.

True or False:

11. A square must be a parallelogram.
12. A rhombus must be a rectangle.
13. A parallelogram must be a rectangle.

Answers: Polygon Problems

1. Pentagon	6. Square	11. True
2. Rectangle	7. Rhombus	12. False
3. Hexagon	8. Quadrilateral	13. False
4. Parallelogram	9. Octagon	
5. Triangle	10. Regular pentagon	

Sum of the Interior Angles of a Polygon

• The *sum of the interior angles* in any polygon can be determined
by using this formula: $(n - 2)180°$, where n is the number of sides
in the polygon. *For example:*

The triangle (3 sides):
$$(n - 2)180°$$
$$(3 - 2)180°$$
$$(1)180° = 180°$$

The quadrilateral (4 sides):
$$(n - 2)180°$$
$$(4 - 2)180°$$
$$(2)180° = 360°$$

The pentagon (5 sides)
$$(n - 2)180°$$
$$(5 - 2)180°$$
$$(3)180° = 540°$$

Practice: Sum of the Interior Angles of a Polygon Problems

1. Find the sum of the interior angles of a hexagon.
2. Find the degree measure of an angle of a regular nonagon.

Answers: Sum of the Interior Angles of a Polygon Problems

1. Since a hexagon has six sides, use n = 6.

$$(n - 2)180°$$
$$(6 - 2)180°$$
$$(4)180° = 720°$$

2. A regular nonagon has nine equal angles. First find the total degree measure.

$$(n - 2)180°$$
$$(9 - 2)180°$$
$$(7)180° = 1260°$$

Now to find one angle, divide the total by 9, the number of angles.

$$\frac{1260°}{9} = 140°$$

Perimeter and Area of Polygons

Perimeter of Polygons

● *Perimeter* means the total distance all the way around the outside of any polygon. The perimeter of any polygon can be determined by adding up the lengths of all the sides. The total distance around will be the sum of all sides of the polygon. No special formulas are really necessary, although two are commonly seen.

● Perimeter of a square = $4s$. (s = length of side)

● Perimeter of a parallelogram (rectangle and rhombus) = $2l + 2w$ or $2(l + w)$. (l = length, w = width)

Area of Polygons

● *Area* (A) means the amount of space inside the polygon. The formulas for each area are as follows:

- Triangle: $A = \frac{1}{2}bh$

or

For example:

$A = \frac{1}{2}bh$
$A = \frac{1}{2}(24)(18) = 216$ sq in

- Square or rectangle: $A = lw$

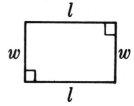

For example:

$A = l(w) = 4(4) = 16$ sq in

$A = l(w) = 12(5) = 60$ sq in

- Parallelogram: $A = bh$

For example:

A = b(h)
A = 10(5) = 50 sq in

- Trapezoid: A = ½(b₁ + b₂)h

For example:

A = ½(b₁ + b₂)h
A = ½(8 + 12)7
  = ½(20)7 = 70 sq in

Practice: Perimeter and Area of Polygons Problems

1. P =
   A =

2. P =
   A =

3. P =
   A =

4. P =
   A =

AB‖DC AD‖BC

5. P =
   A =

6. P =
   A =

AB‖DC

Answers: Perimeter and Area of Polygons Problems

1. $P = 15 + 13 + 14 = 42$
   $A = \frac{1}{2}bh = \frac{1}{2}(14)(12) = 84$

2. $P = 6 + 8 + 10 = 24$
   $A = \frac{1}{2}bh = \frac{1}{2}(8)(6) = 24$

3. $P = 10 + 10 + 2 + 2 = 24$
   $A + bh = 10(2) = 20$

4. $P = 10 + 10 + 5 + 5 = 30$
   $A = bh = 10(4) = 40$

5. $P = 5 + 5 + 5 + 5 = 20$
   $A = bh = 4(5) = 20$

6. $P = 17 + 7 + 10 + 28 = 62$
   $A = \frac{1}{2}(b_1 + b_2)h = \frac{1}{2}(7 + 28)(8) = 4(35) = 140$

Circles

● In a plane the set of all points equidistant from a given point is
called a *circle*. Circles are named by the letter of their center
point.
This is circle M.
M is the center point, since
it is the same distance away
from any point on the circle.

Parts of a Circle

Radius

● The *radius* is a line segment whose endpoints lie one at the center
of the circle and one on the circle. Also, the length of this
segment.

MA is a radius.
MB is a radius.

In any circle, all radii (plural)
are the same length.

Diameter

● The *diameter* of a circle is a
  line segment that contains the
  center and has its end points
  on the circle. Also, the length
  of this segment.

AB is a diameter.
CD is a diameter.

In any circle, all diameters are
the same length. Each diameter
equals two radii in length.

Chord

● A *chord* of a circle is a line segment
  whose endpoints lie on the circle.

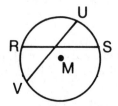

RS is a chord.
UV is a chord.

The diameter is the longest chord
in any circle.

Arc

● An *arc* is the distance between any two points *on* the circle itself.
  An arc is a piece of the circle. The symbol ⌒ is used to denote an
  arc. It is written on top of the two endpoints that form the arc. Arcs
  are measured in degrees (or radians). There are 360° around the
  circle.

This is $\overset{\frown}{EF}$.
Minor $\overset{\frown}{EF}$ is the shorter arc
between E and F.
Major $\overset{\frown}{EF}$ is the longer arc
between E and F.
When $\overset{\frown}{EF}$ is written, the minor arc
is assumed.

Practice: Parts of a Circle Problems

Match the parts of the following circle with center O.

1. Radius   2. Diameter   3. Chord   4. Name of circle

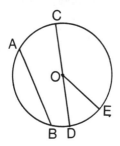

Answers: Parts of a Circle Problems

1. OE   2. CD   3. AB or CD   4. O

Circumference and Area of a Circle

Circumference

- *Circumference* is the distance around the circle. Since the circumference of any circle divided by its diameter yields the same value, the Greek letter π (pi) is used to represent that value. In fractional or decimal form, the commonly used approximations of π are $\pi \simeq$ 3.14 or $\pi \simeq \frac{22}{7}$. Use either value in your calculations. The formula for circumference is: $C = \pi d$ or $C = 2\pi r$. *For example:*

In circle M, d = 8, since r = 4.
$C = \pi d$
$C = \pi(8)$
$C = 3.14(8)$
$C = 25.12$ inches

Area

- The *area* of a circle can be determined by: $A = \pi r^2$. *For example:*

In circle M, r = 5, since d = 10.
$A = \pi r^2$
$A = \pi(5^2)$
$A = 3.14(25)$
$A = 78.5$ sq in

Practice: Circumference and Area of a Circle Problems

Find the area and circumference (leave in terms of π) of each circle from the given radius or diameter.

1. A =
   C =

2. A =
   C =

Find the radius.

3. A = 49π sq in   4. C = 60π in

Answers: Circumference and Area of a Circle Problems

1. A = πr^2
   A = $\pi(3)^2$
   A = 9π sq in

   C = $2\pi r$
   C = $2\pi(3)$
   C = 6π in

2. A = πr^2
   A = $\pi(5)^2$
   A = 25π sq in

   C = $2\pi r$ *or*   C = πd
   C = $2\pi(5)$ C = 10π in
   C = 10π in

3. A = πr^2
   $49\pi = \pi r^2$
   $49 = r^2$
   7 in = r

4. C = $2\pi r$ *or*   C = πd
   $60\pi = 2\pi r$ $60\pi = \pi d$
   $60 = 2r$ 60 = d
   30 in = r   30 in = d

Angles in a Circle

Central Angles

- *Central angles* are angles formed by any two radii in a circle. The vertex is the center of the circle. A central angle is equal to the measure of its intercepted arc. *For example:*

In circle O, AB = 75°.
Therefore, $\angle AOB = 75°$.
(m $\overset{\frown}{AB}$ is sometimes used to denote the measure of arc AB.)

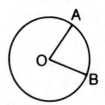

Inscribed Angles

● *Inscribed angles* are angles formed
by any two chords of a circle that
meet on the circle. (The vertex is
on the circle.) An inscribed angle
is equal to one-half the measure of
its intercepted arc. *For example:*

In circle O, $\overset{\frown}{CD}$ = 90°.
Therefore, ∠CED = 45°.

● In general as the vertex moves further away from the arc, the angle
measure gets smaller. The closer the vertex to the arc, the larger
the size of the angle. *For example:*

$$\overset{\frown}{AB} = 80°$$

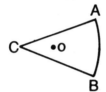

∠AOB = 80°   ∠ACB = 40°   ∠ARB must be smaller than 40°

Practice: Angles in a Circle Problems

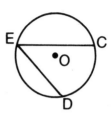

1. Find the measure of ∠x in circle A.

2. Find the measure of ∠y in circle A.

3. Find the measure of ∠z.

4. Find the measure of ∠q.

5. Find the measure of $\overset{\frown}{AB}$ of circle Q.

6. Find the measure of ∠AQB in circle Q.

Answers: Angles in a Circle Problems

1. Since ∠x is a central angle, it equals the measure of the arc it intercepts, or 60°.

2. Since ∠y is an inscribed angle, it equals one-half the arc it intercepts, or 30°.

3. ∠z, an inscribed angle, equals one-half 110°, or 55°.

4. ∠q, an inscribed angle, equals one-half 110°, or 55°.

5. $\overset{\frown}{AB}$ is twice the inscribed angle which intercepts $\overset{\frown}{AB}$. Thus, 2 × 40° = 80°.

6. The measure of central angle AQB equals the measure of the arc it intercepts, or 80°.

Concentric Circles

- Circles with the same center are called *concentric circles*.

Tangents to a Circle

- A line that touches a circle at only one point is called a *tangent* or tangent line. This line cannot be in the interior of the circle. Two tangents to the same circle drawn from the same point are:

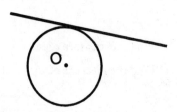

1. Equal in length. (AB = AC)
2. Perpendicular to a radius
   that meets at that point.

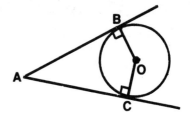

Congruence and Similarity

- Two plane geometric figures are said to be *congruent* if they are identical in size and shape. They are said to be *similar* if they have the same shape but are not identical in size. *For example:*

All squares are similar.

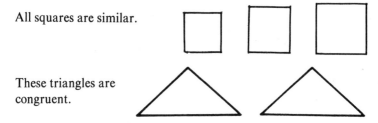

These triangles are
congruent.

Volumes of Solid Figures

- Three of the most common solid geometric figures are the cube, the rectangular solid, and the cylinder. Each of these figures may be thought of as the three-dimensional extensions of three flat two-dimensional figures, namely the square, the rectangle, and the circle.
- The *volume* of a solid is the number of cubic units of space the figure contains. Volume is always labeled *cubic* units. The formula for the volume of each shape is different, but in general, it is the area of the base times the height.

Volume of a Cube

- The formula for the
  volume of a cube is
  $V = s \times s \times s = s^3$

Volume of a Rectangular Solid

- The formula for the volume
  of a rectangular solid is
  $V = (lw)(h) = lwh$

Volume of a Right Circular Cylinder (Circular Bases)

- The formula for the volume of
  a right circular cylinder
  (circular bases) is
  $V = (\pi r^2)h = \pi r^2 h$

Practice: Volumes of Solid Figures Problems

Find the volumes of the solid figures below whose dimensions are indicated.

1. Rectangular Solid

2. Cube

s=8 yds

3. Cylinder

Answers: Volumes of Solid Figures Problems

1. $V = lwh = (10)(5)(4) = 200$ cu in

2. $V = s^3 = 8 \times 8 \times 8 = 512$ cu yd

3. $V = \pi r^2 h = \dfrac{22}{\cancel{7}} \times \dfrac{2}{1} \times \dfrac{2}{1} \times \dfrac{\overset{2}{\cancel{14}}}{1} = 22(8) = 176$ cu in

Surface Areas of Solid Figures

Surface Area of a Rectangular Solid

● To find the *surface area of a rectangular solid,* proceed as follows.

Area of side 1 = 3 × 4 = 12 sq in
Area of side 2 = 5 × 3 = 15 sq in
Area of side 3 = 5 × 4 = 20 sq in

Since there are two of each of these sides:
Surface Area = 2(12) + 2(15) + 2(20)
                = 24 + 30 + 40
                = 94 sq in

Surface Area of a Right Circular Cylinder

● To determine the *surface area of a right circular cylinder,* it is best envisioned "rolled out" onto a flat surface as below.

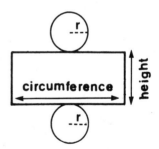

Now find the area of each individual piece. The area of each circle equals πr^2. Note that the length of the rectangle equals the

circumference of the circle. The rectangle's area equals circumference times height. Adding the three parts gives the surface area of the cylinder: *For example:*

Find the surface area
of a cylinder with radius 5'
and height 12'.

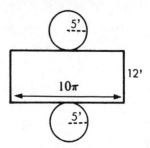

The area of the top circle $= \pi(r^2) = \pi(5^2) = 25\pi$.
The area of the bottom circle is the same, 25π.
The length of the rectangle is the circumference of the circle, or $2\pi r = 2\pi(5) = 10\pi$.
Therefore the area of the rectangle equals its height times $10\pi = 12 \times 10\pi = 120\pi$.
Totaling all the pieces gives $25\pi + 25\pi + 120\pi = 170\pi$.

Practice: Volumes and Surface Areas of Solids Problems

1. What is the volume of a cube whose side is 5½"?

2. If a rectangular solid has a length of 4 inches, a width of 3 inches, and a height of 2 feet, find its volume.

3. Given that a cylinder's height is 42" and its radius is 3", determine its volume.

4. Find the surface area of a rectangular solid that measures 4" by 7" by 6".

5. Find the surface area of a right regular cylinder that has a height of 20" and a radius of 4".

Answers: Volumes and Surface Areas of Solids Problems

1. 166⅜ cu in
   $V = s^3 = 5½ \times 5½ \times 5½ = {}^{11}\!/_2 \times {}^{11}\!/_2 \times {}^{11}\!/_2 = {}^{1331}\!/_8 = 166⅜$ cu in

2. 288 cu in
    $V = l \times w \times h = 4 \times 3 \times 24 = 288$ cu in

    Note: The 2 feet had to be converted to 24 inches so that all dimensions would be expressed in the same units.

3. 1,188 cu in.
    $$V = \pi r^2 h = \frac{22}{\cancel{7}} \times \frac{3}{1} \times \frac{3}{1} \times \frac{\cancel{42}^{6}}{1} = 1,188 \text{ cu in}$$

4. 188 sq in.

    Area of side 1 = $4 \times 6 = 24$ sq in
    Area of side 2 = $6 \times 7 = 42$ sq in
    Area of side 3 = $4 \times 7 = 28$ sq in
    Surface area = $2(24) + 2(42) + 2(28)$
    $\qquad\qquad = 48 + 84 + 56$
    $\qquad\qquad = 188$ sq in

5. 192 π sq in.

    Area of top circle = $\pi r^2 = 16\pi$ sq in
    Area of bottom circle = $\pi r^2 = 16\pi$ sq in
    Area of rectangle = $20 \times$ circumference
    $\qquad\qquad\qquad = 20 \times 2\pi r$
    $\qquad\qquad\qquad = 20 \times 2\pi(4)$
    $\qquad\qquad\qquad = 20 \times 8\pi$ sq in
    $\qquad\qquad\qquad = 160\pi$ sq in

Adding all the pieces, total surface area is 192π sq in.

Geometry Formulas That You Should Be Familiar With

TRIANGLE

Perimeter = $s_1 + s_2 + s_3$
Area = $\frac{1}{2}bh$

SQUARE

Perimeter = $4s$
Area = $s \cdot s$, or s^2

RECTANGLE

Perimeter = $2(l + w)$, or $2l + 2w$
Area = bh, or lw

PARALLELOGRAM

Perimeter = $2(l + w)$, or $2l + 2w$
Area = bh

TRAPEZOID

Perimeter = $b_1 + b_2 + s_1 + s_2$
Area = $\frac{1}{2}h(b_1 + b_2)$, or $h\left(\dfrac{b_1 + b_2}{2}\right)$

CIRCLE

Circumference = $2\pi r$, or πd
Area = πr^2

PYTHAGOREAN THEOREM
(for right triangles)

$a^2 + b^2 = c^2$
The sum of the squares of the legs of a right triangle equals the square of the hypotenuse.

CUBE

Volume = $s \cdot s \cdot s$, or s^3
Surface area = $s \cdot s \cdot 6$

RECTANGULAR PRISM

Volume = $l \cdot w \cdot h$
Surface area = $2(lw) + 2(lh) + (2wh)$

RIGHT CIRCULAR CYLINDER

Volume = $\pi r^2 h$
Surface area = $2(\pi r^2) + h(2\pi r)$

GEOMETRY REVIEW TEST

Questions

1. The study of shapes and figures in two dimensions is called _____ .

2. The study of shapes and figures in three dimensions is called _____ .

3. An angle is formed by two rays that have the same endpoint; that endpoint is called the _____ .

4. Which of the following name the same angle in the triangle? _____ .

   (A) ∠A, ∠ACB, and ∠CAB
   (B) ∠ACB and ∠CAB
   (C) ∠A, ∠1, ∠B
   (D) ∠A, ∠CAB, and ∠1
   (E) ∠ACB, ∠1, and ∠B

5. A right angle measures _____ .

6. An acute angle measures _____ .

7. An obtuse angle measures _____ .

8. A straight angle measures _____ .

9. Two angles next to each other, sharing a common side and vertex, are called _____ .

10. In the diagram _____ .

   (A) ∠1 = ∠3
   (B) ∠1 = ∠2 and ∠3 = ∠4
   (C) ∠2 = ∠4 and ∠2 = ∠3
   (D) ∠1 = ∠2 and ∠3 = ∠2
   (E) ∠1 = ∠4 and ∠2 = ∠3

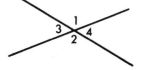

11. Two angles the sum of whose measures is 90° are said to be _____ to each other.

12. Two angles the sum of whose measures is 180° are said to be _____ to each other.

13. An angle bisector _____ .

14. A _____ is often described as the shortest distance between two points; it continues forever in both directions.

15. A part of a line with two endpoints is called _____ .

16. A part of a line that continues in one direction and has only one endpoint is called _____ .

17. If two lines meet at a point they are called _____ lines.

18. Two lines that meet at right angles are _____ to each other.

19. Two or more lines that remain the same distance apart at all times are called _____ .

20. In the diagram _____ . $\ell \parallel m$

  I. $\angle 1 = \angle 2 = \angle 4 = \angle 5$
  II. $\angle 1 = \angle 4 = \angle 5 = \angle 8$
  III. $\angle 2 = \angle 3 = \angle 6 = \angle 7$
  IV. $\angle 5 = \angle 8$ only
  V. $\angle 5 = \angle 6 = \angle 8$

 (A) I and V   (D) II and III
 (B) II   (E) II and IV
 (C) III

For questions 21 through 28, name the following.

21. A three-sided polygon. _____

22. A four-sided polygon. _____

23. A five-sided polygon. _____

24. A six-sided polygon. _____

25. A seven-sided polygon. _____

26. An eight-sided polygon. _____

27. A nine-sided polygon. _____

28. A ten-sided polygon. _____

29. If all sides and angles have the same measure, the polygon is called _____.

30. In a polygon, a line segment that connects one vertex to another but is not the side of the polygon is called a _____.

31. The polygon at the right is called a _____ polygon.

32. The sum of the measures of the angles of any triangle is _____.

33. If all sides of a triangle are equal, the triangle is _____.

34. A triangle that has two equal sides is called _____.

35. A triangle whose three sides are of different lengths is called _____.

36. A triangle having a 90° angle is called _____.

37. A triangle containing an angle greater than 90° is called _____.

38. If all angles in a triangle are less than 90°, then the triangle is called _____.

39. In a triangle, a line segment drawn from a vertex to the midpoint of the opposite side is called _____.

40. If two angles of a triangle measure 43° each, what is the measure of the third angle? _____.

41. The longest side of triangle ABC is _____.

42. A triangle can have sides of length 2, 2, and 5. True or false?

43. Find the measure of angle z in the triangle shown right.

    ∠z = _____

44. Find the length of side c
    in right triangle ABC.

    c = _____

45. Find the length of side r
    in right triangle QRS.

    r = _____

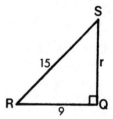

46. Find x, y, and z in
    the triangle shown right.

    x = _____
    y = _____
    z = _____

47. Find a, b, and c in the
    triangle shown right.

    a = _____
    b = _____
    c = _____

For questions 48 through 51, name the following figures.

48. _____

AB ∥ DC
AD ∥ BC

49. _____   AB = BC = DC = AD

50. _____   AB ∥ DC
                      AD ∥ BC

51. _____   AB ∥ DC

52. What is the sum of the measures of the interior angles of a heptagon? _____

53. Find the area of
    triangle ABC.
    area = _____

54. Find the area and perimeter
    of square ABCD.
    area = _____
    perimeter = _____

55. Find the area and perimeter
    of rectangle ABCD.
    area = _____
    perimeter = _____

56. Find the area of
parallelogram ABCD.
area = _____

57. Find the area of
trapezoid ABCD.
area = _____

In the circle below

58. OA is called a
_____ of circle O.

59. BC is called a
_____ of circle O.

60. DC is called a
_____ of circle O.

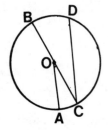

61. Find the area and
circumference of
circle A (in terms
of π).
area = _____
circumference = _____

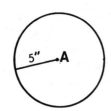

62. In the circle shown below,
if $\widehat{AB} = 50°$, then the measure of the central
angle AOB = _____.

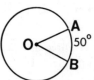

63. In the circle shown right,
    if $\overparen{AB} = 100°$, then the measure
    of the inscribed
    angle ADB = _____.

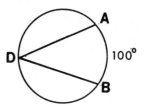

64. Circles with the same center are called _____.

65. A line that touches a circle at one point is called _____.

66. Polygons that are the same shape, but different in size are called
    _____.

67. Polygons that are exactly the same in shape and size are called
    _____.

*For questions 68 through 70, find the volumes and surface areas of
the figures below.*

68. volume = _____
    surface area = _____

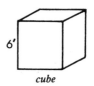

cube

69. volume = _____
    surface area = _____

rectangular solid

70. volume = _____
    surface area = _____

right circular cylinder

Answers

Page numbers following each answer refer to the review section applicable to this problem type.

1. plane geometry (p. 205)

2. solid geometry (p. 205)

3. vertex (p. 205)

4. (D) $\angle A$, $\angle CAB$, $\angle 1$ (p. 205)

5. 90° (p. 206)

6. less than 90° (p. 206)

7. greater than 90° but less than 180° (p. 206)

8. 180° (p. 206)

9. adjacent angles (p. 207)

10. (B) $\angle 1 = \angle 2$ and $\angle 3 = \angle 4$ (p. 208)

11. complementary (p. 208)

12. supplementary (p. 208)

13. divides an angle into two angles of equal measure (p. 209)

14. a line (p. 210)

15. a line segment (p. 210)

16. a ray (p. 211)

17. intersecting (p. 211)

18. perpendicular (p. 212)

19. parallel lines (p. 212)

20. (D) II and III (p. 212)

21. triangle (p. 216)

22. quadrilateral (p. 216)

23. pentagon (p. 216)

24. hexagon (p. 216)

25. heptagon (p. 216)

26. octagon (p. 216)

27. nonagon (p. 216)

28. decagon (p. 216)

29. regular (p. 216)

30. diagonal (p. 216)

31. concave (p. 216)

32. 180° (p. 216)

33. equilateral (p. 217)

34. isosceles (p. 217)

35. scalene (p. 217)

36. a right triangle (p. 217)

37. an obtuse triangle (p. 218)

38. an acute triangle (p. 218)

39. a median (p. 219)

40. 94° (p. 222)

41. AB (p. 220)

42. false (p. 220)

43. 120° (p. 221)

44. 10 (p. 225)

45. 12 (p. 225)

46. $x = 45°, y = 8, z = 8\sqrt{2}$
    (p. 225)

47. $a = 9, b = 9\sqrt{3}, c = 60°$
    (p. 226)

48. rectangle (p. 229)

49. square (p. 229)

50. parallelogram (p. 229)

51. trapezoid (p. 230)

52. 900° (p. 231)

53. 45 sq in (p. 232)

54. area = 49 sq in
    perimeter = 28 in (p. 232)

55. area = 18 sq in
    perimeter = 22 in (p. 232)

56. 36 sq in (p. 232)

57. 35 sq in (p. 232)

58. radius (p. 235)

59. diameter (could be called
    a chord) (p. 236)

60. chord (p. 236)

61. area = 25π sq in
    circumference = 10π in (p. 237)

62. 50° (p. 238)

63. 50° (p. 239)

64. concentric circles (p. 240)

65. a tangent line (p. 240)

66. similar (p. 241)

67. congruent (p. 241)

68. volume = 216 cu ft (p. 241)
    surface area = 216 sq ft
    (p. 243)

69. volume = 60 cu ft (p. 242)
    surface area = 94 sq ft
    (p. 243)

70. volume = 160π cu ft (p. 242)
    surface area = 112π sq ft
    (p. 243)

GEOMETRY GLOSSARY OF TERMS

ACUTE ANGLE: An angle whose measure is less than 90°.

ACUTE TRIANGLE: A triangle containing all acute angles.

ADJACENT ANGLES: Angles that share a common side and a common vertex.

ANGLE: Formed by two rays with a common endpoint.

ARC: The set of points on a circle that lie in the interior of a central angle.

AREA: The space within a shape; measured in square units.

BISECTS: Divides into two equal parts.

CENTRAL ANGLE: An angle whose vertex is the center of the circle. The measure of a central angle is equal to the measure of its arc.

CHORD: A line segment joining any two points on a circle.

CIRCLE: In a plane, the set of points all equidistant from a given point.

CIRCUMFERENCE: The distance around a circle; equals two times π times the radius or π times the diameter ($C = 2\pi r$ or πd).

COMPLEMENTARY ANGLES: Two angles the sum of whose measures is 90°.

CONCAVE POLYGON: A polygon which contains at least one diagonal outside the figure.

CONCENTRIC CIRCLES: Circles with the same center.

CONGRUENT: Exactly alike. Identical in shape and size.

CONSECUTIVE: Next to each other.

CONVEX POLYGON: A polygon in which all diagonals lie within the figure.

CORRESPONDING: In the same position. Coinciding.

CUBE: A six-sided solid. All sides are equal squares and all edges are equal.

DECAGON: A plane closed figure with ten sides and ten angles.

DEGREE: A unit of measurement of an angle.

DIAGONAL OF A POLYGON: A line segment connecting one vertex to another vertex, and not a side of the polygon.

DIAMETER: A line segment that contains the center and has its endpoints on the circle. Also, the length of this segment. (A chord through the center of the circle.)

EQUILATERAL TRIANGLE: A triangle in which all three angles are equal in measure and all three sides have the same length.

EXTERIOR ANGLE: An angle formed outside the polygon by extending one side. In a triangle, the measure of an exterior angle equals the sum of the measures of the two remote interior angles.

HEIGHT: Altitude. From the highest point, a perpendicular drawn to the base.

HEPTAGON: A plane closed figure with seven sides and seven angles.

HEXAGON: A plane closed figure with six sides and six angles.

HYPOTENUSE: In a right triangle, the side opposite the 90° angle.

INSCRIBED ANGLE: In a circle, an angle formed by two chords. Its vertex is on the circle. The measure of an inscribed angle equals one-half the measure of its arc.

INTERIOR ANGLES: Angles formed inside the shape or within two parallel lines.

INTERSECTING LINES: Lines that meet at a point.

ISOSCELES RIGHT TRIANGLE: A triangle having two equal sides, two equal angles, and one 90° angle. Its sides are always in the ratio 1, 1, $\sqrt{2}$.

ISOSCELES TRIANGLE: A triangle having two equal sides (and thus two equal angles across from those sides).

LEGS: In a right triangle, the two sides forming the 90° angle. In a trapezoid, the nonparallel sides.

LINE SEGMENT: A part of a line; has two endpoints.

MEDIAN: In a triangle, a line segment drawn from a vertex to the midpoint of the opposite side.

MEDIAN: In a trapezoid, a line segment parallel to the bases and bisecting the legs.

MIDPOINT: The halfway point of a line segment, equidistant from each endpoint.

MINUTE: A subdivision of an angle, one-sixtieth of a degree.:

NONAGON: A plane closed figure with nine sides and nine angles.

OBTUSE ANGLE: An angle greter than 90° but less than 180°.

OBTUSE TRIANGLE: A triangle containing an obtuse angle.

OCTAGON: A plane closed figure with eight sides and eight angles.

PARALLEL LINES: Two or more lines, always the same distance apart. Parallel lines never meet.

PARALLELOGRAM: A four-sided plane closed figure having opposite sides equal and parallel. (Opposite angles are equal, and consecutive angles are supplementary.)

PENTAGON: A five-sided plane closed figure. The sum of its five angles is 540°.

PERIMETER: The total distance around the outside of any polygon. The total length of all the sides.

PERPENDICULAR LINES: Two lines that intersect at right angles.

PI (π): A constant used in determining a circle's area or circumference. Equals approximately 3.14 or $^{22}/_7$.

PLANE: Often described as a flat surface.

PLANE FIGURE: Shape having only length and width (two dimensional).

PLANE GEOMETRY: The study of shapes and figures in two dimensions.

POINT: A basic element of geometry, a location. If two lines intersect, they do so at a point.

POLYGON: Many-sided plane closed figure. Triangle, quadrilateral, pentagon, etc.

PRISM: A three-dimensional shape bounded by congruent parallel faces and a set of parallelograms formed by joining the corresponding vertices of the bases.

PYTHAGOREAN THEOREM: A theorem which applies to right triangles. The sum of the squares of a right triangle's two legs equals the square of the hypotenuse ($a^2 + b^2 = c^2$).

QUADRILATERAL: A four-sided plane closed figure. The sum of its four angles equals 360°.

RADII: Plural of *radius*.

RADIUS: A line segment whose endpoints lie one at the center of a circle and one on the circle. Also, the length of this segment.

RAY: A half-line. Continues forever in one direction. Has one endpoint.

RECTANGLE: A four-sided plane closed figure having opposite sides equal and parallel and four right angles.

REGULAR POLYGON: A polygon in which sides and angles are all equal. For example, a regular pentagon has five equal angles and five equal sides.

RHOMBUS: A parallelogram with four equal sides.

RIGHT ANGLE: An angle whose measure is equal to 90°.

RIGHT CIRCULAR CYLINDER: A solid shaped like a can. Base meets side at a right angle.

RIGHT TRIANGLE: A triangle containing a 90° angle.

SCALENE TRIANGLE: A triangle having none of its sides equal (or angles equal).

SIMILAR: Having the same shape but not the same size, in proportion.

SOLID GEOMETRY: The study of shapes and figures in three dimensions: length, width, and thickness.

SQUARE: A four-sided plane closed figure having equal sides and four right angles. Its opposite sides are parallel.

STRAIGHT ANGLE: An angle equal to 180°. Often called a line.

STRAIGHT LINE: Often described as the shortest distance between two points. Continues forever in both directions. (*Line* means *straight line*.)

SUPPLEMENTARY ANGLES: Two angles the sum of whose measures is 180°.

SURFACE AREA: The total surface of all sides of a solid, or the total area of faces.

TANGENT TO A CIRCLE: A line, line segment, or ray that touches a circle at one point (cannot go within the circle).

TRANSVERSAL: A line crossing two or more parallel or nonparallel lines in a plane.

TRAPEZOID: A four-sided plane closed figure with only one pair of parallel sides, called bases.

TRIANGLE: A three-sided plane closed figure. Contains three angles the sum of whose measures is 180°.

VERTEX: The point at which two rays meet and form an angle, or the point at which two sides meet in a polygon.

VERTICAL ANGLES: The opposite angles formed by the intersection of two lines. Vertical angles are equal in measure.

VERTICES: Plural of *vertex*.

VOLUME: Capacity to hold, measured in cubic units. Volume of rectangular prism = length times width times height.

WORD PROBLEMS

WORD PROBLEMS DIAGNOSTIC TEST

Questions

1. What is the simple interest on $2,500 invested at 8% annual rate over three years?

2. A map's key shows that 1″ = 25 miles. How many inches apart on the map will two cities be if they are exactly 12 miles apart?

3. A plane flies from Los Angeles to Denver, a distance of 1,120 miles, at 280 miles per hour. A train from Denver to Los Angeles travels at a rate of 70 miles per hour. If a passenger took the plane to Denver and then returned to Los Angeles on the train, how long did the entire trip take?

4. In order to pass an examination, a student must answer exactly thirty questions correctly to obtain the minimum passing grade of 60%. How many questions are on the examination?

5. Last year, Tom's income was $18,000. This year, he was given a new position with the company with a salary of $24,000. What was the percent increase in Tom's salary?

6. If one number is four times as large as another number and the smaller number is decreased by two, the result is fourteen less than the larger number. What are the two numbers?

7. Fred is six years older than Sylvia. In two years, the sum of their ages will be eighteen. How old is Sylvia now?

8. The length of a rectangle is three more than the width. If the perimeter of the rectangle is twenty-six inches, what are the measures of length and width?

9. Adam can do a job in five hours, and Jennifer can do the same job in six hours. If they work together, how long will the job take them?

10. Nuts costing 70¢ per pound are mixed with nuts costing 40¢ per pound to produce twenty pounds of mixture worth 50¢ per pound. How much of each type is used?

Answers

Page numbers following each answer refer to the review section applicable to this problem type.

1. $600 (p. 264)

2. .48 inches (p. 270)

3. 20 hours (p. 274)

4. 50 questions (p. 277)

5. 33⅓% (p. 281)

6. 4 and 16 (p. 285)

7. 4 years old (p. 289)

8. 8 inches and 5 inches (p. 294)

9. 2⁸/₁₁ hours (p. 297)

10. 6⅔ pounds of 70¢ nuts
    13⅓ pounds of 40¢ nuts (p. 302)

WORD PROBLEMS REVIEW

Word problems are often the nemesis of even the best math student. For many, the difficulty is not the computation. The problems stem from what is given and what is being asked.

Solving Technique

There are many types of word problems involving arithmetic, algebra, geometry, and combinations of each with various twists. It is most important to have a systematic technique for solving word problems. Here is such a technique.

1. First, *identify what is being asked.* What are you ultimately trying to find? How far a car has traveled? How fast a plane flies? How many items can be purchased? Whatever it is, find it and then *circle it.* This helps insure that you are solving for what is being asked.

2. Next, *underline and pull out information you are given* in the problem. Draw a picture if you can. This helps you know what you have and will point you to a relationship or equation. Note any key words in the problem (see "Key Words and Phrases" following).

3. If you can, *set up an equation or some straightforward system* with the given information.

4. *Is all the given information necessary to solve the problem?* Occasionally you may be given more than enough information to solve a problem. *Choose what you need* and don't spend needless energy on irrelevant information.

5. *Carefully solve the equation or work the necessary computation.* Be sure you are working in the same units (for example, you may have to change feet into inches, pounds into ounces, etc., in order to keep everything consistent).

6. *Did you answer the question?* One of the most common errors in answering word problems is the failure to answer what was actually being asked.

7. And finally, *is your answer reasonable?* Check to make sure that an error in computation or a mistake in setting up your equation did not give you a ridiculous answer.

Key Words and Phrases

In working with word problems, there are some words or phrases that give clues as to how the problem should be solved. The most common words or phrases are as follows.

Add

Sum—as in *the sum of 2, 4, and 6 . . .*
Total—as in *the total of the first six payments . . .*
Addition—as in *a recipe calls for the addition of five pints . . .*
Plus—as in *three liters plus two liters . . .*
Increase—as in *her pay was increased by $15 . . .*
More than—as in *this week the enrollment was eight more than last week*
Added to—as in *if you added $3 to the cost . . .*
Successive—as in *the total of six successive payments . . .*

Subtract

Difference—as in *what is the difference between . . .*
Fewer—as in *there were fifteen fewer men than women . . .*
Remainder—as in *how many are left* or *what quantity remains . . .*
Less—as in *a number is five less than another number . . .*
Reduced—as in *the budget was reduced by $5,000 . . .*
Decreased—as in *if he decreased the speed of his car by ten miles per hour . . .*
Minus—as in *some number minus 9 is . . .*

Multiply

Product—as in *the product of 8 and 5 is . . .*
Of—as in *one-half of the group . . .*
Times—as in *five times as many girls as boys . . .*
At—as in *the cost of ten yards of material at 70¢ a yard is . . .*
Total—as in *if you spend $15 a week on gas, what is the total for a three week period . . .*
Twice—as in *twice the value of some number . . .*

Divide

Quotient—as in *the final quotient is . . .*
Divided by—as in *some number divided by 12 is . . .*

Divided into—as in *the group was divided into* . . .
Ratio—as in *what is the ratio of* . . .
Half—as in *half the profits are* . . . (dividing by 2)

As you work a variety of word problem types, you will discover more "clue" words.

A Final Reminder:

Be sensitive to what each of these questions is asking. What time? How many? How much? How far? How old? What length? What is the ratio?

Simple Interest

Example:

How much simple interest will an account earn in five years if $500 is invested at 8% interest per year?

First circle what you must find—*interest*. Now use the equation.

$$Interest = principal \text{ times } rate \text{ times } time$$
$$I = prt$$

Simply plug into the equation.

$$I = \$500(.08)5$$
$$I = \$200$$

Note that both rate and time are in yearly terms (annual rate; years).

Practice: Simple Interest Problems

1. What is the simple interest on $5,000 invested at 6% annual rate over four years.

2. What is the simple interest on a loan of $10,000 at a 6½% rate over five years?

3. What is the simple interest on $4,000 at a 4% semiannual rate over three years?

4. A woman invests $30,000 in a mutual stock that pays 3% quarterly. What is her simple interest dividend for nine months?

5. An investment group receives $3,600 simple interest for a three-year investment of $10,000. If the interest rate has remained stable throughout the investment period, what interest rate is the group receiving?

Answers: Simple Interest Problems

1. What is the simple interest on $5,000 invested at 6% annual rate over four years?

First circle what you must find—*simple interest*. Now using the information given in the problem, plug into the equation.

$$I = prt$$
$$I = \$5,000(.06)4$$
$$I = \$300(4)$$
$$I = \$1,200$$

Interest was therefore $1,200.

2. What is the simple interest on a loan of $10,000 at a 6½% rate over five years.

First circle what you must find—*simple interest*. Now using the information given in the problem, plug into the equation.

$$I = prt$$
$$I = \$10,000(.065)5$$
$$I = \$650(5) = \$3,250$$

Therefore simple interest is $3,250.

3. What is the simple interest on $4,000 at a 4% semiannual rate over three years?

First circle what you must find in the problem—*simple interest*. However, note that the 4% figure is a *semiannual* rate. Therefore, before plugging into the I = prt equation, you should change the rate to an annual rate. Since semiannual means every half year, the annual rate would be twice 4%, or 8%, annual rate. Thus,

$$I = prt$$
$$I = \$4,000(.08)3$$
$$I = \$320(3)$$
$$I = \$960$$

The simple interest is thus $960.

4. A woman invests $30,000 in a mutual stock that pays 3% quarterly. What is her simple interest dividend for nine months?

First circle what you must find in the problem—*simple interest dividend*. Now plug into the equation I = prt. Note however that the 3% rate is a quarterly rate; thus the annual rate would be 4(3%), or 12%.

$$I = prt$$
$$I = \$30,000(.12)\frac{3}{4}$$

Note that the time is *nine months,* or ¾ of a year.

$$I = \$3,600\ (\tfrac{3}{4})$$
$$I = \$2,700$$

Simple interest for nine months is $2,700.

5. An investment group receives $3,600 simple interest for a three-year investment of $10,000. If the interest rate has remained stable throughout the investment period, what interest rate is the group receiving?

First circle what you must find—*interest rate*. Now plug into the equation.

$$I = prt$$
$$\$3,600 = \$10,000(r)3$$

$$\frac{\$3,600}{3} = \frac{\$10,000(r)3}{3}$$

$$\$1,200 = \$10,000r$$

$$\frac{\$1,200}{\$10,000} = \frac{\$10,000r}{10,000}$$

$$.12 = r$$

The simple interest rate is thus 12%.

Compound Interest

Example:

What will be the final total after three years on an original investment of $1,000 if a 12% annual interest rate is compounded yearly?

First circle what you must find—*final total.* Note also that interest will be *compounded each year.* Therefore, the solution has three parts, one for each year.

Total for first year: *interest = principal* times *rate* times *time*
$$I = prt$$
$$I = \$1,000 \times .12 \times 1$$
$$I = \$120$$

Thus, the *total* after one year is $1,000 + $120 = $1,120.

Total for second year: I = prt
$$I = \$1,120(.12)1$$
$$I = \$134.40$$

Note that the principal at the beginning of the second year was $1,120. Thus, the total after two years is $1,120 + $134.40 = $1,254.40.

Total for third year: I = prt
$$I = \$1,254.40(.12)1$$
$$I = \$150.53$$

Note that the principal at the beginning of the second year was $1,254.40. Thus, the total after three years is $1,254.40 + $150.53 = $1,404.93

Practice: Compound Interest Problems

1. Find the total interest on $140 at a 5% annual rate for two years if interest is compounded annually.

2. Dana deposited $1,000 in the Great Island Savings for her trip to Tahiti. If interest is compounded annually at 8%, how much will be in her account at the end of two years?

3. If the beginning balance of a savings account is $200 and interest is paid semiannually at a 5% semiannual rate, what is the ending balance after two years?

4. Arnie invests $5,000 in a stock which pays dividends of 20% annually. Arnie always reinvests his dividends into his stock. How much stock will Arnie have after four years?

5. Stacy invests $3,000 for three years at an annual rate of 8%. Find her total after three years if the interest is compounded annually.

Answers: Compound Interest Problems

1. Find the total interest on $140 at a 5% annual rate for two years if interest is compounded annually.

First circle what you must find—*total interest.*

Interest for first year: $I = prt$
                            $I = \$140(.05)1$
                            $I = \$7.00$

Now add that interest to the second year principal to find the second year interest.

Interest for second year: $I = prt$
                             $I = \$147(.05)1$
                             $I = \$7.35$

Now add the first year interest, $7.00, to the second year interest, $7.35, to get total interest paid, $14.35.

2. Dana deposited $1,000 in the Great Island Savings for her trip to Tahiti. If interest is compounded annually at 8%, how much will be in her account at the end of two years?

First circle what you must find—*how much in her account after two years* (or total principal after two years).

Interest for first year: $I = prt$
                            $I = \$1,000(.08)1$
                            $I = \$80$

Thus, the amount in savings after one year will be $1,000 + $80 = $1,080. A faster way to find the total (with interest) is to simply multiply the principle by 1.08 (if the interest rate is 8%). If the interest rate were, say, 12%, then simply multiply the principal by 1.12, and so on. Therefore, using this method to find amount at the end of the second year:

$$p \times 1.08 =$$
$$\$1,080(1.08) = \$1,166.40$$

There will be $1,166.40 in the account at the end of two years.

3. If the beginning balance of a savings account is $200 and interest is paid semiannually at a 5% semiannual rate, what is the ending balance after two years?

First circle what you must find—*ending balance after two years*. Note how interest is paid (semiannually at 5%). Thus,

After ½ year:	$200(1.05) = $210 in account
After 1 year:	$210(1.05) = $220.50 in account
After 1½ years:	$220.50(1.05) = $231.53 in account
After 2 years:	$231.53(1.05) = $243.11 in account

Ending balance is thus $243.11 after two years.

4. Arnie invests $5,000 in a stock which pays dividends of 20% annually. Arnie always reinvests his dividends into his stock. How much stock will Arnie have after four years?

First circle what you must find—*how much stock . . . after four years* (total). Arnie will have

After the first year:	$5,000(1.20) = $6,000 worth of stock
After the second year:	$6,000(1.20) = $7,200 worth of stock
After the third year:	$7,200(1.20) = $8,640 worth of stock
After the fourth year:	$8,640(1.20) = $10,368 worth of stock

Therefore, after four years, Arnie will have $10,368 worth of stock.

5. Stacy invests $3,000 for three years at an annual rate of 8%. Find her total after three years if the interest is compounded annually.

First circle what you must find—*total after three years*. Stacy will have

After the first year: $3,000(1.08) = $3,240
After the second year: $3,240(1.08) = $3,499.20
After the third year: $3,499.20(1.08) = $3,779.14

Therefore, Stacy will have a total of $3,779.14 after three years.

Ratio and Proportion

Example:

If Arnold can type 600 pages of manuscript in twenty-one days, how many days will it take him to type 230 pages if he works at the same rate?

First circle what you're asked to find—*how many days*. One simple way to work this problem is to set up a "framework" (proportion) using the categories given in the equation. Here the categories are *pages* and *days*. Therefore a framework may be

$$\frac{\text{Pages}}{\text{Days}} = \frac{\text{Pages}}{\text{Days}}$$

Note that you also may have used

$$\frac{\text{Days}}{\text{Pages}} = \frac{\text{Days}}{\text{Pages}}$$

The answer will still be the same. Now simply plug into the equation for each instance.

$$\frac{600}{21} = \frac{230}{x}$$

Cross multiplying

$$600x = 21(230)$$
$$600x = 4,830$$

$$\frac{600x}{600} = \frac{4,830}{600}$$

$$x = 8\tfrac{1}{20}$$

Therefore it will take $8\frac{1}{20}$ days to type 230 pages. (Some of you may have simplified the original proportion before solving.)

Practice: Ratio and Proportion Problems

1. A map's key shows that $1'' = 35$ miles. How many inches apart on the map will two cities be if they are exactly seven miles apart?

2. If eight pounds of apples cost 98¢, at the same rate, how much will twelve pounds of apples cost?

3. If a girl can run m miles in h hours, at the same rate, how fast will she run k miles?

4. It takes q hours to drain a pool containing x gallons of water. If the pool contains y gallons of water, how long will it take to drain at the same rate?

5. In six years a man was able to build fifty-eight violins. Considering that he works at the same speed, how many complete violins can he build in eleven years?

Answers: Ratio and Proportion Problems

1. A map's key shows that $1'' = 35$ miles. How many inches apart on the map will two cities be if they are exactly seven miles apart?

First circle what you must find in the problem—*how many inches apart*. Now using the information given in the problem, construct a framework for a proportion and plug into it.

$$\frac{\text{miles}}{\text{inches}} = \frac{\text{miles}}{\text{inches}}$$

$$\frac{35}{1} = \frac{7}{x}$$

Cross multiplying

$$35x = 7$$

$$\frac{35x}{35} = \frac{7}{35}$$

$$x = \frac{1}{5}$$

The two cities will be $\frac{1}{5}$ of an inch apart.

2. If eight pounds of apples cost 98¢, at the same rate, how much will twelve pounds of apples cost?

First circle what you must find—*how much will twelve pounds of apples cost*. Now using the information given in the problem, set up a framework for a proportion and plug into it.

$$\frac{\text{pounds}}{\text{price}} = \frac{\text{pounds}}{\text{price}}$$

$$\frac{8}{98¢} = \frac{12}{x}$$

Cross multiplying

$$8x = 98(12)$$
$$8x = 1,176$$

$$\frac{8x}{8} = \frac{1,176}{8}$$

$$x = 147¢$$

The answer is 147¢ or $1.47.

3. If a girl can run m miles in h hours, at the same rate, how fast will she run k miles?

First circle what you must find—*how fast will she run k miles* (how many hours). Now using the information given in the problem, set up a framework for a proportion and plug into it.

$$\frac{\text{miles}}{\text{hours}} = \frac{\text{miles}}{\text{hours}}$$

$$\frac{m}{h} = \frac{k}{x}$$

Cross multiplying

$$mx = kh$$

$$\frac{mx}{m} = \frac{kh}{m}$$

$$x = \frac{kh}{m} \text{ or } \frac{hk}{m}$$

4. It takes q hours to drain a pool containing x gallons of water. If the pool contains y gallons of water, how long will it take to drain at the same rate?

First circle what you must find—*how long* (time). Now using the information given in the problem, set up a proportion and plug in.

$$\frac{\text{hours}}{\text{gallons}} = \frac{\text{hours}}{\text{gallons}}$$

$$\frac{q}{x} = \frac{?}{y}$$

Cross multiplying $qy = x(?)$

$$\frac{qy}{x} = \frac{x(?)}{x}$$

$$\frac{qy}{x} \text{ or } \frac{yq}{x} = ?$$

Careful: Notice that since x was in the problem, we used ? for the unknown quantity.

5. In six years a man was able to build fifty-eight violins. Considering that he works at the same speed, how many complete violins can he build in eleven years?

First circle what you must find in the problem—*how many complete violins* (note the word *complete*). Now using the information given in the problem, set up a proportion and plug in.

$$\frac{\text{violins}}{\text{years}} = \frac{\text{violins}}{\text{years}}$$

$$\frac{58}{6} = \frac{x}{11}$$

Cross multiplying $638 = 6x$

$$\frac{638}{6} = \frac{6x}{6}$$

$$106.33 \cong x$$

Therefore he can build 106 complete violins.

Motion

Example:

How long will it take a bus traveling 72 km/hr to go 36 kms? First circle what you're trying to find—*how long will it take* (time). Motion problems are solved by using the equation

$$\text{distance} = \text{rate times time}$$
$$d = rt$$

Therefore, simply plug in: 72 km/hr is the rate (or speed) of the bus, and 36 km is the distance.

$$d = rt$$
$$36 \text{ km} = (72 \text{ km/hr})(t)$$

$$\frac{36}{72} = \frac{72t}{72}$$

$$\frac{1}{2} = t$$

Therefore, it will take one-half hour for the bus to travel 36km at 72 km/hr.

Practice: Motion Problems

1. How many miles will a speedboat travel going 80 mph for 2½ hours?

2. How long will it take a car averaging 55 mph to travel a distance of 594 miles?

3. What is the average speed of a train if it takes three complete days to travel 3,600 miles?

4. A plane flies from New York to Chicago (a distance of 1,600 miles) at 400 mph. Returning from Chicago to New York it flies into a headwind and averages only 320 mph. How many hours total was the plane in the air for the entire trip?

5. Frank rows a boat at 5 mph but travels a distance of only 7 miles in two hours. How fast was the current moving against him?

Answers: Motion Problems

1. How many miles will a speedboat travel going 80 mph for 2½ hours?

First circle what you must find—*how many miles*. Now, using the information given in the problem, plug into the equation.

$$d = rt$$
$$d = (80)(2.5)$$
$$d = 200 \text{ miles}$$

Thus the speedboat will travel 200 miles.

2. How long will it take a car averaging 55 mph to travel a distance of 594 miles?

First circle what you must find—*how long will it take* (time). Now, using the information given in the problem, plug into the equation.

$$d = rt$$
$$594 = 55t$$
$$\frac{594}{55} = \frac{55t}{55}$$
$$10.8 = t$$

Therefore, it will take 10.8 hours.

3. What is the average speed of a train if it takes three complete days to travel 3,600 miles?

First circle what you must find—*average speed*. Now, using the information given in the problem, plug into the equation.

$$d = rt$$
$$3,600 = r(3 \text{ days})$$

Note that three days equals 3 times 24 hours, or 72 hours.

$$3,600 = r(72)$$
$$\frac{3,600}{72} = \frac{r(72)}{72}$$
$$50 = r$$

The average speed of the train is 50 mph.

4. A plane flies from New York to Chicago (a distance of 1,600 miles) at 400 mph. Returning from Chicago to New York it flies into a headwind and averages only 320 mph. How many hours total was the plane in the air for the entire trip?

First circle what you must find—*how many hours was the plane in the air* (time). Note that this is a two-part question, as the time each way will be different. First to find the time going to Chicago, plug into the equation.

$$d = rt$$
$$1,600 = 400t$$
$$\frac{1,600}{400} = \frac{400t}{400}$$
$$4 = t$$

Thus it took four hours to fly from New York to Chicago. Now, returning to New York:

$$d = rt$$
$$1,600 = 320t$$
$$\frac{1,600}{320} = \frac{320t}{320}$$
$$5 = t$$

Since returning took five hours of flying time, the total time in the air was 4 hours + 5 hours = 9 hours.

5. Frank rows a boat at 5 mph but travels a distance of only 7 miles in two hours. How fast was the current moving against him?

First circle what you must find—*how fast was the current moving against him.* Using the information given in the problem, plug into the equation. Note that Frank traveled 7 miles in two hours. Thus

$$d = rt$$
$$7 = r(2)$$
$$3.5 = r$$

Therefore, Frank's actual speed in the water was 3½ mph. If Frank rows at 5 mph, to find the current against him simply subtract.

Frank's speed − actual speed in water
5 mph − 3.5 mph = 1.5 mph

The current was going 1.5 mph against him.

Percent

Example:

Thirty students are awarded doctoral degrees at the graduate school, and this number comprises 40% of the total graduate student body. How many graduate students were enrolled?

First circle what you must find in the problem—*how many graduate students*. Now, in order to plug into the percentage equation

$$\frac{is}{of} = \%$$

try rephrasing the question into a simple sentence. For example, in this case

30 is 40% of what total?

Note that the 30 sits next to the word *is;* therefore, 30 is the "is" number. 40 is the percent. Notice that *what total* sits next to the word *of*. Therefore, plugging into the equation,

$$\frac{is}{of} = \%$$

$$\frac{30}{x} = \frac{40}{100}$$

Cross multiplying $40x = 3,000$

$$\frac{40x}{40} = \frac{3,000}{40}$$

$$x = 75$$

Therefore, the total graduate enrollment was 75 students.

Practice: Percent Problems

1. In a school of three hundred students, sixty do not sign up for after-school sports. What percent of the school signs up for after-school sports?

2. In order to pass an examination, a student must answer exactly nine questions in order to receive the lowest passing grade, a 75%. How many questions are on the examination?

3. Seventy million Americans are registered voters. Sixty percent are registered Democrats, and the rest are either registered Republicans or uncommitted. If ten percent of the total registered voters are uncommitted, how many registered voters are registered Republicans?

4. Slightly more than half (or 55%) of eight hundred people polled answered vanilla when asked their favorite ice-cream flavor. What percent of those polled answered chocolate as their favorite?

5. A two-hundred-square-yard playground is to be constructed. Exactly 40% must be grass, 30% must be sand, and the remaining percentage asphalt. What are the square-yard specifications for grass, sand, and asphalt?

6. A United States postage stamp collection was offered for sale at a stamp show for $800 but went unsold. Its owner resubmitted the collection for sale at the next stamp show but dropped his asking price 30%. The collection, however, still did not sell, so the owner offered an additional discount of 25% off the new asking price. What was the final price of the postage stamp collection?

Answers: Percent Problems

1. In a school of three hundred students, sixty do not sign up for after-school sports. What percent of the school signs up for after-school sports?

First circle what you must find in this problem—*what percent . . . signs up*. Now, using the information given in the problem, plug into the equation. Note that since sixty students do *not* sign up for after-school sports, the number that *does* sign up must be the total number of students minus sixty, or $300 - 60 = 240$ students. The problem may now be reworded as *240 students is what percent of 300.*

$$\frac{\text{is}}{\text{of}} = \%$$

$$\frac{240}{300} = \frac{x}{100}$$

Cross multiplying $24,000 = 300x$

$$\frac{24,000}{300} = \frac{300x}{300}$$

$$80 = x$$

Therefore, 80% of the school signs up for after-school sports.

2. In order to pass an examination, a student must answer exactly nine questions in order to receive the lowest passing grade, a 75%. How many questions are on the examination?

First circle what you are looking for—*how many questions are on the examination.* To plug into the equation, this problem may be reworded as *nine questions is 75% of how many questions.* Now plug in.

$$\frac{\text{is}}{\text{of}} = \%$$

$$\frac{9}{x} = \frac{75}{100}$$

Cross multiplying $900 = 75x$

$$\frac{900}{75} = \frac{75x}{75}$$

$$12 = x$$

Therefore, there are twelve questions on the test.

3. Seventy million Americans are registered voters. Sixty percent are registered Democrats, and the rest are either registered Republicans or uncommitted. If ten percent of the total registered voters are uncommitted, how many registered voters are registered Republicans?

First circle what you are asked to find—*how many . . . are registered Republicans*. Note that if 60% are Democrats and 10% are uncommitted, then 30% must be Republicans. Now you may restate the question as *how much is 30% of seventy million voters*. You may now plug into the equation.

$$\frac{\text{is}}{\text{of}} = \%$$

$$\frac{x}{70 \text{ million}} = \frac{30}{100}$$

Cross multiplying $100x = 2,100 \text{ million}$

$$x = 21 \text{ million}$$

In this problem, since you are finding 30% of seventy million, you could simply multiply: $.30 \times 70$ million = 21 million. Therefore, there are 21 million registered Republicans.

4. Slightly more than half (or 55%) of eight hundred people polled answered vanilla when asked their favorite ice-cream flavor. What percent of those polled answered chocolate as their favorite?

Be careful. Note here that just because 55% like vanilla, that doesn't mean that *all* the remaining 45% like chocolate. There are many ice-cream flavors to choose from, and the remaining 45% could be divided among chocolate, strawberry, pistachio, etc. There is thus not enough information to determine an answer. This type of question appears occasionally.

5. A two-hundred-square-yard playground is to be constructed. Exactly 40% must be grass, 30% must be sand, and the remaining percentage asphalt. What are the square-yard specifications for grass, sand, and asphalt?

Note that this "three-part" question may be rephrased as:

> *For the grass, what is 40% of 200?*
> *For the sand, what is 30% of 200?*
> *For the asphalt, what is 30% of 200?*
> (30% is the remaining percentage for the asphalt)

Using the equation, for the grass:

$$\frac{is}{of} = \%$$

$$\frac{x}{200} = \frac{40}{100}$$

Cross multiplying $100x = 8,000$
$x = 80$ sq yds grass

For the sand:

$$\frac{x}{200} = \frac{30}{100}$$

Cross multiplying $100x = 6,000$
$x = 60$ sq yds sand

For the asphalt: 60 sq yds asphalt (same percentage as for sand)

6. A United States postage stamp collection was offered for sale at a stamp show for $800 but went unsold. Its owner resubmitted the collection for sale at the next stamp show but dropped his asking price 30%. The collection, however, still did not sell, so the owner offered an additional discount of 25% off the new asking price. What was the final price of the postage stamp collection?

The original price was $800. Thirty percent drop in price is:

$$30\% \text{ of } 800 = .30 \times 800 = \$240 \text{ off}$$

The new price therefore is $800 − $240 = $560. Since the collection still did not sell (at $560), an additional 25% discount was offered:

$$25\% \text{ of } \$560 = .25 \times 560 = \$140 \text{ off}$$

Therefore the final asking price is $560 − $140 = $420.

Percent Change

Example:

Last year Harold earned $250 a month at his after-school job. This year his after-school earnings have increased to $300 per month. What is the percent increase in his monthly after-school earnings?

First circle what you're looking for—*percent increase*.

Percent change (percent increase, percentage rise, % difference, percent decrease, etc.) is always found by using the equation

$$\text{percent change} = \frac{\text{change}}{\text{starting point}}$$

Therefore, $$\text{percent change} = \frac{\$300 - \$250}{\$250}$$

$$= \frac{\$50}{\$250}$$

$$= \frac{1}{5} = .20 = 20\%$$

The percent increase in Harold's after-school salary was 20%.

Practice: Percent Change Problems

1. Last year Hank's income was $12,000. This year it rose to $15,000. What was the percent increase in Hank's salary?

2. A five-year study showed that the population of Hicksville, New York, fell from 65,000 in 1975 to 48,750 in 1980. What was the percent decrease in population over those five years?

3. Last year's Dow Jones averaged 900. This year's index averaged 1080. What was the percentage rise in the average Dow Jones index over those years?

4. Economic indicators predict 12% inflation over the next 12 months. If that's true, how much must a $20,000 salary be increased to keep up with inflation?

5. Due to 5% inflation, a woman's monthly salary was increased $80 to exactly keep up with the economy. What is the woman's new monthly salary? (Hint: First find her initial monthly salary.)

Answers: Percent Change Problems

1. Last year Hank's income was $12,000. This year it rose to $15,000. What was the percent increase in Hank's salary?

First circle what you must find—*percent increase*. Now, using the information given in the problem, plug into the equation.

$$\text{percent increase} = \frac{\text{change}}{\text{starting point}}$$

$$= \frac{\$15{,}000 - \$12{,}000}{\$12{,}000}$$

$$= \frac{\$3{,}000}{\$12{,}000}$$

$$= .25, \text{ or } 25\%$$

The percent increase was 25%.

2. A five-year study showed that the population of Hicksville, New York, fell from 65,000 in 1975 to 48,750 in 1980. What was the percent decrease in population over those five years?

First circle what you must find—*percent decrease*. Now, using the information given in the problem, plug into the equation.

$$\text{percent decrease} = \frac{\text{change}}{\text{starting point}}$$

$$= \frac{65{,}000 - 48{,}750}{65{,}000}$$

$$= \frac{16{,}250}{65{,}000}$$

$$= .25, \text{ or } 25\%$$

The percent decrease was 25%. Note that the fact that the study was a five-year study had no bearing on the answer.

3. Last year's Dow Jones averaged 900. This year's index averaged 1080. What was the percentage rise in the average Dow Jones index over those years?

First circle what you must find—*percentage rise*. Now, using the information given in the problem, plug into the equation.

$$\text{percentage rise} = \frac{\text{change}}{\text{starting point}}$$

$$= \frac{1,080 - 900}{900}$$

$$= \frac{180}{900}$$

$$= .20, \text{ or } 20\%$$

The percentage rise in the average Dow Jones was 20%.

4. Economic indicators predict 12% inflation over the next 12 months. If that's true, how much must a $20,000 salary be increased to keep up with inflation?

First circle what you must find—*how much must a . . . salary be increased*. Now, using the information given in the problem, you could simply multiply: .12 × 20,000 = 2,400. Or, if you want to plug into the standard equation,

$$\text{percent increase} = \frac{\text{change}}{\text{starting point}}$$

$$12\% = \frac{x}{\$20,000}$$

$$\frac{.12}{1} = \frac{x}{\$20,000}$$

$$.12(\$20,000) = x$$

$$\$2,400 = x$$

The salary must be increased $2,400.

5. Due to 5% inflation, a woman's monthly salary was increased $80 to exactly keep up with the economy. What is the woman's new monthly salary? (Hint: First find her initial monthly salary.)

First circle what you must find—*new monthly salary*. Now, using the information given in the problem, plug into the equation.

$$\text{percent increase} = \frac{\text{change}}{\text{starting point}}$$

$$5\% = \frac{\$80}{x}$$

$$\frac{.05}{1} = \frac{\$80}{x}$$

$$.05x = \$80$$

$$\frac{.05x}{.05} = \frac{\$80}{.05}$$

$$x = \$1,600$$

Thus, $1,600 is her *starting* salary. Adding the change of $80 (increase), her *new* salary is $1,680.

Number

Examples:

1. One number exceeds another number by 5. If the sum of the two numbers is 39, find the smaller number.

First circle what you are looking for—*the smaller number.* Now let the smaller number equal x. Therefore, the larger number equals x + 5. Now use the problem to set up an equation.

$$\underbrace{\text{If the sum of the two numbers}}_{x + (x + 5)} \underbrace{\text{is}}_{=} \underbrace{39}_{39} \ldots$$

$$2x + 5 = 39$$
$$2x + 5 - 5 = 39 - 5$$
$$2x = 34$$

$$\frac{2x}{2} = \frac{34}{2}$$

$$x = 17$$

Therefore, the smaller number is 17.

2. If one number is three times as large as another number and the smaller number is increased by 19, the result is 6 less than twice the larger number. What is the larger number?

First circle what you must find—*the larger number*. Let the smaller number equal x. Therefore, the larger number will be 3x. Now using the problem, set up an equation.

The $\underbrace{\text{smaller number}}$ $\underbrace{\text{increased by}}$ $\underbrace{19}$ is $\underbrace{\text{6 less than twice the larger number.}}$

$$x \qquad + \qquad 19 = \qquad 2(3x) - 6$$

$$x + 19 = 6x - 6$$
$$-x + x + 19 = -x + 6x - 6$$
$$19 = 5x - 6$$
$$19 + 6 = 5x - 6 + 6$$
$$25 = 5x$$
$$5 = x$$

Therefore, the larger number, 3x, will be 3(5), or 15.

3. The sum of three consecutive integers is 306. What is the largest integer?

First circle what you must find—*the largest integer*. Let the smallest integer equal x; let the next integer equal x + 1; let the largest integer equal x + 2. Now use the problem to set up an equation.

The $\underbrace{\text{sum of three consecutive integers}}$ $\underbrace{\text{is}}$ $\underbrace{\text{306.}}$

$$x + (x + 1) + (x + 2) \qquad = 306$$

$$3x + 3 = 306$$
$$3x + 3 - 3 = 306 - 3$$
$$3x = 303$$

$$\frac{3x}{3} = \frac{303}{3}$$

$$x = 101$$

Therefore, the largest integer, x + 2, will be 101 + 2, or 103.

Practice: Number Problems

1. The sum of three consecutive integers is 51. What is the largest integer?

2. The sum of three consecutive even integers is 612. What is the smallest integer?

3. Two integers total 35. One integer is 23 larger than the other. What are the two integers?

4. The difference between ½ of a number and ⅓ of the same number is 8. What is the number?

5. If one number is twice as large as another number and the smaller number is increased by 8, the result is 4 less than the larger number. What is the larger number?

Answers: Number Problems

1. The sum of three consecutive integers is 51. What is the largest integer?

First circle what it is you must find—*the largest integer*. Let the consecutive integers equal x, x + 1, and x + 2. Now use the problem to set up an equation.

$$\underbrace{\text{The sum of three consecutive integers}}_{x + (x + 1) + (x + 2)} \underbrace{\text{is}}_{=} \underbrace{51.}_{51}$$

$$3x + 3 = 51$$
$$3x + 3 - 3 = 51 - 3$$
$$3x = 48$$

$$\frac{3x}{3} = \frac{48}{3}$$

$$x = 16$$

Therefore, the largest integer, x + 2, will be 16 + 2 = 18.

2. The sum of three consecutive even integers is 612. What is the smallest integer.

First circle what you must find—*the smallest integer*. Let the three integers equal x, x + 2, and x + 4 (since consecutive even numbers increase by 2). Now use the problem to set up an equation.

$$\underbrace{\text{The sum of three consecutive even integers}}_{x + (x + 2) + (x + 4)} \underbrace{\text{is}}_{=} \underbrace{612.}_{612}$$

$$3x + 6 = 612$$
$$3x + 6 - 6 = 612 - 6$$
$$3x = 606$$
$$\frac{3x}{3} = \frac{606}{3}$$
$$x = 202$$

The smallest integer, x, is therefore 202.

3. Two integers total 35. One integer is 23 larger than the other. What are the two integers?

First circle what you must find—*the two integers*. Let the smaller integer equal x. Therefore, the larger integer equals x + 23. Now use the problem to set up an equation.

$$\underbrace{\text{Two integers}} \ \underbrace{\text{total}} \ \underbrace{35.}$$
$$x + (x + 23) = 35$$

$$2x + 23 = 35$$
$$2x + 23 - 23 = 35 - 23$$
$$2x = 12$$
$$\frac{2x}{2} = \frac{12}{2}$$
$$x = 6$$

Therefore, one integer, x, is 6 and the other integer, x + 23, is 29.

4. The difference between ½ of a number and ⅓ of the same number is 8. What is the number?

First circle what you must find—*the number*. Therefore, let the number equal x. Now use the problem to set up an equation.

$$\underbrace{\text{The difference between ½ of a number and ⅓ of the same number}} \ \underbrace{\text{is}} \ \underbrace{8.}$$
$$(½)x - (⅓)x = 8$$

$$\frac{x}{2} - \frac{x}{3} = 8$$

Using a common denominator $\dfrac{3x}{6} - \dfrac{2x}{6} = 8$

$$\frac{x}{6} = 8$$

$$(6)\frac{x}{6} = (6)8$$

$$x = 48$$

The number is 48.

5. If one number is twice as large as another number and the smaller number is increased by 8, the result is 4 less than the larger number. What is the larger number?

First circle what you must find—*the larger number.* Now let x denote the smaller number. Therefore the larger number will be 2x, since it is twice as large as x. Now use the problem to set up an equation.

If the smaller number is increased by 8, the result is 4 less than the larger number.

$$x + 8 \qquad = \qquad 2x - 4$$

$$-x + x + 8 = 2x - x - 4$$
$$8 = x - 4$$
$$8 + 4 = x - 4 + 4$$
$$12 = x$$

Thus, the larger number, 2x, is 24.

Age

Examples:

1. Tom and Phil are brothers. Phil is thirty-five years old. Three years ago Phil was four times as old as his brother was then. How old is Tom now?

First circle what it is you must ultimately find—*Tom now.* Therefore, let t be Tom's age now. Then three years ago Tom's age would be t − 3. Four times Tom's age three years ago would be 4(t − 3). Phil's age three years ago would be 35 − 3 = 32. A simple chart may also be helpful.

	NOW	3 YEARS AGO
Phil	35	32
Tom	t	t − 3

Now use the problem to set up an equation.

Three years ago Phil was four times as old as his brother was then.

$$\underbrace{32}_{} = \underbrace{4 \text{ times}}_{} \qquad \underbrace{(t - 3)}_{}$$

$$\frac{32}{4} = \frac{4(t - 3)}{4}$$

$$8 = t - 3$$
$$8 + 3 = t - 3 + 3$$
$$11 = t$$

Therefore, Tom is now 11.

2. Lisa is 16 years younger than Kathy. If the sum of their ages is 30, how old is Lisa?

First circle what you must find—*Lisa.* Let Lisa equal x. Therefore, Kathy is x + 16. (Note that since Lisa is 16 years *younger* than Kathy, we must *add* 16 years to Lisa to denote Kathy's age.) Now use the problem to set up an equation.

$$\underbrace{\text{If the sum of their ages}}_{} \underbrace{\text{is}}_{} \underbrace{30}_{} \ldots$$

$$\text{Lisa} + \text{Kathy} = 30$$

$$x + (x + 16) = 30$$
$$2x + 16 = 30$$
$$2x + 16 - 16 = 30 - 16$$
$$2x = 14$$

$$\frac{2x}{2} = \frac{14}{2}$$

$$x = 7$$

Therefore, Lisa is 7 years old.

Practice: Age Problems

1. Clyde is four times as old as John. If the difference between their ages is 39 years, how old is Clyde?

2. Sylvia is twenty years older than Jan. If the sum of their ages is 48 years, how old is Jan?

3. Sheila is three times as old as Kim. The sum of their ages is 24 years. How old is Sheila?

4. In eight years, Joy will be three times as old as she is now. How old is Joy now?

5. Matt is six years older than Hector. In two years Matt will be twice as old as Hector. How old is Hector now?

Answers: Age Problems

1. Clyde is four times as old as John. If the difference between their ages is 39 years, how old is Clyde?

First circle what you must find in this problem—*Clyde*. Let John (the smaller of the two ages) equal x. Therefore, Clyde equals 4x. Now use the problem to set up an equation.

If the difference between their ages is 39 . . .

$$Clyde - John = 39$$
$$4x - x = 39$$
$$3x = 39$$
$$\frac{3x}{3} = \frac{39}{3}$$
$$x = 13$$

Therefore, Clyde, 4x, will be 4(13), or 52 years old.

2. Sylvia is twenty years older than Jan. If the sum of their ages is 48 years, how old is Jan?

First circle what you must find in this problem—*Jan*. Let Jan (the younger of the two ages) equal x. Therefore, Sylvia equals x + 20. Now use the problem to set up an equation.

If the sum of their ages is 48 . . .

$$Jan + Sylvia = 48$$

$$x + (x + 20) = 48$$
$$2x + 20 = 48$$
$$2x + 20 - 20 = 48 - 20$$
$$2x = 28$$
$$\frac{2x}{2} = \frac{28}{2}$$
$$x = 14$$

Therefore, Jan is 14 years old.

3. Sheila is three times as old as Kim. The sum of their ages is 24 years. How old is Sheila?

First circle what you must find in the problem—*Sheila*. Now let Kim (the younger of the two ages) equal x. Therefore, Sheila equals 3x. Now use the problem to set up an equation.

$$\underbrace{\text{The sum of their ages}} \underbrace{\text{is}} \ \underbrace{24} \ldots$$

$$\text{Sheila} + \text{Kim} = 24$$
$$3x + x = 24$$
$$4x = 24$$
$$\frac{4x}{4} = \frac{24}{4}$$
$$x = 6$$

Therefore, Sheila, 3x, is 3(6), or 18 years old.

4. In eight years, Joy will be three times as old as she is now. How old is Joy now?

First circle what you must find—*Joy now*. You may wish to set up a chart for this problem.

	NOW	IN 8 YEARS
Joy	x	x + 8

Let Joy's age now equal x. Therefore Joy's age eight years from now will be x + 8. Now use the problem to set up an equation.

$$\underbrace{\text{In eight years, Joy}}_{x + 8} \underbrace{\text{will be}}_{=} \underbrace{\text{three}}_{3} \underbrace{\text{times as}}_{\text{times}} \underbrace{\text{old as she is now.}}_{x}$$

$$x + 8 - x = 3x - x$$
$$8 = 2x$$

$$\frac{8}{2} = \frac{2x}{2}$$

$$4 = x$$

Therefore, Joy's age now is 4 years old.

5. Matt is six years older than Hector. In two years Matt will be twice as old as Hector. How old is Hector now?

First circle what you must find—*Hector now*. Let Hector now equal x. Therefore, Matt now equals x + 6. You may wish to set up a chart.

	NOW	IN 2 YEARS
Hector	x	x + 2
Matt	x + 6	x + 8

Now use the problem to set up an equation.

$$\underbrace{\text{In two years Matt}}_{x + 8} \underbrace{\text{will be}}_{=} \underbrace{\text{twice}}_{2} \underbrace{\text{as}}_{\text{times}} \text{old as} \underbrace{\text{Hector.}}_{(x + 2)}$$

$$x + 8 = 2x + 4$$
$$x + 8 - x = 2x + 4 - x$$
$$8 = x + 4$$
$$8 - 4 = x + 4 - 4$$
$$4 = x$$

Therefore, Hector now is 4 years old.

Geometry

Example:

If a rectangle's length is twice its width and its area is 200 square inches, find its length and width.

First circle what you must find—*length and width*. Now let x denote the rectangle's width. Therefore, its length will be twice the width, or 2x. Now set up an equation.

$$\underbrace{\text{Width}}_{(x)} \text{ times } \underbrace{\text{length}}_{(2x)} \underbrace{\text{equals}}_{=} \underbrace{\text{area.}}_{200}$$

$$2x^2 = 200$$

$$\frac{2x^2}{2} = \frac{200}{2}$$

$$x^2 = 100$$
$$x = 10 \text{ then } 2x = 20$$

Therefore, the width is 10 inches and the length is 20 inches.
(*Note: Drawing diagrams in geometry problems is often helpful*)

Practice: Geometry Problems

1. In a triangle, the smallest angle is 20° less than the largest angle. The third angle is 10° more than the smallest angle. What is the measure of each angle?

2. The length of a rectangle is 6 inches less than four times the width. If the perimeter of the rectangle is 28 inches, find its length and width.

3. Each of the equal sides of an isosceles triangle is 5 inches more than twice the third side. If the perimeter of the triangle is 45 inches, find the sides of the triangle.

4. One angle of a triangle is 44°. The second angle is 4° larger than the third angle. How many degrees are in the measure of the other two angles?

5. Find the measure of the sides of a rectangle if the length is 5 inches longer than the width and the perimeter is 50 inches.

Answers: Geometry Problems

1. In a triangle, the smallest angle is 20° less than the largest angle. The third angle is 10° more than the smallest angle. What is the measure of each angle?

First circle what you must find—*the measure of each angle*. Now let the largest angle be known as x. Therefore, the smallest angle, since it is 20° less than the largest, will be x − 20°. The third angle is 10° more than the smallest, or x − 20° + 10°, which equals x − 10°. Now set up the equation.

The sum of the degrees in each angle of a triangle equals 180°.

$$x + (x - 20) + (x - 10) = 180$$

$$3x - 30 = 180$$
$$3x - 30 + 30 = 180 + 30$$
$$3x = 210$$

$$\frac{3x}{3} = \frac{210}{3}$$

$$x = 70$$

The largest angle is 70°; the smallest angle is 70 − 20, or 50°; the third angle is 70 − 10, or 60°.

2. The length of a rectangle is 6 inches less than four times the width. If the perimeter of the rectangle is 28 inches, find its length and width.

First circle what you must find—*length and width*. Now let x denote the width of the rectangle. Therefore, its length will be 4x − 6 (6 less than four times the width). Now set up the equation.

The perimeter of the rectangle equals 28 inches.

or

2 widths plus 2 lengths equal 28 inches

$$2x + 2(4x - 6) = 28$$

$$2x + 8x - 12 = 28$$
$$10x - 12 = 28$$

$$10x - 12 + 12 = 28 + 12$$
$$10x = 40$$

$$\frac{10x}{10} = \frac{40}{10}$$

$$x = 4$$

Therefore, the width of the rectangle is 4; the length of the rectangle, $4x - 6$, is $4(4) - 6$, or 10.

3. Each of the equal sides of an isosceles triangle is 5 inches more than twice the third side. If the perimeter of the triangle is 45 inches, find the sides of the triangle.

First circle what you must find—*sides of the triangle*. Therefore, each of the equal sides will be $2x + 5$. Now set up the equation.

$$\underbrace{\text{The sum of the sides of a triangle}}\ \underbrace{\text{equals}}\ \underbrace{\text{the perimeter}}$$
$$x + (2x + 5) + (2x + 5) \qquad = \qquad 45$$

$$5x + 10 = 45$$
$$5x + 10 - 10 = 45 - 10$$
$$5x = 35$$

$$\frac{5x}{5} = \frac{35}{5}$$

$$x = 7$$

Therefore, one side is 7 and the other two sides are $2x + 5$ each, or $2(7) + 5$, which equals 19 for each of the other two sides.

4. One angle of a triangle is 44°. The second angle is 4° larger than the third angle. How many degrees are in the measure of the other two angles?

First circle what you must find—*the other two angles*. Now let the third angle be denoted as x. Then the second angle will be $x + 4$. Now set up an equation.

$$\underbrace{\text{The sum of the angles in a triangle}}\ \underbrace{\text{equals}}\ \underbrace{180°.}$$
$$44 + x + (x + 4) \qquad = \qquad 180$$

$$2x + 48 = 180$$
$$2x + 48 - 48 = 180 - 48$$
$$2x = 132$$

$$\frac{2x}{2} = \frac{132}{2}$$

$$x = 66$$
$$x + 4 = 70$$

Therefore, the other two angles of the triangle are 66° and 70°.

5. Find the measure of the sides of a rectangle if the length is 5 inches longer than the width and the perimeter is 50 inches.

First circle what you must find in the problem—*the measure of the sides*. Now let the width be denoted as x. Therefore, the length will be x + 5. Now set up the equation.

2 widths plus 2 lengths equal the perimeter.

$$2x \quad + \quad 2(x + 5) \quad = \quad 50$$

$$2x + 2x + 10 = 50$$
$$4x + 10 = 50$$
$$4x + 10 - 10 = 50 - 10$$
$$4x = 40$$

$$\frac{4x}{4} = \frac{40}{4}$$

$$x = 10$$

Therefore, the width is 10 and the length is x + 5, or 15.

Work

Example:

Ernie can plow a field alone in four hours. It takes Sid five hours to plow the same field alone. If they work together (and each have a plow), how long will it take to plow the field?

First circle what you must find—*how long ... together*. Work problems of this nature may be solved by using the following equation.

$$\frac{1}{\text{1st person's rate}} + \frac{1}{\text{2nd person's rate}} + \frac{1}{\text{3rd person's rate}} + \text{etc.} = \frac{1}{\text{rate together}}$$

Therefore,

$$\frac{1}{\text{Ernie's rate}} + \frac{1}{\text{Sid's rate}} = \frac{1}{\text{rate together}}$$

$$\frac{1}{4} + \frac{1}{5} = \frac{1}{t}$$

Finding a common denominator

$$\frac{5}{20} + \frac{4}{20} = \frac{1}{t}$$

$$\frac{9}{20} = \frac{1}{t}$$

Cross multiplying $9t = 20$

$$\frac{9t}{9} = \frac{20}{9} = 2\tfrac{2}{9} \text{ hours}$$

Therefore, it will take them $2\tfrac{2}{9}$ hours working together.

Practice: Work Problems

1. Tom can mow Harry's lawn in exactly three hours. Bill can mow Harry's lawn in exactly six hours. If Harry hires Bill and Tom to work together using two lawn mowers, how fast can they mow the lawn?

2. Tom can paint a house in eight hours. Dick can paint the house in six hours. Harry can also paint the house in six hours. How long will it take to paint the house if they all work together?

3. Working alone, Bill can do a job in 4 hours. With Fred's help, it takes only $2\tfrac{2}{9}$ hours. How long would it take Fred working alone to do the job?

4. A tank is being filled at a rate of ten gallons per hour. However, a hole in the tank allows water to run off at a rate of two gallons per hour. How long will it take to fill an empty fifty-gallon tank?

5. Sue, Maria, and Lucy decide to type Lucy's term paper. Sue can type three chapters per hour; Lucy can type five chapters per hour; Maria can type six chapters per hour. If Lucy's paper consists of thirty chapters, how long will it take them working together to type the entire paper?

Answers: Work Problems

1. Tom can mow Harry's lawn in exactly three hours. Bill can mow Harry's lawn in exactly six hours. If Harry hires Bill and Tom to work together using two lawn mowers, how fast can they mow the lawn?

First circle what you must find—*how fast . . . together.* Now, using the information given in the problem, plug into the equation.

$$\frac{1}{A} + \frac{1}{B} = \frac{1}{T}$$

$$\frac{1}{3} + \frac{1}{6} = \frac{1}{T}$$

$$\frac{2}{6} + \frac{1}{6} = \frac{1}{T}$$

$$\frac{3}{6} = \frac{1}{T}$$

$$\frac{1}{2} = \frac{1}{T}$$

Cross multiplying $T = 2$

It will take 2 hours working together.

2. Tom can paint a house in eight hours. Dick can paint the house in six hours. Harry can also paint the house in six hours. How long will it take to paint the house if they all work together?

First circle what you must find—*how long . . . together.* Now, using the information given in the problem, plug into the equation.

$$\frac{1}{A} + \frac{1}{B} + \frac{1}{C} = \frac{1}{T}$$

$$\frac{1}{8} + \frac{1}{6} + \frac{1}{6} = \frac{1}{T}$$

$$\frac{3}{24} + \frac{4}{24} + \frac{4}{24} = \frac{1}{T}$$

$$\frac{11}{24} = \frac{1}{T}$$

Cross multiplying $\quad 11T = 24$

$$\frac{11T}{11} = \frac{24}{11}$$

$$T = 2\frac{2}{11} \text{ hours}$$

Therefore, it will take $2\frac{2}{11}$ hours working together.

3. Working alone, Bill can do a job in 4 hours. With Fred's help, it takes only $2\frac{2}{9}$ hours. How long would it take Fred working alone to do the job?

First circle what you must find—*how long . . . Fred . . . alone.* Now, using the information given in the problem, plug into the equation.

$$\frac{1}{A} + \frac{1}{B} = \frac{1}{T}$$

$$\frac{1}{x} + \frac{1}{4} = \frac{1}{2\frac{2}{9}}$$

$$\frac{1}{x} + \frac{1}{4} = \frac{1}{\frac{20}{9}}$$

$$\frac{1}{x} + \frac{1}{4} = \frac{9}{20}$$

$$\frac{1}{x} = \frac{9}{20} - \frac{1}{4}$$

$$\frac{1}{x} = \frac{9}{20} - \frac{5}{20}$$

$$\frac{1}{x} = \frac{4}{20}$$

Cross multiplying $4x = 20$

$x = 5$ hours

Therefore, it will take Fred 5 hours working alone.

4. A tank is being filled at a rate of ten gallons per hour. However, a hole in the tank allows water to run off at a rate of two gallons per hour. How long will it take to fill an empty fifty-gallon tank?

First circle what you must find in the problem—*how long . . . to fill an empty fifty-gallon tank*. Note that since the hole allows water to leave at two gallons per hour, the tank is being filled at only $10 - 2$, or eight gallons per hour. Therefore, a fifty-gallon tank will take $50/8 = 6.25$ hours to fill.

50 gallons ÷ gallons filled per hour =
$50 \div 8 =$

$$\frac{50}{8} = 6.25, \text{ or } 6\tfrac{1}{4} \text{ hours}$$

5. Sue, Maria, and Lucy decide to type Lucy's term paper. Sue can type three chapters per hour; Lucy can type five chapters per hour; Maria can type six chapters per hour. If Lucy's paper consists of thirty chapters, how long will it take them working together to type the entire paper?

First circle what you must find in the problem—*how long . . . working together*. In this type of problem, their combined rate may be found by *adding* their chapters typed each hour.

$3 + 5 + 6 = 14$ chapters typed each hour

Now, simply divide 30 by 14.

$$14 \overline{)30} \quad \tfrac{2^2\!/_{14}}{} = 2\tfrac{1}{7} \text{ hours}$$
$$\underline{28}$$
$$2$$

Therefore, together it will take them $2\tfrac{1}{7}$ hours.

Mixture

Example:

Coffee worth $1.05 per pound is mixed with coffee worth 85¢ per pound to obtain twenty pounds of a mixture worth 90¢ per pound. How many pounds of each type are used?

First circle what you are trying to find—*how many pounds of each type.* Now let the number of pounds of $1.05 coffee be denoted as x. Therefore, the number of pounds of 85¢-per-pound coffee must be the remainder of the twenty pounds, or 20 − x. Now make a chart for the cost of each type and the total cost.

	COST PER LB. ×	AMOUNT IN LBS. =	TOTAL COST OF EACH
$1.05 coffee	$1.05	x	$1.05x
$ .85 coffee	$ .85	20 − x	$ .85(20 − x)
Mixture	$ .90	20	$ .90(20)

Now set up the equation.

Total cost of one type plus total cost of other type equal total cost of mixture.

$$\underbrace{\$1.05x} \quad + \quad \underbrace{.85(20 - x)} \quad = \quad \underbrace{.90(20)}$$

$$1.05x + 17.00 - .85x = 18.00$$
$$17.00 + .20x = 18.00$$
$$-17.00 + 17.00 + .20x = 18.00 - 17.00$$
$$.20x = 1.00$$

$$\frac{.20x}{.20} = \frac{1.00}{.20}$$

$$x = 5$$

Therefore, 5 pounds of coffee worth $1.05 are used. And 20 − x, or 20 − 5, or 15 pounds of 85¢-per-pound coffee are used.

Practice: Mixture Problems

1. Tea worth 75¢ per pound is mixed with tea worth 90¢ per pound to produce ten pounds of a mixture worth 85¢ per pound. How much of each type is used?

2. One solution is 75% salt water and another solution is 50% salt water. How many gallons of each should be used to make ten gallons of a solution that is 60% salt water?

3. Ms. Gomez invests $1,000—part of it in a bank paying 8% interest and the remainder in a bank paying 10% interest annually. If her total income for one year was $94, how much has she invested at each rate?

4. Ellen has collected nickels and dimes worth a total of $6.30. If she has collected seventy coins in all and each is worth face value, how many of each kind does she have?

5. At a game, adult tickets sold for $2.50 and children's tickets sold for $1.50. If 400 tickets were sold and the income was $900, how many of each type were sold?

Answers: Mixture Problems

1. Tea worth 75¢ per pound is mixed with tea worth 90¢ per pound to produce ten pounds of a mixture worth 85¢ per pound. How much of each type is used?

First circle what you are trying to find—*how much of each type.* Now let the number of pounds of 75¢ tea be denoted by x. Then the number of pounds of 90¢ tea is what's left of the total, or 10 − x. Now make a chart.

	COST PER LB.	×	AMOUNT IN LBS.	=	TOTAL COST OF EACH
$ .75 tea	.75		x		.75x
$ .90 tea	.90		(10 − x)		.90(10 − x)
Mixture	.85		10		10(.85)

Now set up the equation.

Total cost of one type plus total cost of the other type equal cost of mixture

$$.75x \quad + \quad .90(10 - x) \quad = \quad 10(.85)$$
$$.75x + 9 - .90x = 8.5$$
$$-.15x + 9 - 9 = 8.5 - 9$$

$$-.15x = -.5$$

$$\frac{-.15x}{-.15} = \frac{-.5}{-.15}$$

$$x = 3\frac{1}{3}$$

Therefore, $3\frac{1}{3}$ pounds of 75¢ tea was used. And the amount of the 90¢ tea is $10 - x$, or $10 - 3\frac{1}{3}$, or $6\frac{2}{3}$ pounds.

2. One solution is 75% salt water and another solution is 50% salt water. How many gallons of each should be used to make ten gallons of a solution that is 60% salt water?

First circle what you are trying to find—*how many gallons of each.* Now let the number of gallons of 75% salt water be x. Then the remainder—the amount of the 50% solution—will be what's left from the total of ten gallons, or $10 - x$. Now set up a chart.

	RATE	×	AMOUNT OF SOLUTION	=	AMOUNT OF SALT
75% solution	.75		x		.75x
50% solution	.50		$10 - x$		$.50(10 - x)$
Mixture	.60		10		$.60(10)$

Now set up the equation.

Salt in one solution plus salt in other solution equal salt in mixture.

$$.75x \quad + \quad .50(10 - x) \quad = \quad .60(10)$$

$$.75x + 5 - .50x = 6$$
$$.25x + 5 = 6$$
$$.25x + 5 - 5 = 6 - 5$$
$$.25x = 1$$

$$\frac{.25x}{.25} = \frac{1}{.25}$$

$$x = 4$$

Therefore, 4 gallons of 75% solution are used and $10 - 4$, or 6 gallons, of 50% solution are used.

3. Ms. Gomez invests $1,000—part of it in a bank paying 8% interest and the remainder in a bank paying 10% interest annually. If her total income for one year was $94, how much has she invested at each rate?

First circle what you're trying to find—*how much . . . invested at each rate*. Now let the amount invested at 8% be denoted as x. Therefore, the remainder invested at 10% will be $1,000 − x. Now set up a chart.

AMOUNT INVESTED	×	INTEREST RATE	=	INTEREST INCOME
x		.08		.08x
(1,000 − x)		.10		(1,000 − x).10

Now set up the equation.

Interest income from 8% plus interest income from 10% equal total income.

$$.08x \quad + \quad (1,000 - x).10 \quad = \quad 94$$

$$.08x + 100 - .10x = 94$$
$$-.02x + 100 = 94$$
$$-.02x + 100 - 100 = 94 - 100$$
$$-.02x = -6$$

$$\frac{-.02x}{-.02} = \frac{-6}{-.02}$$

$$x = 300$$

Therefore, the amount invested at 8% was $300, and the remainder of the $1,000, or $700, was invested at 10%.

4. Ellen has collected nickels and dimes worth a total of $6.30. If she has collected seventy coins in all and each is worth face value, how many of each kind does she have?

First circle what you must find—*how many of each kind*. Now let x denote the number of nickels. Therefore, the remainder of the coins (70 − x) will be the number of dimes. Now set up a chart.

	NUMBER OF COINS	×	VALUE OF EACH	=	TOTAL VALUE
Nickels	x		.05		.05x
Dimes	70 − x		.10		(70 − x).10

Now set up the equation.

Total value of nickels plus total value of dimes equal total worth.

$$.05x \quad + \quad (70 - x).10 \quad = \quad 6.30$$

$$.05x + 7 - .10x = 6.30$$
$$-.05x + 7 = 6.30$$
$$-.05x + 7 - 7 = 6.30 - 7$$
$$-.05x = -.70$$

$$\frac{-.05x}{-.05} = \frac{-.70}{-.05}$$

$$x = 14$$

Therefore, Ellen has 14 nickels and (70 − 14), or 56, dimes.

5. At a game, adult tickets sold for \$2.50 and children's tickets sold for \$1.50. If 400 tickets were sold and the income was \$900, how many of each type were sold?

First circle what you must find—*how many of each type*. Now let x denote the number of adult tickets sold. Therefore, the remainder (400 − x) will denote the number of children's tickets sold. Now set up a chart.

	NUMBER OF TICKETS	×	COST PER TICKET	=	INCOME
Adult tickets	x		2.50		2.50x
Children's tickets	(400 − x)		1.50		1.50(400 − x)

Now set up the equation.

Income from adult tickets plus income from children's tickets equal total income

$$2.50x \qquad + \qquad 1.50(400 - x) \qquad = \qquad 900$$

$$2.50x + 600 - 1.50x = 900$$
$$x + 600 = 900$$
$$x + 600 - 600 = 900 - 600$$
$$x = 300$$

Therefore, 300 adult tickets were sold and 100 children's tickets were sold.

WORD PROBLEMS REVIEW TEST

Questions

1. What is the simple interest on a loan of $5,000 for eight years at an annual interest rate of 14%?

2. If a woman earns $2,000 simple interest over four years on an investment of $5,000, what is the annual interest rate she receives?

3. Mr. Lincoln deposits $4,000 in a savings account that pays 12% annually, but interest is compounded quarterly. What is the total in his account after one year? (Remember, 3% interest will be paid each quarter.)

4. If Jim can bake twenty-seven pies in twelve days, how many pies can he bake in twenty days?

5. If p pencils cost k cents, at the same price how much will q pencils cost?

6. How long will it take a train traveling at an average speed of 80 miles per hour to travel a distance of 5,600 miles?

7. Two automobiles, A and B, leave at the same time and travel the same route. Automobile A goes at a rate of 55 miles per hour. Automobile B travels at a rate of 40 miles per hour. How many hours after they begin their trip will automobile A be 60 miles ahead of automobile B?

8. Mrs. Baum won $5,600 on a television quiz show. If she has to pay 20% of her winnings to the Internal Revenue Service, how much of her winnings will she have left?

9. A prized Amazon yellow nape parrot is placed on sale at a bird show for $900. It doesn't sell immediately, so its owner discounts the bird 30%. When the parrot still does not interest any buyers, the owner offers another 20% discount off the new price. What is the final price of the bird?

10. Last year's Los Angeles Dodgers attendance was 2,800,000. This year the Dodgers' attendance figures topped three million (exactly 3,200,000). What was the Dodgers' percent increase in attendance?

11. If Arnold's 1985 salary reflects a percent drop of 15% from the previous year, what was his 1985 salary if in 1984 he earned $30,000?

12. Three consecutive odd integers add up to total 33. What is the smallest of the three integers?

13. A green flag costs ten times the price of a blue flag. A red flag costs half the price of a green flag. An orange flag costs ten dollars less than a red flag. If the four different color flags cost a total of $200, what is the price of an orange flag?

14. Judith is exactly 18 years older than Brad. If today the sum of their ages is 52, how old will Brad be in 1 year?

15. Carole is 7 years older than Lenn. Ann is twice as old as Lenn, and her mother is 65. If the total age of all four persons is 116, how old was Lenn 5 years ago.

16. One angle of a triangle is twice as big as the smallest angle, and the third angle is three times as big as the smallest angle. What are the three angles of the triangle?

17. If in quadrilateral ABCD, side AB is twice side BC, side BC is twice side CD, and side CD is twice side DA, what is the length of side DA if the perimeter of ABCD is 75 inches?

18. Bob can cut a lawn in four hours. Bette can cut the same lawn in three hours. If they both use lawn mowers and work together, how long will it take them to cut the lawn?

19. Gina can build a house in twelve months alone. Bart can build a house in six months alone. How long will it take them to build a house if they work together?

20. A chemistry teacher has two quarts of 25% acid solution and one quart of 40% acid solution. If she mixes these, what will be the concentration of acid in the final mixture?

21. Programs sell at a baseball game for $2.00 each, and scorecards sell for $.75 each. If a total of 200 items was sold (programs *and* scorecards) for a cash income of $250, how many of each were sold?

Answers

Page numbers following each answer refer to the review section applicable to this problem type.

1. $5,600 (p. 264)

2. 10% (p. 264)

3. $4,502.04 (p. 267)

4. 45 pies (p. 270)

5. qk/p or kq/p (p. 270)

6. 70 hours (p. 274)

7. 4 hours (p. 274)

8. $4,480 (p. 274)

9. $504 (p. 267)

10. approximately 14.2% (p. 281)

11. $25,500 (p. 281)

12. 9 (p. 285)

13. $40 (p. 285)

14. 18 years old (p. 289)

15. 6 years old (p. 289)

16. 30°, 60°, 90° (p. 294)

17. 5 inches (p. 294)

18. 1⁵⁄₇ hours (p. 297)

19. 4 months (p. 297)

20. 30% acid concentration (p. 302)

21. 80 programs, 120 scorecards (p. 302)

WORD PROBLEMS GLOSSARY OF TERMS

ANNUAL: Once per year.

BALANCE: Beginning balance is the principal in interest problems. Ending balance is the principal plus interest acquired.

BIANNUAL: Twice per year, or every six months.

COMPOUNDED: In interest problems, means the interest is to be added to the principal at specific intervals.

CONSECUTIVE: What comes immediately after. For example, consecutive numbers are 1, 2, 3, 4, etc. Consecutive odd numbers are 1, 3, 5, 7, 9, etc.

DIFFERENCE: The result obtained by subtracting.

DIVIDEND: In interest problems, signifies the amount of interest paid.

EQUATION: A number sentence *with a balance relationship between numbers or symbols.*

EVALUATE: To determine the value or numerical amount.

EXCEEDS: Is more than.

INEQUALITY: A number sentence in which the *relationships between numbers or symbols are not equal.*

INTEGER: Whole number. For example, 6, 109, 0, -52.

PERCENTAGE CHANGE: Expressed also as percent rise, percent difference, percentage increase, % decrease, percent drop, etc. Found by dividing the actual amount of change by the numerical starting point.

PRINCIPAL: The amount of money invested or loaned upon which interest is paid.

PRODUCT: The result obtained by multiplying.

QUARTERLY: Four times per year, or every three months.

QUOTIENT: The result obtained by dividing.

RATE: How fast an object moves (speed).

RATIO: A comparison between items. For example, the ratio of 2 to 3 may be written as 2:3 or $\frac{2}{3}$.

SEMIANNUAL: Twice per year, or every six months.

SIMPLE INTEREST: Compounded at intervals determined by the rate. For interest, annual rate compounds every year. Quarterly rate compounds at each quarter, etc.

SIMPLIFY: To combine several terms into fewer terms.
SPEED: The rate at which an object moves.
SUM: The result obtained by adding.
VALUE: The numerical amount.
VELOCITY: The speed, or rate, at which an object moves.

Part III: Strategies and Practice

This section is designed to introduce you to important test-taking strategies and to some typical problem types encountered on many standardized exams. Although some of these question types do not appear on all standardized tests, you will find it valuable to practice them, as such practice will increase your understanding and strengthen your mastery of concepts.

Your most effective plan of attack to best prepare for the test you must take is to first ensure that you have a firm grasp of the "basics," which will enable you to answer the easy or average-in-difficulty problems correctly. Only then should you move on to the more difficult problems.

Because standardized tests vary greatly in difficulty and because the purpose of this guide is to be instructional for as wide a range of test takers as possible, some extremely easy and extremely difficult problem types are not given. The practice problems on the following pages encompass many problem types and are meant to give a sampling of a variety of questions.

Answer Key pages are cross referenced to the appropriate review section. If you wish to review the concepts again after working the practice problems, turn to the page indicated after that question number.

It is a good idea to accustom yourself to answering questions on a scoring sheet, as that is what you must do when taking the standardized tests. When you practice be sure to blacken the space completely, and if you change an answer, erase thoroughly.

For these practice sections, the arithmetic, algebra, and geometry questions have been separated to help you strengthen your skills and pinpoint your problem areas. BE AWARE THAT STANDARDIZED TESTS DO NOT SEPARATE ARITHMETIC, ALGEBRA, AND GEOMETRY SECTIONS IN THIS WAY. Rather, all of these areas are combined under one question type (such as Data Sufficiency).

ANSWER SHEET FOR PRACTICE SECTIONS
(Remove This Sheet and Use It to Mark Your Answers)

Mathematical Ability

Arithmetic	Algebra	Geometry	Procedure Problems
1 Ⓐ Ⓑ Ⓒ Ⓓ Ⓔ	1 Ⓐ Ⓑ Ⓒ Ⓓ Ⓔ	1 Ⓐ Ⓑ Ⓒ Ⓓ Ⓔ	1 Ⓐ Ⓑ Ⓒ Ⓓ Ⓔ
2 Ⓐ Ⓑ Ⓒ Ⓓ Ⓔ	2 Ⓐ Ⓑ Ⓒ Ⓓ Ⓔ	2 Ⓐ Ⓑ Ⓒ Ⓓ Ⓔ	2 Ⓐ Ⓑ Ⓒ Ⓓ Ⓔ
3 Ⓐ Ⓑ Ⓒ Ⓓ Ⓔ	3 Ⓐ Ⓑ Ⓒ Ⓓ Ⓔ	3 Ⓐ Ⓑ Ⓒ Ⓓ Ⓔ	3 Ⓐ Ⓑ Ⓒ Ⓓ Ⓔ
4 Ⓐ Ⓑ Ⓒ Ⓓ Ⓔ	4 Ⓐ Ⓑ Ⓒ Ⓓ Ⓔ	4 Ⓐ Ⓑ Ⓒ Ⓓ Ⓔ	4 Ⓐ Ⓑ Ⓒ Ⓓ Ⓔ
5 Ⓐ Ⓑ Ⓒ Ⓓ Ⓔ	5 Ⓐ Ⓑ Ⓒ Ⓓ Ⓔ	5 Ⓐ Ⓑ Ⓒ Ⓓ Ⓔ	5 Ⓐ Ⓑ Ⓒ Ⓓ Ⓔ
6 Ⓐ Ⓑ Ⓒ Ⓓ Ⓔ	6 Ⓐ Ⓑ Ⓒ Ⓓ Ⓔ	6 Ⓐ Ⓑ Ⓒ Ⓓ Ⓔ	6 Ⓐ Ⓑ Ⓒ Ⓓ Ⓔ
7 Ⓐ Ⓑ Ⓒ Ⓓ Ⓔ	7 Ⓐ Ⓑ Ⓒ Ⓓ Ⓔ	7 Ⓐ Ⓑ Ⓒ Ⓓ Ⓔ	7 Ⓐ Ⓑ Ⓒ Ⓓ Ⓔ
8 Ⓐ Ⓑ Ⓒ Ⓓ Ⓔ	8 Ⓐ Ⓑ Ⓒ Ⓓ Ⓔ	8 Ⓐ Ⓑ Ⓒ Ⓓ Ⓔ	8 Ⓐ Ⓑ Ⓒ Ⓓ Ⓔ
9 Ⓐ Ⓑ Ⓒ Ⓓ Ⓔ	9 Ⓐ Ⓑ Ⓒ Ⓓ Ⓔ	9 Ⓐ Ⓑ Ⓒ Ⓓ Ⓔ	9 Ⓐ Ⓑ Ⓒ Ⓓ Ⓔ
10 Ⓐ Ⓑ Ⓒ Ⓓ Ⓔ	10 Ⓐ Ⓑ Ⓒ Ⓓ Ⓔ	10 Ⓐ Ⓑ Ⓒ Ⓓ Ⓔ	10 Ⓐ Ⓑ Ⓒ Ⓓ Ⓔ
11 Ⓐ Ⓑ Ⓒ Ⓓ Ⓔ	11 Ⓐ Ⓑ Ⓒ Ⓓ Ⓔ	11 Ⓐ Ⓑ Ⓒ Ⓓ Ⓔ	
12 Ⓐ Ⓑ Ⓒ Ⓓ Ⓔ	12 Ⓐ Ⓑ Ⓒ Ⓓ Ⓔ	12 Ⓐ Ⓑ Ⓒ Ⓓ Ⓔ	
13 Ⓐ Ⓑ Ⓒ Ⓓ Ⓔ	13 Ⓐ Ⓑ Ⓒ Ⓓ Ⓔ	13 Ⓐ Ⓑ Ⓒ Ⓓ Ⓔ	
14 Ⓐ Ⓑ Ⓒ Ⓓ Ⓔ	14 Ⓐ Ⓑ Ⓒ Ⓓ Ⓔ	14 Ⓐ Ⓑ Ⓒ Ⓓ Ⓔ	
15 Ⓐ Ⓑ Ⓒ Ⓓ Ⓔ	15 Ⓐ Ⓑ Ⓒ Ⓓ Ⓔ	15 Ⓐ Ⓑ Ⓒ Ⓓ Ⓔ	
16 Ⓐ Ⓑ Ⓒ Ⓓ Ⓔ	16 Ⓐ Ⓑ Ⓒ Ⓓ Ⓔ	16 Ⓐ Ⓑ Ⓒ Ⓓ Ⓔ	
17 Ⓐ Ⓑ Ⓒ Ⓓ Ⓔ	17 Ⓐ Ⓑ Ⓒ Ⓓ Ⓔ	17 Ⓐ Ⓑ Ⓒ Ⓓ Ⓔ	
18 Ⓐ Ⓑ Ⓒ Ⓓ Ⓔ	18 Ⓐ Ⓑ Ⓒ Ⓓ Ⓔ	18 Ⓐ Ⓑ Ⓒ Ⓓ Ⓔ	
19 Ⓐ Ⓑ Ⓒ Ⓓ Ⓔ	19 Ⓐ Ⓑ Ⓒ Ⓓ Ⓔ	19 Ⓐ Ⓑ Ⓒ Ⓓ Ⓔ	
20 Ⓐ Ⓑ Ⓒ Ⓓ Ⓔ	20 Ⓐ Ⓑ Ⓒ Ⓓ Ⓔ	20 Ⓐ Ⓑ Ⓒ Ⓓ Ⓔ	
21 Ⓐ Ⓑ Ⓒ Ⓓ Ⓔ	21 Ⓐ Ⓑ Ⓒ Ⓓ Ⓔ	21 Ⓐ Ⓑ Ⓒ Ⓓ Ⓔ	
22 Ⓐ Ⓑ Ⓒ Ⓓ Ⓔ	22 Ⓐ Ⓑ Ⓒ Ⓓ Ⓔ	22 Ⓐ Ⓑ Ⓒ Ⓓ Ⓔ	
23 Ⓐ Ⓑ Ⓒ Ⓓ Ⓔ	23 Ⓐ Ⓑ Ⓒ Ⓓ Ⓔ	23 Ⓐ Ⓑ Ⓒ Ⓓ Ⓔ	
24 Ⓐ Ⓑ Ⓒ Ⓓ Ⓔ	24 Ⓐ Ⓑ Ⓒ Ⓓ Ⓔ	24 Ⓐ Ⓑ Ⓒ Ⓓ Ⓔ	
25 Ⓐ Ⓑ Ⓒ Ⓓ Ⓔ	25 Ⓐ Ⓑ Ⓒ Ⓓ Ⓔ	25 Ⓐ Ⓑ Ⓒ Ⓓ Ⓔ	
26 Ⓐ Ⓑ Ⓒ Ⓓ Ⓔ			
27 Ⓐ Ⓑ Ⓒ Ⓓ Ⓔ			
28 Ⓐ Ⓑ Ⓒ Ⓓ Ⓔ			
29 Ⓐ Ⓑ Ⓒ Ⓓ Ⓔ			
30 Ⓐ Ⓑ Ⓒ Ⓓ Ⓔ			

ANSWER SHEET FOR PRACTICE SECTIONS
(Remove This Sheet and Use It to Mark Your Answers)

Quantitative Comparison

Arithmetic	Algebra	Geometry

Arithmetic

1 Ⓐ Ⓑ Ⓒ Ⓓ Ⓔ
2 Ⓐ Ⓑ Ⓒ Ⓓ Ⓔ
3 Ⓐ Ⓑ Ⓒ Ⓓ Ⓔ
4 Ⓐ Ⓑ Ⓒ Ⓓ Ⓔ
5 Ⓐ Ⓑ Ⓒ Ⓓ Ⓔ
6 Ⓐ Ⓑ Ⓒ Ⓓ Ⓔ
7 Ⓐ Ⓑ Ⓒ Ⓓ Ⓔ
8 Ⓐ Ⓑ Ⓒ Ⓓ Ⓔ
9 Ⓐ Ⓑ Ⓒ Ⓓ Ⓔ
10 Ⓐ Ⓑ Ⓒ Ⓓ Ⓔ
11 Ⓐ Ⓑ Ⓒ Ⓓ Ⓔ
12 Ⓐ Ⓑ Ⓒ Ⓓ Ⓔ
13 Ⓐ Ⓑ Ⓒ Ⓓ Ⓔ
14 Ⓐ Ⓑ Ⓒ Ⓓ Ⓔ
15 Ⓐ Ⓑ Ⓒ Ⓓ Ⓔ

Algebra

1 Ⓐ Ⓑ Ⓒ Ⓓ Ⓔ
2 Ⓐ Ⓑ Ⓒ Ⓓ Ⓔ
3 Ⓐ Ⓑ Ⓒ Ⓓ Ⓔ
4 Ⓐ Ⓑ Ⓒ Ⓓ Ⓔ
5 Ⓐ Ⓑ Ⓒ Ⓓ Ⓔ
6 Ⓐ Ⓑ Ⓒ Ⓓ Ⓔ
7 Ⓐ Ⓑ Ⓒ Ⓓ Ⓔ
8 Ⓐ Ⓑ Ⓒ Ⓓ Ⓔ
9 Ⓐ Ⓑ Ⓒ Ⓓ Ⓔ
10 Ⓐ Ⓑ Ⓒ Ⓓ Ⓔ
11 Ⓐ Ⓑ Ⓒ Ⓓ Ⓔ
12 Ⓐ Ⓑ Ⓒ Ⓓ Ⓔ
13 Ⓐ Ⓑ Ⓒ Ⓓ Ⓔ
14 Ⓐ Ⓑ Ⓒ Ⓓ Ⓔ
15 Ⓐ Ⓑ Ⓒ Ⓓ Ⓔ

Geometry

1 Ⓐ Ⓑ Ⓒ Ⓓ Ⓔ
2 Ⓐ Ⓑ Ⓒ Ⓓ Ⓔ
3 Ⓐ Ⓑ Ⓒ Ⓓ Ⓔ
4 Ⓐ Ⓑ Ⓒ Ⓓ Ⓔ
5 Ⓐ Ⓑ Ⓒ Ⓓ Ⓔ
6 Ⓐ Ⓑ Ⓒ Ⓓ Ⓔ
7 Ⓐ Ⓑ Ⓒ Ⓓ Ⓔ
8 Ⓐ Ⓑ Ⓒ Ⓓ Ⓔ
9 Ⓐ Ⓑ Ⓒ Ⓓ Ⓔ
10 Ⓐ Ⓑ Ⓒ Ⓓ Ⓔ
11 Ⓐ Ⓑ Ⓒ Ⓓ Ⓔ
12 Ⓐ Ⓑ Ⓒ Ⓓ Ⓔ
13 Ⓐ Ⓑ Ⓒ Ⓓ Ⓔ
14 Ⓐ Ⓑ Ⓒ Ⓓ Ⓔ
15 Ⓐ Ⓑ Ⓒ Ⓓ Ⓔ

Data Sufficiency

Arithmetic	Algebra	Geometry

Arithmetic

1 Ⓐ Ⓑ Ⓒ Ⓓ Ⓔ
2 Ⓐ Ⓑ Ⓒ Ⓓ Ⓔ
3 Ⓐ Ⓑ Ⓒ Ⓓ Ⓔ
4 Ⓐ Ⓑ Ⓒ Ⓓ Ⓔ
5 Ⓐ Ⓑ Ⓒ Ⓓ Ⓔ
6 Ⓐ Ⓑ Ⓒ Ⓓ Ⓔ
7 Ⓐ Ⓑ Ⓒ Ⓓ Ⓔ
8 Ⓐ Ⓑ Ⓒ Ⓓ Ⓔ
9 Ⓐ Ⓑ Ⓒ Ⓓ Ⓔ
10 Ⓐ Ⓑ Ⓒ Ⓓ Ⓔ
11 Ⓐ Ⓑ Ⓒ Ⓓ Ⓔ
12 Ⓐ Ⓑ Ⓒ Ⓓ Ⓔ
13 Ⓐ Ⓑ Ⓒ Ⓓ Ⓔ
14 Ⓐ Ⓑ Ⓒ Ⓓ Ⓔ
15 Ⓐ Ⓑ Ⓒ Ⓓ Ⓔ

Algebra

1 Ⓐ Ⓑ Ⓒ Ⓓ Ⓔ
2 Ⓐ Ⓑ Ⓒ Ⓓ Ⓔ
3 Ⓐ Ⓑ Ⓒ Ⓓ Ⓔ
4 Ⓐ Ⓑ Ⓒ Ⓓ Ⓔ
5 Ⓐ Ⓑ Ⓒ Ⓓ Ⓔ
6 Ⓐ Ⓑ Ⓒ Ⓓ Ⓔ
7 Ⓐ Ⓑ Ⓒ Ⓓ Ⓔ
8 Ⓐ Ⓑ Ⓒ Ⓓ Ⓔ
9 Ⓐ Ⓑ Ⓒ Ⓓ Ⓔ
10 Ⓐ Ⓑ Ⓒ Ⓓ Ⓔ
11 Ⓐ Ⓑ Ⓒ Ⓓ Ⓔ
12 Ⓐ Ⓑ Ⓒ Ⓓ Ⓔ
13 Ⓐ Ⓑ Ⓒ Ⓓ Ⓔ
14 Ⓐ Ⓑ Ⓒ Ⓓ Ⓔ
15 Ⓐ Ⓑ Ⓒ Ⓓ Ⓔ

Geometry

1 Ⓐ Ⓑ Ⓒ Ⓓ Ⓔ
2 Ⓐ Ⓑ Ⓒ Ⓓ Ⓔ
3 Ⓐ Ⓑ Ⓒ Ⓓ Ⓔ
4 Ⓐ Ⓑ Ⓒ Ⓓ Ⓔ
5 Ⓐ Ⓑ Ⓒ Ⓓ Ⓔ
6 Ⓐ Ⓑ Ⓒ Ⓓ Ⓔ
7 Ⓐ Ⓑ Ⓒ Ⓓ Ⓔ
8 Ⓐ Ⓑ Ⓒ Ⓓ Ⓔ
9 Ⓐ Ⓑ Ⓒ Ⓓ Ⓔ
10 Ⓐ Ⓑ Ⓒ Ⓓ Ⓔ
11 Ⓐ Ⓑ Ⓒ Ⓓ Ⓔ
12 Ⓐ Ⓑ Ⓒ Ⓓ Ⓔ
13 Ⓐ Ⓑ Ⓒ Ⓓ Ⓔ
14 Ⓐ Ⓑ Ⓒ Ⓓ Ⓔ
15 Ⓐ Ⓑ Ⓒ Ⓓ Ⓔ

CUT HERE

MATHEMATICAL ABILITY

MATHEMATICAL ABILITY STRATEGIES

Mathematical ability problems are a standard question type appearing on many different examinations. Typically you must answer a question or solve an equation using the information given in the problem and your knowledge of mathematics. Complex computation is usually not required. Five answer choices are commonly given and you must choose the correct answer from the five. Some exams will have problems that will require you to derive information from graphs and charts.

Information Provided in the Test Booklet

On many standardized exams (SAT, PSAT, and CBEST), some basic mathematical formulas and information may be provided. Although this information may appear at the beginning of the test, test-takers should already have a working knowledge of these facts even if they have not completely committed them to memory.

Data That May Be Used as Reference for the Test

The area formula for a circle of radius r is: $A = \pi r^2$
The circumference formula is: $C = 2\pi r$
A circle is composed of 360°.
A straight angle measures 180°.

Triangle: The sum of the angles of a triangle is 180°.
If angle ADB is a right angle, then

(1) The area of triangle ABC is $\dfrac{AC \times BD}{2}$

(2) $AD^2 + BD^2 = AB^2$

Symbol References:

= is equal to	≧ is greater than or equal to
≠ not equal to	≦ is less than or equal to
> is greater than	‖ is parallel to
< is less than	⊥ is perpendicular to

Suggested Approach with Examples

Here are a number of approaches that can be helpful in attacking many types of mathematics problems. Of course, these strategies will not work on *all* problems, but if you become familiar with them, you'll find they'll be helpful in answering quite a few questions.

Mark Key Words

Circling and/or underlining key words in each question is an effective test-taking technique. Many times you may be misled because you may overlook a key word in a problem. By circling or underlining these key words, you'll help yourself focus on what you are being asked to find. Remember, you are allowed to mark and write on your testing booklet. Take advantage of this opportunity.

Examples:

1. In the following number, which digit is in the ten-thousandths place?

$$56,874.12398$$

(A) 5   (B) 7   (C) 2   (D) 3   (E) 9

The key word here is *ten-thousandths*. By circling it you will be paying closer attention to it. This is the kind of question which, under time pressure and testing pressure, may often be misread. It may be easily misread as *ten-thousands* place. Your circling the important words will minimize the possibility of misreading. Your completed question may look like this after you mark the important words or terms.

1. Which ⟨digit⟩ is in the ⟨ten-thousandths⟩ place?

$$56,874.123⑨8$$

(A) 5   (B) 7   (C) 2   (D) 3   (E) 9

2. If six yards of ribbon cost \$3.96, what is the price per foot?
   (A) \$.22   (B) \$.66   (C) \$1.32   (D) \$1.96   (E) \$3.96

The key word here is *foot*. Dividing \$3.96 by six will tell you only the price per *yard*. Notice that \$.66 is one of the choices, (B). You must still divide by three (since there are three feet per yard) to find the cost per foot. \$.66 ÷ 3 = \$.22, which is choice (A). Therefore, it would be very helpful to circle the words *price per foot* in the problem.

3. If $3x + 1 = 16$, what is the value of $x - 4$?
   (A) -1 (B) 1   (C) 5   (D) 16   (E) 19

The key here is find the value of $x - 4$. Therefore, circle $x - 4$. Note that solving the original equation will tell only the value of x.

$$3x + 1 = 16$$
$$3x = 15$$
$$x = 5$$

Here again notice that 5 is one of the choices, (C). But the question asks for the value of $x - 4$, not just x. To continue, replace x with 5 and solve.

$$x - 4 =$$
$$5 - 4 = 1$$

The correct answer choice is (B).

4. Together a hat and coat cost \$125. The coat costs \$25 more than the hat. What is the cost of the coat?
   (A) \$25   (B) \$50   (C) \$75   (D) \$100   (E) \$125

The key words here are *cost of the coat,* so circle those words. If we solve this algebraically

$$x = hat$$
$$x + 25 = coat \text{ (cost \$25 more than the hat)}$$

Together they cost \$125.

$$(x + 25) + x = 125$$
$$2x + 25 = 125$$
$$2x = 100$$
$$x = 50$$

But this is the cost of the *hat*. Notice that $50 is one of the answer choices, (B). Since x = 50, then x + 25 = 75. Therefore, the coat costs $75, which is choice (C). *Always answer the question that is being asked.* Circling the key word or words will help you do that.

Pull out Information

Pulling information out of the wording of a word problem can make the problem more workable for you. Pull out the given facts and identify which of those facts will help you to work the problem. Not all facts will always be needed to work out the problem.

Examples:

1. Bill is ten years older than his sister. If Bill was twenty-five years of age in 1983, in what year could he have been born?
   (A) 1948   (B) 1953   (C) 1958   (D) 1963   (E) 1968

The key words here are *in what year* and *could he have been born*. Thus the solution is simple: 1983 − 25 = 1958, answer (C). Notice that you pulled out the information *twenty-five years of age* and *in 1983*. The fact about Bill's age in comparison to his sister's age was not needed, however, and was not pulled out.

2. Bob is twenty years old. He works for his father for ¾ of the year, and he works for his brother for the rest of the year. What is the ratio of the time Bob spends working for his brother to the time he spends working for his father per year?
   (A) ¼   (B) ⅓   (C) ¾   (D) ⁴⁄₃   (E) ⁴⁄₁

The key word *rest* points to the answer:

$1 - \frac{3}{4} =$

$\frac{4}{4} - \frac{3}{4} = \frac{1}{4}$ (the part of the year Bob works for his brother)

Also, a key is the way in which the ratio is to be written. The problem becomes that of finding the ratio of ¼ to ¾.

$$\frac{\frac{1}{4}}{\frac{3}{4}} = \frac{1}{4} \div \frac{3}{4} = \frac{1}{{}_1\cancel{4}} \times \frac{\cancel{4}^1}{3} = \frac{1}{3}$$

Therefore the answer is choice (B). Note that here Bob's age is not needed to solve the problem.

Sometimes you may not have sufficient information to solve the problem. *For example:*

3. The average rainfall for the first few months of 1985 was four inches. The next month's average rainfall was five inches. What was the average rainfall per month for all those months?
   (A) 4″   (D) 4¾″
   (B) 4¼″   (E) not enough information
   (C) 4½″

To calculate an average, you must have the total amount and then divide by the number of items. The difficulty here, however, is that *first few months* does not specify exactly *how many* months averaged 4″. Does *few* mean two? Or does it mean three? *Few* is not a precise mathematical term. Therefore, there is not enough information to pull out to calculate an average. The answer is (E).

4. If gasohol is ⅔ alcohol by volume and ⅞ gasoline by volume, what is the ratio of the volume of gasoline to the volume of alcohol?
   (A) ⅔   (B) 2/7   (C) 7/9   (D) 7/2   (E) 9/2

The first bit of information that you should pull out should be what you are looking for, *ratio of the volume of gasoline to the volume of alcohol.* Rewrite it as G:A and then into its mathematical working form G/A. Next you should pull out the volumes of each. G = 7/9 and A = 2/9 Now the answer can be easily figured by inspection or substitution. Using

$$\frac{(7/9)}{(2/9)} = ?$$

which is the same as 7/9 ÷ 2/9 = ?

invert the second fraction and multiply to get

$$7/9 \times 9/2 = ?$$

The answer is 7/2 (the ratio of gasoline to alcohol). The correct answer is (D). When pulling out information, actually write out the numbers and/or letters to the side of the problem, putting them into some form and eliminating some of the wording.

Plug in Numbers

When a problem involving variables (unknowns, or letters) seems difficult and confusing, simply *replace those variables with numbers*. Simple numbers will make the arithmetic easier for you to do. Usually problems using numbers are easier to understand. Be sure to make logical substitutions. Use a positive number, a negative number, or zero when applicable to get the full picture.

Examples:

1. If x is a positive integer in the equation $12x = q$, then q must be
   (A) a positive even integer
   (B) a negative even integer
   (C) zero
   (D) a positive odd integer
   (E) a negative odd integer

At first glance, this problem appears quite complex. But let's plug in some numbers and see what happens. For instance, first plug in 1 (the simplest positive integer) for x.

$$12x = q$$
$$12(1) = q$$
$$12 = q$$

Now try 2.

$$12x = q$$
$$12(2) = q$$
$$24 = q$$

Try it again. No matter what positive integer is plugged in for x, q will always be positive and even. Therefore, the answer is (A).

2. If a, b, and c are all positive integers greater than 1 such that $a < b < c$, which of the following is the largest quantity

   (A) $a(b + c)$ (D) they are all equal
   (B) $ab + c$ (E) cannot be determined
   (C) $ac + b$

Substitute 2, 3, and 4 for a, b, and c, respectively.

$a(b + c) =$	$ab + c =$	$ac + b =$
$2(3 + 4) =$	$2(3) + 4 =$	$2(4) + 3 =$
$2(7) = 14$	$6 + 4 = 10$	$8 + 3 = 11$

Since 2, 3, and 4 meet the conditions stated in the problem and choice (A) produces the largest numerical value, it will consistently be the largest quantity. Therefore, a(b + c) is the correct answer, (A). Remember to substitute simple numbers, since *you* have to do the work.

3. If $x > 1$, which of the following decreases as x decreases?

$$\text{I. } x + x^2$$

$$\text{II. } 2x^2 - x$$

$$\text{III. } \frac{1}{x + 1}$$

(A) I   (B) II   (C) III   (D) I and II   (E) II and III

This problem is most easily solved by taking each situation and substituting simple numbers. However, in the first situation, I, $x + x^2$, you should recognize that this expression will decrease as x decreases. Trying $x = 2$, gives $2 + (2)^2$, which equals 6. Now trying $x = 3$, gives $3 + (3)^2 = 12$. Notice that choices (B), (C), and (E) are already eliminated because they do not contain I. You should also realize that now you only need to try the values in II; since III is not paired with I as a possible choice, III cannot be one of the answers. Trying $x = 2$ in the expression $2x^2 - x$, gives $2(2)^2 - 2$, or $2(4) - 2$, which leaves 6. Now trying $x = 3$ gives $2(3)^2 - 3$, or $2(9) - 3 = 18 - 3 = 15$. This expression also decreases as x decreases. Therefore the correct answer is choice (D). Once again notice that III was not even attempted, because it was not one of the possible choices.

Work from the Answers

At times, the solution to a problem will be obvious to you. At other times it may be helpful to *work from the answers*. This technique is even more efficient when some of the answer choices are easily eliminated.

Examples:

1. Approximate $\sqrt{1{,}596}$
   (A) 10   (B) 20   (C) 30   (D) 40   (E) 50

Without the answer choices this would be a very difficult problem, requiring knowledge of a special procedure to calculate square roots. With the answer choices, however, the problem is easily solvable. How? By working up from the answer choices. Since $\sqrt{1,596}$ means *what number times itself equals 1,596,* you can take any answer choice and multiply it by itself. As soon as you find the answer choice that when multiplied by itself approximates 1,596, you've got the correct answer.

But here's another strategy. Start to work up from the *middle answer choice.* Why? Watch.

1. Approximate $\sqrt{1,596}$
   (A) 10   (B) 20   (C) 30   (D) 40   (E) 50

First try choice (C), 30. Multiplying it by itself, you get $30 \times 30 = 900$. Since 900 is too small (you are looking for approximately 1,596), you may eliminate choice (C). But notice that you may *also eliminate choices (A) and (B),* since they are also too small.

Working up from the middle choice will often allow you to eliminate more than one answer choice, since the answers are usually in increasing order. This should save you valuable time.

2. If $(x/4) + 2 = 22$, find x.
   (A) 40   (B) 80   (C) 100   (D) 120   (E) 160

If you cannot solve this algebraically, you may use the *work up from your choices* strategy. But start with (C), 100. What if x = 100?

$$(x/4) + 2 = 22$$
$$(100/4) + 2 \overset{?}{=} 22$$
$$25 + 2 \overset{?}{=} 22$$
$$27 \neq 22$$

Note that since 27 is too large, choices (D) and (E) will also be too large. Therefore, try (A). If (A) is too small, then you know the answer is (B). If (A) works, the answer is (A).

$$(x/4) + 2 = 22$$
$$(40/4) + 2 \overset{?}{=} 22$$
$$10 + 2 \overset{?}{=} 22$$
$$12 \neq 22$$

Since (A) is too small, the answer must be (B).

3. If Barney can mow the lawn in five hours and Fred can mow the lawn in four hours, how long will it take them to mow the lawn together?

(A) 1 hour
(B) 2⅖ hours
(C) 4 hours
(D) 4½ hours
(E) 5 hours

Suppose that you are unfamiliar with the type of equation for this problem. Try the "reasonable" method. Since Fred can mow the lawn in four hours by himself, he will take less than four hours if Barney helps him. Therefore choices (C), (D), and (E) are ridiculous. Taking this method a little further, suppose that Barney could also mow the lawn in four hours. Then together it would take Barney and Fred two hours. But, since Barney is a little slower than this, the total time should be a little more than two hours. The correct answer is (B), 2⅖ hours. Using the equation for this problem would give the following calculations.

$$\frac{1}{\text{person A's rate}} + \frac{1}{\text{person B's rate}} = \frac{1}{\text{rate together}}$$

$$\frac{1}{5} + \frac{1}{4} = \frac{1}{x}$$

In 1 hour, Barney could do ⅕ of the job and in 1 hour Fred could do ¼ of the job; unknown $(1/x)$ is that part of the job they could do together in one hour. Now solving, you calculate as follows:

$$\frac{4}{20} + \frac{5}{20} = \frac{1}{x}$$

$$\frac{9}{20} = \frac{1}{x}$$

Cross multiplying gives $9x = 20$
Therefore, $x = {}^{20}\!/_9$, or 2⅖.

4. Find the counting number between 11 and 30 that when divided by 3 has a remainder of 1 but when divided by 4 has a remainder of 2.

(A) 12   (B) 13   (C) 16   (D) 21   (E) 22

By working from the answers, you can eliminate wrong answer choices. For instance, (A) and (C) can be immediately eliminated because they are divisable by 4, leaving no remainder. Choices (B) and (D) can also be eliminated because they leave a remainder of 1 when divided by 4. Therefore, the correct answer is (E). 22 leaves a remainder of 1 when divided by 3 and a remainder of 2 when divided by 4.

Approximate

If a problem involves calculations with numbers that seem tedious and time consuming, scan your answer choices to see if you can *round off or approximate* those numbers. If so, replace those numbers with numbers easier to work with. Find the answer choice closest to your approximated answer.

Examples:

1. The value for $(.889 \times 55)/9.97$ to the nearest tenth is
   (A) .5   (B) 4.63   (C) 4.9   (D) 17.7   (E) 49.1

Before starting any computations, take a glance at the answers to see how far apart they are. Notice that the only close answers are (B) and (C), but (B) is not a possible choice, since it is to the nearest hundredth, not tenth. Now, making some quick approximations, $.889 \simeq 1$ and $9.97 \simeq 10$, leaving the problem in this form.

$$\frac{1 \times 55}{10} = \frac{55}{10} = 5.5$$

The closest answer is (C); therefore it is the correct answer. Notice that choices (A) and (E) are not reasonable.

2. The value of $\sqrt{\dfrac{9,986}{194}}$ is approximately

   (A) 7   (B) 18   (C) 35   (D) 40   (E) 50

Round off both numbers to the hundreds place. The problem then becomes

$$\sqrt{\frac{10,000}{200}}$$

This is much easier to work. By dividing, the problem now becomes

$$\sqrt{50} = \text{slightly more than 7}$$

The closest answer choice is choice (A).

Make Comparisons

At times, questions will require you to *compare* the sizes of several decimals, or of several fractions. If decimals are being compared, make sure that the numbers being compared have the same number of digits. (Remember: Zeros to the far right of a decimal point can be inserted or eliminated without changing the value of the number.)

Examples:

1. Put these in order from smallest to largest: .6, .16, .66⅔, .58
   (A) .6, .16, .66⅔, .58   (D) .66⅔, .6, .58, .16
   (B) .58, .16, .6, .66⅔   (E) .58, .6, .66⅔, .16
   (C) .16, .58, .6, .66⅔

Rewrite .6 as .60; therefore all of the decimals now have the same number of digits: .60, .16, .66⅔, .58. Treating these as though the decimal point were not there (this can be done only when all the numbers have the same number of digits to the right of the decimal), the order is as follows: .16, .58, .60, .66⅔. The correct answer is (C). Remember to circle *smallest to largest* in the question.

2. Put these in order from smallest to largest: 75%, ⅔, ⅝
   (A) ⅔, 75%, ⅝   (D) 75%, ⅝, ⅔
   (B) ⅔, ⅝, 75%   (E) 75%, ⅔, ⅝
   (C) ⅝, ⅔, 75%

Using common denominators, we find

$$\tfrac{2}{3} = {}^{16}\!/_{24}$$
$$\tfrac{5}{8} = {}^{15}\!/_{24}$$
$$75\% = \tfrac{3}{4} = {}^{18}\!/_{24}$$

Therefore the order becomes ⅝, ⅔, 75%. Using decimal equivalents

$$\tfrac{5}{8} = .625$$
$$\tfrac{2}{3} = .666\tfrac{2}{3}$$
$$75\% = .750$$

The order again is ⅝, ⅔, 75%. The answer is (C).

Mark Diagrams

When a figure is included with the problem, *mark the given facts on the diagram*. This will help you visualize all the facts that have been given.

Examples:

1. If each square in the figure has a side of length 3, what is the perimeter?
   (A) 12
   (B) 14
   (C) 21
   (D) 30
   (E) 36

Mark the known facts.

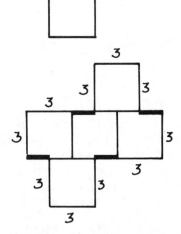

We now have a calculation for the perimeter: 30 *plus* the darkened parts. Now look carefully at the top two darkened parts. They will add up to 3. (Notice how the top square may slide over to illustrate that fact.)

The same is true for the bottom darkened parts. They will add to 3.

Thus, the total perimeter is 30 + 6 = 36, choice (E).

2. What is the maximum number of pieces of birthday cake of size 4″ × 4″ that can be cut from the cake above?
   (A) 5   (B) 10   (C) 16   (D) 20   (E) 25

Marking in as follows makes this a fairly simple problem.

Notice that five pieces of cake will fit along each side; therefore 5 × 5 = 25. The correct answer is (E). Finding the total area of the cake and dividing it by the area of one of the 4 × 4 pieces would have also given you the correct answer, but beware of this method because it may not work if the pieces do not fit evenly into the original area.

3. The perimeter of the isosceles triangle is 44″. The two equal sides are each five times as long as the third side. What are the lengths of each side?
   (A) 21, 21, 21
   (B) 6, 6, 18
   (C) 18, 21, 3
   (D) 20, 20, 4
   (E) 4, 4, 36

△ ABC is isosceles
AB = AC

Mark the equal sides
on the diagram.

AB and AC are each five
times as long as BC.

The equation for perimeter is

$$5x + 5x + x = 44$$
$$11x = 44$$
$$x = 4$$

becomes

The answer is (D). Note: This problem could have been solved by working from the answers given.

4. In the following triangle, CD is an angle bisector, angle ACD is 30°, and angle ABC is a right angle. What is the measurement of angle x in degrees?

(A) 30°   (D) 75°
(B) 45°   (E) 180°
(C) 60°

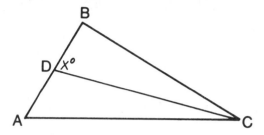

You should have read the problem and marked as follows:

In the triangle above, CD is an angle bisector (STOP AND MARK IN THE DRAWING), angle ACD is 30° (STOP AND MARK IN THE DRAWING), and angle ABC is a right angle (STOP AND MARK IN THE DRAWING). What is the measurement of angle x in degrees? (STOP AND MARK IN OR CIRCLE WHAT YOU ARE LOOKING FOR IN THE DRAWING.)

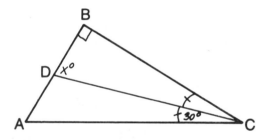

Now with the drawing marked in, it is evident that, since angle ACD is 30°, then angle BCD is also 30° because they are formed by an angle bisector (divides an angle into two equal parts). Since angle ABC is 90° (right angle) and BCD is 30°, then angle x is 60° because there are 180° in a triangle, 180 − (90 + 30) = 60. The correct answer is (C). ALWAYS MARK IN DIAGRAMS AS YOU READ DESCRIPTIONS AND INFORMATION ABOUT THEM. THIS INCLUDES WHAT YOU ARE LOOKING FOR.

Draw Diagrams

Drawing diagrams to meet the conditions set by the word problem can often make the problem easier for you to work. Being able to "see" the facts is more helpful than just reading the words.

Examples:

1. If all sides of a square are halved, the area of that square
    (A) is halved   (D) remains the same
    (B) is divided by 3   (E) not enough information to tell
    (C) is divided by 4

One way to solve this problem is to draw a square and then halve all
its sides. Then compare the two areas.

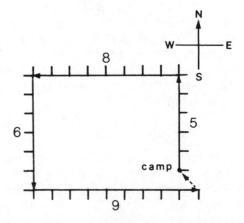

Notice that the total area of the new square will now be one-fourth
the original square. The correct answer is (C).

2. A hiking team begins at camp and hikes 5 miles north, then 8
    miles west, then 6 miles south, then 9 miles east. In what direction
    must they now travel in order to return to camp?
    (A) north   (D) west
    (B) northeast   (E) They already are at camp.
    (C) northwest

For this question,
your diagram would look
something like this:

Thus, they must travel
northwest (C) to return
to camp. Note that in
this case it is important
to draw your diagram
very accurately.

Procedure Problems

Some problems (commonly on the PPST and CBEST) may not ask you to solve and find a correct numerical answer. Rather, you may be asked *how to work* the problem.

Examples:

1. To find the area of the following figure, a student would use which formula?
    (A) I   (D) I and II
    (B) II   (E) I and III
    (C) III

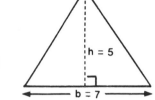

I. area = base times height
II. area = ½ times base times height
III. area = one side squared

Notice that it is not necessary to use any of the numerical values given in the diagram. You are to simply answer how the problem is to be worked. In such cases don't bother working the problem; it is merely a waste of time. The correct answer is (B) II.

2. 108 ÷ 4 could be quickly mentally calculated by
    (A) 100 ÷ 4 + 8   (D) (54 ÷ 4) × 2
    (B) 27 + 27 + 27 + 27   (E) 4 into 108
    (C) (100 ÷ 4) + (8 ÷ 4)

Answer (C) is correct. The quickest method of calculating 108 ÷ 4 is to first break down 108 into 100 + 8. Then divide each value by 4, finally adding them together. Answer choices (D) and (E) will give the correct answer but are not the best ways to *quickly* calculate the answer. And choices (A) and (B) are simply incorrect.

Sometimes, however, actually working the problem can be helpful, as follows.

3. The fastest method to solve ⁹⁄₄₈ × ⁸⁄₉ would be to
    (A) invert the second fraction and then multiply
    (B) multiply each column across and then reduce to lowest terms
    (C) find the common denominator and then multiply across
    (D) divide 9 into the numerator and denominator, divide 8 into numerator and denominator, and then multiply across
    (E) reduce the first fraction to lowest terms and then multiply across

In this problem, the way to determine the fastest procedure may be to actually work the problem as you would if you were working toward an answer. Then see if that procedure is listed among the choices. You should then compare it to the other methods listed. Is one of the other *correct* methods faster than the one you used? If so, select the fastest.

These types of problems are not constructed to test your knowledge of *obscure* tricks in solving mathematical equations. Rather, they test your knowledge of common procedures used in standard mathematical equations. Thus, the fastest way to solve this problem would be to first divide 9 into the numerator and denominator.

$$\frac{\overset{1}{\cancel{9}}}{48} \times \frac{8}{\underset{1}{\cancel{9}}} =$$

Then divide 8 into the numerator and denominator.

$$\frac{\overset{1}{\cancel{9}}}{\underset{6}{\cancel{48}}} \times \frac{\overset{1}{\cancel{8}}}{\underset{1}{\cancel{9}}} =$$

Then multiply across.

$$\frac{\overset{1}{\cancel{9}}}{\underset{6}{\cancel{48}}} \times \frac{\overset{1}{\cancel{8}}}{\underset{1}{\cancel{9}}} = \frac{1}{6}$$

The correct answer is (D).

> Holiday bouquets cost the Key Club $2.00 each. The Key Club sells them for $4.75 each

4. Based on the above information, how could Clark determine how many bouquets must be sold (Q) to make a profit of $82.50?

   (A) Q = $82.50 ÷ $2.00   (D) Q = $82.50 ÷ $4.75 − $2.00
   (B) Q = $82.50 − $2.00   (E) Q = $82.50 ÷ $2.75
   (C) Q = $4.75 − $2.00(Q)

The correct answer is (E). Notice that, since the bouquets are bought for $2.00 each but sold at $4.75 each, the profit on each bouquet is $2.75. Therefore, to determine how many bouquets equal a profit of $82.50, one need only divide $82.50 by $2.75.

Multiple-Multiple-Choice

Some mathematical ability questions use a *"multiple-multiple-choice"* format. At first glance, these appear more confusing and more difficult than normal five-choice (A, B, C, D, E) multiple-choice problems. Actually, once you understand "multiple-multiple-choice" problem types and technique, they are often easier than a comparable standard multiple-choice question.

Example:

If X is a positive integer, then which of the following *must* be true?

  I. $X > 0$
 II. $X = 0$
III. $X < 1$

(A) I only (B) II only (C) III only (D) I and II (E) I and III

Since X is a positive integer, it must be a counting number. Note that possible values of X could be 1, or 2, or 3, or 4, and so on. Therefore, statement I, $X > 0$, is always true. So next to I on your question booklet place a *T* for *true*.

$$T \quad \begin{array}{l} \text{I.} X > 0 \\ \text{II.} X = 0 \\ \text{III.} X < 1 \end{array}$$

Now realize that the correct final answer choice (either A, B, C, D, or E) *must* contain *true statement I*. This eliminates (B) and (C) as possible correct answer choices, as they do *not* contain true statement I. You should cross out (B) and (C) on your question booklet.

Statement II is *incorrect*. If X is positive, X cannot equal zero. Thus, next to II, you should place an *F* for false.

$$\begin{array}{l} T \quad \text{I.} X > 0 \\ F \quad \text{II.} X = 0 \\ \quad\;\; \text{III.} X < 1 \end{array}$$

Knowing that II is false allows you to eliminate any answer choices that contain *false statement II*. Therefore, you should cross out (D), as it contains a false statement II. Only (A) and (E) are left as possible correct answers. Finally you realize that statement III is also false, as X must be 1 or greater. So you place an F next to III, thus eliminating choice (E) and leaving (A), I only.

This technique often saves some precious time and allows you to take a better educated guess should you not be able to complete all parts (I, II, III, IV, etc.) of a multiple-multiple-choice question.

A PATTERNED PLAN OF ATTACK

Math Ability

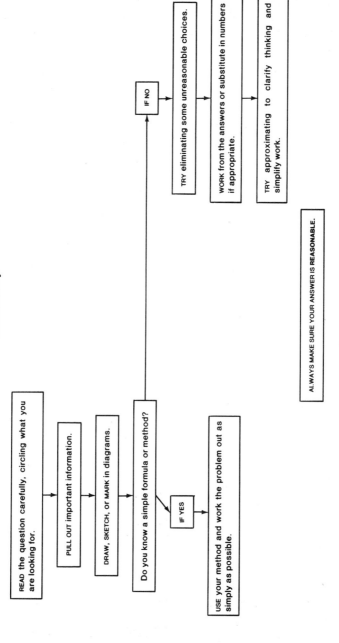

READ the question carefully, circling what you are looking for.

PULL OUT important information.

DRAW, SKETCH, or MARK in diagrams.

Do you know a simple formula or method?

IF YES

USE your method and work the problem out as simply as possible.

IF NO

TRY eliminating some unreasonable choices.

WORK from the answers or substitute in numbers if appropriate.

TRY approximating to clarify thinking and simplify work.

ALWAYS MAKE SURE YOUR ANSWER IS REASONABLE.

MATHEMATICAL ABILITY PRACTICE

Arithmetic

Questions

1. Which of the following pairs are *not* equal?
   (A) $\frac{2}{5}$, .4   (D) $13\frac{1}{4}$, $3\frac{1}{4}$
   (B) $\frac{1}{3}$, $\frac{11}{33}$ (E) $\frac{7}{11}$, $\frac{72}{112}$
   (C) $\frac{5}{4}$, $1\frac{1}{4}$

2. The number 103,233,124 is divisible by
   (A) 3   (B) 4   (C) 5   (D) 6   (E) 8

3. The product of 1.5 and .4 expressed as a fraction is
   (A) $\frac{2}{5}$ (B) $\frac{1}{2}$ (C) $\frac{3}{5}$ (D) $\frac{2}{3}$ (E) $\frac{4}{5}$

4. The greatest common factor of 32, 48, and 64 is
   (A) 4   (B) 6   (C) 8   (D) 16   (E) 32

5. Dividing a number by $\frac{8}{2}$ is the same as multiplying by
   (A) 4   (B) 2   (C) $\frac{1}{4}$ (D) $\frac{1}{6}$ (E) $\frac{1}{8}$

6. What is .25 percent of 2,000?
   (A) 500   (B) 50   (C) 5   (D) .5   (E) .05

7. $(9.3 \times 10^7) - (2.1 \times 10^2) =$
   (A) 92,000,790   (D) 93,000,790
   (B) 92,999,790   (E) 93,999,790
   (C) 93,000,210

8. A national birth rate of 72,000 newborn babies each day is equal to how many births per minute?
   (A) 5   (B) 10   (C) 50   (D) 120   (E) 500

9. If the average of 30 numbers is 50, what is the sum of the numbers?
   (A) 300   (B) 600   (C) 1,500   (D) 3,050   (E) 5,030

10. The number 24 is 20 percent of what number?
    (A) 12   (B) 28   (C) 100   (D) 120   (E) 480

11. If the ratio of males to females at a party is 4 to 5 and the ratio of adults to children at the party is 3 to 2, which of the following could be the number of people at the party?
    (A) 18   (B) 25   (C) 35   (D) 45   (E) 60

12. A television regularly selling for $85 is discounted 20%. What is the new selling price of the television?

(A) $65   (B) $67   (C) $68   (D) $70   (E) $75

DOW JONES AVERAGE

1980	830.0
1981	870.0
1982	910.0
1983	950.0
1984	990.0
1985	1030.0

13. In the table above, the greatest percent increase was between which years?

(A) 1980 and 1981   (D) 1983 and 1984
(B) 1981 and 1982   (E) 1984 and 1985
(C) 1982 and 1983

14. Find the sum of $\frac{1}{3}$, $\frac{1}{8}$, and $\frac{5}{6}$.

(A) $\frac{13}{24}$ (B) $\frac{15}{14}$ (C) $\frac{31}{24}$ (D) $\frac{33}{24}$ (E) $\frac{35}{24}$

15. Approximate the value for $.26 \times .67 \times .5 \times .9$

(A) .08   (B) .13   (C) .8   (D) .32   (E) .04

16. A teacher gave a test to a class and all the boys averaged 82% while all the girls averaged 85%. If there were twenty boys and ten girls in the class, what was the average for the entire class?

(A) $82\frac{1}{2}$%   (B) 83%   (C) $83\frac{1}{2}$%   (D) 84%   (E) 85%

17. If the average (arithmetic mean) of 10, 14, 16, and q is 14, then q =

(A) 10   (B) 12   (C) 14   (D) 16   (E) 18

18. If the price of apples is decreased from two dozen for $5 to three dozen for $6, how many more apples can be purchased for $30 now than could be purchased before?

(A) 36   (B) 48   (C) 72   (D) 144   (E) 180

19. If 28 millimeters is equivalent to 2.8 centimeters, how many millimeters are in 50 centimeters?

(A) .5   (B) 5   (C) 50   (D) 500   (E) 5,000

20. Which of the following is (are) equal to ⅜?

    I. .375   II. 37½%   III. $\dfrac{37½}{100}$ IV. $\dfrac{375}{100}$

    (A) I and II   (D) II and III
    (B) I, II, and III   (E) IV
    (C) I, II, and IV

21. What is the arithmetic mean of six Tigers each averaging .280 and four Padres averaging .250 each?
    (A) .268   (B) .270   (C) .272   (D) .274   (E) .276

22. Find the simple interest on $3,000 if it is left in an account for four months paying a 2% quarterly rate of interest.
    (A) $8   (B) $60   (C) $80   (D) $120   (E) $600

23. How many paintings were displayed at the County Museum of Art if 30% of them were by Monet and Monet was represented by 24 paintings?
    (A) 48   (B) 50   (C) 60   (D) 76   (E) 80

24. A motorist travels 120 miles to his destination at the average speed of 60 miles per hour and returns to the starting point at the average speed of 40 miles per hour. His average speed for the entire trip is
    (A) 40 mph   (D) 50 mph
    (B) 45 mph   (E) 53 mph
    (C) 48 mph

25. A special race is held in which runners may stop to rest. However, if a runner stops, he may then run only half as far as his previous distance between stops, at which point he must stop to rest again. If a runner finishes running when stopping for the fifth time, what's the farthest distance Albert can run if he takes his first rest stop after .8 kilometers?
    (A) 1.5 km   (D) 1.80 km
    (B) 1.55 km   (E) 2.0 km
    (C) 1.75 km

26. A used bicycle pump, for sale originally at $7.00, is discounted 20%. Because it doesn't sell, it is discounted an additional 10%.

What is its new selling price?
(A) $4.90   (B) $5.00   (C) $5.04   (D) $5.21   (E) $5.60

27. A student scored 80% on each of two tests. What does he have to score on the third test in order to raise his overall average to 85%?
(A) 90%   (B) 93%   (C) 95%   (D) 98%   (E) 100%

28. Successive discounts of 40% and 20% are equal to a single discount of
(A) 20%   (B) 30%   (C) 52%   (D) 60%   (E) 80%

29. A solution must contain at least 30% orange juice but not more than 20% ginger ale in addition to its other ingredients. If the punch bowl is to hold 400 cups of this solution, which of the following are allowable amounts of orange juice and ginger ale?
(A) 120 cups of orange juice, 130 cups of ginger ale
(B) 130 cups of orange juice, 140 cups of ginger ale
(C) 150 cups of orange juice, 70 cups of ginger ale
(D) 20 cups of orange juice, 80 cups of ginger ale
(E) 14 cups of orange juice, 100 cups of ginger ale

30. What percent is $\frac{1}{2^3}$ of 2^3?

(A) 0.016%   (B) 0.16%   (C) 1.6%   (D) 16%   (E) 160%

Algebra

Questions

1. If $x = -3$ and $y = (x + 5)(x - 5)$, then the value of y is
(A) 64   (B) 16   (C) 9   (D) -9   (E) -16

2. If $9x + 4 = -32$, then what is $x + 1$?
(A) -5   (B) -4   (C) -3   (D) 4   (E) 5

3. If $(4)(4)(4)(4) = \frac{(8)(8)}{p}$, then p must equal

(A) ¼   (B) ½   (C) 1   (D) 2   (E) 4

4. Find the value of a^{bc} if $a = 2$, $b = 3$, and $c = 2$.
(A) 8   (B) 16   (C) 32   (D) 64   (E) 128

$$\sqrt{(9 - x)^2} = 9 - x$$

5. In the real number system, which of the following cannot be a value for x in the statement above?

(A) −10   (B) −9   (C) 0   (D) 9   (E) 10

6. If $\dfrac{1}{t} + \dfrac{1}{p} = \dfrac{1}{2}$, then t + p =

(A) 8   (D) ½
(B) 2   (E) cannot be determined
(C) 1

7. If a and b are positive integers and $a^2 - b^2 = 11$, then 2a + 2b must equal

(A) 11   (B) 12   (C) 22   (D) 26   (E) 36

8. If x + 2 = y, what is the value of x − 2 in terms of y?
(A) y − 4   (D) y + 4
(B) y − 2   (E) y + 6
(C) y + 2

9. If ab = −5 and $(a + b)^2 = 16$, then $a^2 + b^2$ =
(A) 11   (B) 15   (C) 21   (D) 25   (E) 26

10. If x is an even integer, which of the following must also be an even integer?
(A) 9x + 1   (D) $\dfrac{x}{2}$
(B) 9x − 1
(C) $\dfrac{x}{2} + 1$ (E) 4x + 6

11. For all m, $m^2 + 11m + 30 = (m + y)(m + z)$. What is the value of yz?
(A) 5   (D) 30
(B) 6   (E) cannot be determined
(C) 11

12. If 2x + 5y = 32, then 4x + 10y =
(A) 16   (D) 128
(B) 34   (E) cannot be determined
(C) 64

13. If $25q^2p^2 = 8x$, then $\dfrac{q^2p^2}{4} =$

(A) 16x   (B) 4x   (C) 2x   (D) $\dfrac{2x}{25}$ (E) $\dfrac{x}{25}$

14. If n is a positive integer, then which of the following must be true about (n) and (n + 1)?
(A) n is odd
(B) (n + 1) is odd
(C) the product of the two terms is odd
(D) the sum of the two terms is even
(E) the product of the two terms is even

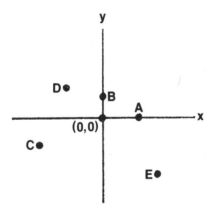

15. On the coordinate grid above, for which point must the product of its x and y coordinates be positive?
(A) A   (B) B   (C) C   (D) D   (E) E

16. If x, y, and z are all positive integers and $x < y < z$, then which of the following must be true?
(A) $(x + y) > z$
(B) $xy > z$
(C) $(z - y) > x$
(D) $(z - 2) = x$
(E) $z > \dfrac{y}{x}$

17. If $0.002 \le a \le 0.05$ and $0.01 \le b \le 0.50$, then what is the greatest possible value of $(a/b)^2$?
(A) .25   (B) .5   (C) 1   (D) 5   (E) 25

18. If $\dfrac{x^2yz + xyz^2}{xyz} = x + z$, then a necessary condition for this to be true is

   I. $x + z < y$ II. $x^2 > z$ III. $xyz \neq 0$

   (A) I   (D) III
   (B) I and II   (E) II and III
   (C) I and III

19. If $\dfrac{1}{5} + \dfrac{1}{2} + \dfrac{1}{x} = 7$, then x =

   (A) $\dfrac{10}{63}$ (B) $\dfrac{60}{7}$ (C) $\dfrac{63}{10}$ (D) $\dfrac{3}{19}$ (E) $\dfrac{7}{60}$

20. A fruit drink made from orange juice and water is diluted with more water so that the final solution is ¼ water. If the original solution was 90% orange juice and two liters of water were added, how many liters are in the final solution of fruit drink?
   (A) 6   (B) 8   (C) 10   (D) 12   (E) 14

21. Ernie purchased some apples from a grocer for $5.00 and later learned that if he had purchased 20% more apples he would have been given a 20% discount in price per apple. What would the difference have been in total cost if he had purchased 20% more apples?
   (A) 20¢ less   (D) 20¢ more
   (B) 10¢ less   (E) cannot be determined
   (C) the same cost

22. A college student invests $2,000, part at 7% in a savings account and some at 12% in a special money market account. The annual income from this investment is $200. How much was invested in the money market account?
   (A) $400   (D) $1,200
   (B) $600   (E) $1,350
   (C) $1,000

23. If p pencils cost c cents, n pencils at the same price will cost

(A) $\dfrac{pc}{n}$ cents   (D) $\dfrac{np}{c}$ cents

(B) $\dfrac{cn}{p}$ cents   (E) $\dfrac{pc}{np}$ cents

(C) npc cents

24. A woman bought a set of porch furniture at a 40 percent reduction sale held late in the summer. The furniture cost her $165. What was the original price of the furniture?
    (A) $66   (D) $412.50
    (B) $231   (E) $510
    (C) $275

25. The midpoint of line segment AB is
    (A) (8, 4)   (D) (5, 6)
    (B) (3, 6)   (E) (4, 8)
    (C) (6, 5)

Geometry

Questions

1. If, in the figure, $line_1$ is parallel to $line_2$, then $x + y$ must equal
   (A) 40°
   (B) 120°
   (C) 160°
   (D) 180°
   (E) 320°

2. In the figure, find the degree
   measure of angle y.
   (A) 40
   (B) 50
   (C) 80
   (D) 90
   (E) 110

3. In the figure, what is
   the value of p?
   (A) 18
   (B) 36
   (C) 72
   (D) 108
   (E) 135

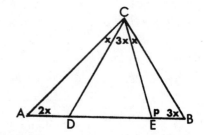

4. In circle O, arc AD = 80°.
   Find the measure of
   inscribed angle MDA.
   (A) 40°
   (B) 50°
   (C) 60°
   (D) 80°
   (E) 100°

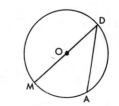

5. In triangle ABC, side AB =
   side BC. Therefore, angles
   r and p each equal
   (A) 50°
   (B) 25°
   (C) 20°
   (D) 10°
   (E) cannot be determined

6. In the figure, x =
   (A) 15
   (B) 10
   (C) 9
   (D) 5
   (E) 4

7. What is the maximum number of
   cubes 3 inches on an edge that
   can be packed into a carton
   with dimensions as shown?
   (A) 70
   (B) 74
   (C) 80
   (D) 84
   (E) 88

8. Find the volume of a cube in cubic inches if the area of one of its
   faces is 49 square inches.
   (A) 49   (B) 64   (C) 125   (D) 144   (E) 343

9. Square ABCD is inscribed in circle O with a radius of $\sqrt{2}$, as
   shown. Find the area of square ABDC.
   (A) 1
   (B) 2
   (C) 4
   (D) 8
   (E) 16

10. If the five angles of a pentagon are in the ratio 1:2:3:4:5, what is
    the degree measure of the largest angle?
    (A) 100   (B) 120   (C) 150   (D) 180   (E) 210

11. Circle O intersects circle Q
    at point K. Line segment PQ = 13,
    and the radius of circle O is 5.
    What is the area of circle Q?
    (A) 144π
    (B) 100π
    (C) 81π
    (D) 64π
    (E) 49π

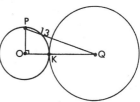

12. In the diagram, circle O
    inscribed in square ABCD
    has an area of 36π square
    inches. Find the perimeter
    of square ABCD.
    (A) 24
    (B) 48
    (C) 60
    (D) 144
    (E) 200

13. A regular cylindrical tank is to be ⅔ filled with water. If its
    height is 9 feet and its diameter is 12 feet, how many cubic feet of
    water will be needed?
    (A) 144π (D) 324π
    (B) 216π (E) 720π
    (C) 256π

14. In the figure, what is
    the area of the shaded
    region?
    (A) 15
    (B) 18
    (C) 20
    (D) 21
    (E) 25

15. Using the figure to
    determine the values of
    q and p, the product qp
    must equal
    (A) ½
    (B) 1
    (C) 2
    (D) $2\sqrt{3}$
    (E) $3\sqrt{2}$

16. If a square has the same perimeter as a rectangle with sides 2 and
    16, what is the area of the square?
    (A) 4   (B) 9   (C) 16   (D) 36   (E) 81

17. In the diagram, if one side of
the regular hexagon ABCDEF is 10,
find the area of the entire
hexagon.

(A) 75
(B) $75\sqrt{3}$
(C) 150
(D) $150\sqrt{2}$
(E) $150\sqrt{3}$

18. If, at point P, line$_2$ bisects the
angle formed by line$_1$ and line $_3$,
what is the degree measure of x
if z equals 100°?

(A) 30
(B) 40
(C) 45
(D) 80
(E) 90

19. In Circle O, if chord SP = 6
and radius of circle O = 5,
find the length of chord RS.

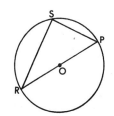

(A) 3
(B) $\sqrt{11}$
(C) 6
(D) 8
(E) cannot be determined

20. In the figure, side AB = 6 and
side BC = 8. Find the area of
triangle ADC.

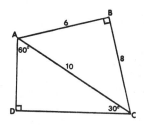

(A) $25\sqrt{3}$
(B) 24
(C) $\dfrac{25\sqrt{3}}{2}$
(D) 20
(E) $20\sqrt{2}$

21. On the coordinate grid, what is the length of line AB if the coordinates at point A are (7, 9) and the coordinates at point B are (13, 17)?

(A) 7½ units
(B) 8½ units
(C) 9 units
(D) 10 units
(E) 12½ units

22. The figure shown represents the end of a garage. Find, in feet, the length of one of the equal rafters AB or CB if each extends 12 inches beyond the eaves.

(A) 10
(B) 11
(C) 13
(D) 22
(E) 33

23. The figure represents a rectangle, whose dimensions are l and w, surmounted by a semicircle, whose radius is r. Express the area of this figure in terms of l, w, r, and π.

(A) $wl + \dfrac{\pi r^2}{2}$

(B) $lw + \pi r$

(C) $lw + \pi r^2$

(D) $\dfrac{\pi}{2} - r^2 lw$

(E) wlr^2

24. The width of the ring (shaded portion of the figure) is exactly equal to the radius of the inner circle. What percent of the entire area is the area of the shaded portion?

(A) 25   (D) 75
(B) 50   (E) 90
(C) 66⅔

25. By what number is the area of a circle multiplied if its radius is doubled?

(A) 2πr   (B) 2   (C) 3.1416   (D) 4   (E) 6

Procedure Problems

1. Jose purchased three items for his new car—a steering wheel grip, a floor mat, and a seat cushion. The steering wheel grip cost three times the seat cushion. The floor mat cost exactly $5.75 with tax. Which of the following can be derived from the above information?

   I. the cost of all three items
  II. the cost of the seat cushion
  III. the cost of the steering wheel grip
  IV. the cost of the floor mat without the tax

(A) I only   (D) IV only
(B) II only   (E) none of these
(C) III only

> John's car is a year older than Sue's car.
> Maria's truck is one year newer than John's car.
> Sue's car, a 1983 model, is newer than Maria's truck.

2. Fred is given the information above in a problem in his math class. With just the information given, Fred should be able to determine the approximate age(s) of

(A) Sue's car
(B) Sue's car and Maria's truck
(C) Sue's car and John's car
(D) Sue's car, Maria's truck, and John's car
(E) Maria's truck

3. Harold is given the following information about the class treasury.

   I. The current balance is five dollars less than last year's final balance, which was $10.

  II. This year's balance of $10 is $5 more than last year's balance.

 III. Ten percent is half of this year's goal, which is $100.

Which of these statements can be calculated by subtracting 5 from 10?

(A) I

(B) II

(C) III

(D) I and II

(E) I, II, and III

Arnold's Scores on Four Tests
Test 1—83%
Test 2—85%
Test 3—100%
Test 4— ?

---

4. If Arnold's score on test 4 was weighted double that of each of the previous three tests, and if his overall average was 90%, how could Arnold determine his score on test 4?

(A) $(83 + 85 + 100 + ?) = 90$

(B) $(83 + 85 + 100 + ? + ?) = 90$

(C) $\dfrac{(83 + 85 + 100 + ?)}{4} = 90$

(D) $\dfrac{(83 + 85 + 100 + ? + ?)}{4} = 90$

(E) $\dfrac{(83 + 85 + 100 + ? + ?)}{5} = 90$

> 27,456 may be represented as **P**.
> 845 may be represented as **Q**.

5. Based on the above information, 27,456 times 846 may be expressed as
   (A) PQ + 1   (D) (P + 1)(Q + 1)
   (B) (P + 1)(Q)   (E) (P)(Q + 845)
   (C) P(Q + 1)

6. When Francisco multiplies $(x + 1)(x + 2)$ he gets $x^2 + 3x + 2$ as an answer. One way to check this answer would be to
   (A) divide $(x + 1)$ by $(x + 2)$
   (B) divide $(x + 2)$ by $(x + 1)$
   (C) plug in a positive integer for x
   (D) square $(x + 1)$
   (E) use reciprocals

> The sum of two numbers equals
> one of the numbers.

7. If the above statement is true, which of the following best represents the relationship?
   (A) $x + y = y + x$ (D) $x + y = y$
   (B) $(x)(y) = 1$ (E) $x + y = x + 1$
   (C) $x + y = 1$

8. Last year Jorge was three years less than twice Teresa's age now. If Jorge is ten years old now, which equation will enable Jorge to correctly find Teresa's present age, T?
   (A) $10 + 1 = 2T - 3$ (D) $11 = 2T - 3$
   (B) $9 - 3 = 2T$ (E) $10 = -3 + 2T$
   (C) $9 = 2T - 3$

9. If a tie costs T dollars and a suit jacket costs four times the price of the tie, which of the following best expresses the cost of two ties and three suit jackets?
   (A) 4T   (D) T + 3(4T)
   (B) T + 4(T)   (E) 2(T) + 3(4T)
   (C) 2(T) + 3(T)

Rossanna knows that a geometric
figure is a rectangle and that it has sides of 18 and 22.

10. How can Rossanna compute the area of a square that has the
    same perimeter as the rectangle above?
    (A) Add 18 and 22, double this sum, divide by four, then
        multiply by two.
    (B) Add 18 and 22, double this sum, divide by four, then
        multiply by four.
    (C) Add 18 and 22, double this sum, divide by four, then square
        the quotient.
    (D) Add 18 and 22, double this sum, then multiply by four.
    (E) Add twice 18 to twice 22, divide by 2, then square the
        quotient.

ANSWER KEY FOR MATHEMATICAL ABILITY PRACTICE

The first page number following each answer will direct you to the
complete explanation for that specific problem. *Read this explanation first.* The page numbers in parentheses refer to the suggested
basic review section.

Arithmetic

  1. (E) p. 356 (29, 51)   16. (B) p. 358 (76)
  2. (B) p. 356 (25)   17. (D) p. 358 (76)
  3. (C) p. 356 (48, 50)   18. (A) p. 358 (83)
  4. (D) p. 356 (32)   19. (D) p. 359 (83)
  5. (C) p. 356 (44)   20. (B) p. 359 (54)
  6. (C) p. 356 (55)   21. (A) p. 359 (76)
  7. (B) p. 356 (60)   22. (C) p. 359 (264)
  8. (C) p. 357 (83)   23. (E) p. 360 (56)
  9. (C) p. 357 (76)   24. (C) p. 360 (274)
 10. (D) p. 357 (55)   25. (B) p. 360 (49)
 11. (D) p. 357 (33)   26. (C) p. 361 (55, 277)
 12. (C) p. 358 (55)   27. (C) p. 361 (77)
 13. (A) p. 358 (59)   28. (C) p. 361 (55)
 14. (C) p. 358 (34)   29. (C) p. 361 (55)
 15. (A) p. 358 (20, 50)   30. (C) p. 361 (56, 63)

Algebra

1. (E) p. 362 (110)	14. (E) p. 364 (322)
2. (C) p. 362 (113)	15. (C) p. 364 (163)
3. (A) p. 362 (113, 120)	16. (E) p. 364 (322)
4. (D) p. 363 (110)	17. (E) p. 364 (110)
5. (E) p. 363 (170)	18. (D) p. 365 (150)
6. (E) p. 363 (122, 322)	19. (A) p. 365 (113)
7. (C) p. 363 (322)	20. (D) p. 365 (113, 302)
8. (A) p. 363 (113)	21. (A) p. 366 (270)
9. (E) p. 363 (110)	22. (D) p. 366 (113, 302)
10. (E) p. 364 (110, 322)	23. (B) p. 366 (113, 270)
11. (D) p. 364 (141)	24. (C) p. 366 (113, 277)
12. (C) p. 364 (113)	25. (D) p. 367 (163)
13. (D) p. 364 (113, 150)	

Geometry

1. (E) p. 367 (212)	14. (A) p. 369 (163, 232)
2. (E) p. 367 (206, 216)	15. (C) p. 370 (226)
3. (D) p. 367 (216)	16. (E) p. 370 (232)
4. (B) p. 367 (239)	17. (E) p. 370 (216, 226)
5. (E) p. 368 (216, 217)	18. (B) p. 370 (207)
6. (D) p. 368 (207)	19. (D) p. 370 (223, 235)
7. (C) p. 368 (242)	20. (C) p. 370 (223, 226)
8. (E) p. 368 (242)	21. (D) p. 371 (163, 223)
9. (C) p. 368 (235)	22. (B) p. 371 (223)
10. (D) p. 368 (231)	23. (A) p. 371 (232, 237)
11. (E) p. 369 (223, 237)	24. (D) p. 372 (237)
12. (B) p. 369 (232, 237)	25. (D) p. 372 (237)
13. (B) p. 369 (242)	

Procedure Problems

1. (E) p. 372 (285)	6. (C) p. 373 (322)
2. (D) p. 372 (289)	7. (D) p. 373 (108)
3. (D) p. 372 (108)	8. (C) p. 373 (289)
4. (E) p. 373 (77)	9. (E) p. 374 (108)
5. (C) p. 373 (108)	10. (C) p. 374 (232)

MATHEMATICAL ABILITY ANSWERS AND EXPLANATIONS

Arithmetic

1. (E) Dividing 7 by 11 gives .63+. Dividing 72 by 112 gives .64+.

2. (B) Since the last two digits are divisible by 4, the number is divisible by 4. Note that since the last *three* digits are not divisible by 8, the number is not divisible by 8.

3. (C) Change the terms into fractions and then multiply.

$$\frac{3}{2} \times \frac{2}{5} = \frac{6}{10} = \frac{3}{5}$$

4. (D) The greatest common factor is the largest factor which divides into all of the numbers. Of the choices, 16 is the largest number which can divide evenly into 32, 48, and 64.

5. (C) To divide by a fraction, you may invert the divisor and then multiply. Thus, say, 5 divided by $\frac{8}{2}$ is

$$5 \div \frac{8}{2} =$$

$$5 \times \frac{2}{8} =$$

$$5 \times \frac{1}{4} =$$

which is the same as multiplying by $\frac{1}{4}$.

6. (C) .25 percent is .0025. Therefore, .25 percent of 2,000 equals .0025 × 2,000 = 5.

7. (B) $(9.2 \times 10^7) - (2.1 \times 10^2) = 93,000,000 - 210 = 92,999,790.$

8. **(C)** Divide 72,000 births by 24 (hours per day) to find the number every hour (3,000). Divide this by 60 (minutes per hour) to find the number of births per minute (50).

9. **(C)** Since the average equals the sum divided by the number of items

$$\text{average} = \frac{\text{sum}}{\text{number of items}}$$

to find the sum, simply multiply the average times the number of items.

$$\frac{\text{average}}{1} = \frac{\text{sum}}{\text{number of items}}$$

Cross multiplying

$$(\text{average})(\text{number of items}) = 1(\text{sum})$$
$$50 \times 30 = \text{sum}$$
$$1,500 = \text{sum}$$

10. **(D)** To find any part of a simple percentage problem, use

$$\frac{\text{is}}{\text{of}} = \%$$

Plugging in the givens

$$\frac{24}{?} = 20\%$$

$$\frac{24}{x} = \frac{20}{100}$$

Cross multiplying

$$20x = 2,400$$

$$x = 120$$

11. **(D)** Since the ratio of males to females is 4 to 5, the males must be a multiple of 4 and the females must be a multiple of 5. Therefore, the total number of people at the party must have been $4 + 5 = 9$, or a multiple of 9. Similarly, adding adults and children means that $3 + 2 = 5$. The number of party goers must also be a multiple of 5. The only choice that is both a multiple of 5 and a multiple of 9 is choice (D), 45.

12. **(C)** Twenty percent off the original price of $85 is a discount of (.20)($85), or $17. Therefore the new selling price is $85 − $17 = $68.

13. **(A)** Notice that each change was an increase of 40 points. Therefore, the largest percent increase will have the smallest starting point (denominator). Thus, 830.0 will be the smallest denominator or starting point.

$$\text{percent increase} = \frac{\text{change}}{\text{starting point}} = \frac{40}{830.0}$$

14. **(C)** Use a common denominator of 24.

$$\frac{1}{3} + \frac{1}{8} + \frac{5}{6} = \frac{8}{24} + \frac{3}{24} + \frac{20}{24} = \frac{31}{24}$$

15. **(A)** Changing the decimals to the nearest fraction gives

$$.26 \times .67 \times .5 \times .9 = \frac{1}{4} \times \frac{2}{3} \times \frac{1}{2} \times \frac{9}{10}$$

Canceling leaves $\frac{1}{4} \times \frac{3}{10} = \frac{3}{40} = .075$ or $.08$

16. **(B)** One method to solve this problem is to compute total points. For the boys, 20×82 points each = 1,640. For the girls, 10×85 points each = 850. Adding gives 2,490 total points. 2,490 total points divided by 30 students gives an average of 83% per student. Another method is to realize that for every two boys averaging 82% there is one girl averaging 85%. So the problem is simply, what is the average of 82, 82, and 85? Again, the answer is 83%.

17. **(D)** If the average of four numbers is 14, then their sum must be 4(14) or 56. Since three of the numbers (10, 14, and 16) sum to 40, the fourth number must be 56 − 40, or 16.

18. **(A)** Thirty dollars previously would purchase six times two dozen apples, or $6 \times 2 \times 12 = 144$. Now, thirty dollars will buy five times three dozen apples, or $5 \times 3 \times 12 = 180$. Therefore, $180 - 144 = 36$ more apples can be purchased now.

19. (D) Setting up a proportion using ratios is one way to solve this problem.

$$\frac{mm}{cm} = \frac{mm}{cm}$$

$$\frac{28}{2.8} = \frac{x}{50}$$

Cross multiplying $1{,}400 = 2.8(x)$

Dividing each side by 2.8 $1{,}400/2.8 = x$
                             $500 = x$

Another way to solve this problem is to realize that the number of millimeters is ten times the number of centimeters. Thus, 10 times 50 centimeters equals 500 millimeters.

20. (B) To determine an equivalent for ⅜, simply divide 3 by 8.

$$8{\overline{\smash{\big)}\,3.000}}^{\,.375}$$

Therefore, ⅜ is equal to .375, which may also be expressed as

$$\frac{37\frac{1}{2}}{100} \text{ or } 37\frac{1}{2}\%$$

21. (A) To determine the arithmetic mean (composite averages) of the items in question, simply determine total points for all players, then divide by the total number of players. For instance,

6 Tigers each averaging .280 = 1.680 total points
4 Padres each averaging .250 = 1.000 total points
          all together = 2.680 total points

Now, divide the final total of 2.680 points by the total number of players (10).

$$\frac{2.680}{10} = .268 \text{ average for all 10 players}$$

22. (C) To determine simple interest, use the equation

interest = (principal) (annual rate) (time in years)
I = prt

Now plug in given values.

I = ($3,000) (.08) (⅓ yr)

Note that the *annual* rate would be four times the quarterly rate.

I = ($1,000) (.08)
I = $80

23. (E) To find the total number of paintings, use the equation

$$\frac{is}{of} = \%$$

and simply plug in the given values. The question is essentially, 24 is 30% of how many? Therefore, 24 is the "is", 30 is the percent, and "how many" (the unknown) is the "of." Plugging into the equation, we get

$$\frac{24}{x} = \frac{30}{100}$$

(note the fractional percent is used to simplify the math)

Cross multiplying $30x = 2,400$

Dividing both sides by 30 $\dfrac{30x}{30} = \dfrac{2,400}{30}$

$$x = 80$$

24. (C) 120 miles = 2 hours (60 mph)
     <u>120 miles</u> = <u>3 hours</u> (40 mph)
     240 miles = 5 hours = average of 48 mph

25. (B) Since Albert stops after .8 km, he may then run half that distance, .4 km, before stopping again, after which he may run .2, then .1, then .05 km. After his .05 km distance, he will make his fifth stop and must cease running. Adding the distances: .8 + .4 + .2 + .1 + .05 = 1.55 km.

26. (C) The original price, $7.00, is first discounted 20%.

$7.00 − .20(7.00) =
$7.00 − $1.40 = $5.60

Then the price is discounted an additional 10%.

$5.60 − .10($5.60) =
$5.60 − $.56 = $5.04

27. (C) Since the student scored 80% on each of two tests, his total scored so far equals 160 points. In order to average 85% for three tests, his total points must be 3 × 85, or 255 total points. Therefore, he needs an additional 95 points to bring his total up from 160 to 255. Thus, he needs to score a 95% on the next test.

28. (C)

$100	list price		$60	first selling price
× .40			× .20	
$ 40	first discount		$12	second discount

$60
− $12
$48 second selling price

$100 list
− $ 48 selling price
$ 52 total discount

$$\frac{\$52}{\$100} = 52\%$$

29. (C) In this problem, the words *at least* and *not more than* play an important role. Note that *at least 30%* of the total means 30% *or more*. And *not more than 20%* means 20% *or less*. Requirement for orange juice = 30% of 400 cups = (.30) (400) = 120 cups of orange juice. Note, however, that this is only the minimum. The punch bowl may contain 120 *or more* cups of orange juice. Ginger ale may be 80 cups or less.

30. (C) $\dfrac{\text{is}}{\text{of}} = \text{percent}$

$\text{is} = \dfrac{1}{2^3} \text{ or } \dfrac{1}{8}$

of $= 2^3$ or 8

$$\frac{\text{is}}{\text{of}} = \frac{\frac{1}{8}}{8} = \frac{1}{64} = .016 = 1.6\%$$

Algebra

1. (E) Substituting x $= -3$ leaves
$$y = (-3 + 5)(-3 - 5)$$
$$y = (2)(-8)$$
$$y = -16$$

2. (C) First circle x $+ 1$, as that is what the ultimate question is. Solving the given equation, subtract 4 from both sides.

$$
\begin{array}{r}
9x + 4 = -32 \\
-4 \quad -4 \\
\hline
9x \quad\;\; = -38
\end{array}
$$

Divide both sides by 9.

$$\frac{9x}{9} = \frac{-36}{9}$$

$$x = -4$$

Therefore, plugging in the value -4 for x gives x $+ 1 = -4 + 1 = -3$.

3. (A) Notice that $(4)(4)(4) = 64$. Therefore,

$$(4)(4)(4)(4) = \frac{(8)(8)}{p}$$

$$(64)(4) = \frac{64}{p}$$

Canceling 64s $4 = \dfrac{1}{p}$

Cross multiplying 4p $= 1$
$$p = \frac{1}{4}$$

4. **(D)** Plugging in the given values for a, b, and c

$$a^{bc} =$$
$$2^{(3)(2)} =$$
$$2^6 = 64$$

5. **(E)** If x is 10, then the value under the radical will be the square root of a negative squared. Negative radicals are "imaginary numbers," not permitted to exist in the real number system.

6. **(E)** If t and p both equal 4, then $\frac{1}{4} + \frac{1}{4} = \frac{1}{2}$. In this case, t + p would equal 8. But t could equal 1 and p could equal -2, which would also make

$$\frac{1}{t} + \frac{1}{p} = \frac{1}{2}$$

$$\frac{1}{1} + \frac{1}{-2} = \frac{1}{2}$$

In this case, t + p would equal -1. No definitive sum of **t + p** can be determined.

7. **(C)** Since a and b are positive integers, they must be 6 and 5, respectively, since they are the only integers whose difference of their squares will equal 11 ($36 - 25 = 11$). Therefore, twice 6 plus twice 5 is $12 + 10$, or 22.

8. **(A)** $x - 2$ is exactly four less than $x + 2$. Since $x + 2$ equals y, then $x - 2$ will be four less, or $y - 4$.

9. **(E)** $(a + b)^2 = a^2 + 2ab + b^2$. If $ab = -5$, then $2ab = -10$.

Plugging this in for 2ab

$$(a + b)^2 = a^2 - 10 + b^2$$

Plugging in the given $(a + b)^2 = 16$

$$16 = a^2 + b^2 - 10$$
$$26 = a^2 + b^2$$

10. (E) A multiple of an even integer will result in an even number. Thus, adding or subtracting 1 from any even multiple will result in an odd number, choices (A) and (B). Choice (C) may be an odd integer if x is 4 or 8 or 16, etc. And choice (D) may be an odd integer if x is 2 or 6 or 10, etc. Choice (E) will always give an even integer.

11. (D) Factoring the quadratic expression $m^2 + 11m + 30$ gives $(m + 5)(m + 6)$. Noting that the 5 and 6 represent y and z (or z and y), therefore, $yz = 5(6)$, which equals 30.

12. (C) Notice that $4x + 10y$ is exactly twice $2x + 5y$. Therefore, the answer is twice 32, or 64.

13. (D) Notice that $\dfrac{q^2p^2}{4}$ is $\dfrac{25q^2p^2}{100}$, which equals $\dfrac{8x}{100}$ and which reduces to $\dfrac{2x}{25}$.

14. (E) Since n and $(n + 1)$ are consecutive numbers, they may be 1 and 2, or 2 and 3, or 3 and 4, or 4 and 5, etc. Notice that their product will always be an even integer.

15. (C) The coordinates of point C are both negative. Thus, the product of two negative numbers will be positive. All the other points will either have a negative or a zero product.

16. (E) First try using 1, 2, and 3 as the three integers, as they usually illustrate the exception to the rule. Using these three integers reveals that choices (A), (B), and (C) are incorrect, as they will not be true with 1, 2, and 3. Choice (D) will be true with 1, 2, and 3, but it may not be true with many other integers (say, 5, 10, and 15). Notice that no matter what positive integers are inserted in choice (E), the largest of the integers will always be greater than the middle integer divided by the smallest.

17. (E) To find the greatest possible value of $\left(\dfrac{a}{b}\right)^2$, use the largest

possible value for a (as the numerator) and the *smallest* possible value for b (as the denominator). Thus $\frac{a}{b}$ would equal $\frac{.05}{.01}$, which equals 5. Therefore, $\left(\frac{a}{b}\right)^2$ will be 5^2, or 25.

18. (D) The necessary condition refers to the denominator not equaling 0, as you cannot divide by 0. Therefore, $xyz \neq 0$.

19. (A) Multiplying the equation $\frac{1}{5} + \frac{1}{2} + \frac{1}{x} = 7$ by the common denominator 10x gives

$$\frac{10x}{5} + \frac{10x}{2} + \frac{10x}{x} = 7(10x)$$

Reduced

$$2x + 5x + 10 = 70x$$
$$7x + 10 = 70x$$

Subtracting 7x from both sides

$$\begin{array}{r} 7x + 10 = 70x \\ -7x \qquad\quad -7x \\ \hline 10 = 63x \end{array}$$

Dividing by 63

$$\frac{10}{63} = x$$

20. (D) Set up an equation.

original solution + amount of pure water = new solution

Let x be the unknown amount of original solution. Solutions will be expressed in terms of concentration of water.

$$.10(x) + 2 = .25(x + 2)$$
$$.10x + 2 = .25x + .50$$
$$1.5 = .15x$$
$$10 = x$$

x is the number of liters in the original solution. Since the final solution is two additional liters of water, the final solution will contain 12 liters.

21. (A) Ernie first purchased a certain number of apples (x) for a certain price per apple (y). Therefore, he paid xy, which equals $5. He later learned that by purchasing 20% more apples (1.2x) he would have been given 20% off the per item price (.8y). Therefore, he would have paid (1.2x)(.8y) = .96xy. Since xy = $5, Ernie would have paid a new total of .96($5) = $4.80, which equals 20¢ less than the original total.

22. (D) Setting up an equation, let x be the amount at 12%. Then ($2,000 − x) is the amount at 7%.

$$.12x + .07(2,000 - x) = 200$$
$$.12x + 140 - .07x = 200$$
$$.05x + 140 = 200$$
$$.05x = 60$$

$$\frac{.05x}{.05} = \frac{60}{.05}$$

$$x = \$1,200$$

23. (B) Formula: $\dfrac{\text{number}}{\text{cost}} = \dfrac{\text{number}}{\text{cost}}$

If x represents the cost of n pencils, we have, by substitution,

$$\frac{p}{c} = \frac{n}{x}$$

$$px = cn$$

$$x = \frac{cn}{p} \text{ cents}$$

24. (C) Formula: selling price = original price − discount

If x = the original price, we substitute

$$165 = x - .40x$$

$$\frac{165}{.60} = \frac{.60x}{.60}$$

$$275 = x$$

25. (D) Adding the x values together and y values together of points A and B

$$
\begin{array}{r}
(1, 8) \\
+ \ (9, 4) \\
\hline
(10, 12)
\end{array}
$$

Dividing each by 2 to find the midpoint leaves (5, 6).

Geometry

1. (E) If line$_1$ and line$_2$ are parallel, then $z = 20°$. Therefore, supplementary angle x equals 160°, as does vertical angle y. Therefore, $160 + 160 = 320°$.

2. (E) Since angle x and angle 5x are supplementary (their sum is straight line, or 180°), then $5x + x = 180°$, and therefore, $x = 30°$. So the third angle of the triangle within the inter-secting lines is the vertical angle of x, or 30°. The three angles of the triangle are thus 30°, 40° and y. Therefore, $30 + 40 + y = 180$. So $y = 110°$.

3. (D) Totaling the sum of the three angles in large triangle ABC

$$2x + 3x + (x + 3x + x) = 10x$$

Since there are 180° in a triangle, $10x = 180°$. Then $x = 18°$. Thus, in small triangle CEB

$$
\begin{array}{r}
x + 3x + p = 180° \\
4x + p = 180° \\
4(18) + p = 180° \\
72 + p = 180° \\
p = 108°
\end{array}
$$

Since x is 18°

4. (B) Chord MOD is a diameter bisecting the circle in half. Therefore, arc MAD is 180°. Since arc AD is 80°, that leaves

100° in arc MA. Angle MDA is an inscribed angle intercepting arc MA, 100°. Since an inscribed angle equals half its intercepted arc, angle MDA is 50°.

5. (E) Although ABC is an isosceles triangle and therefore the base angles are equal, nothing in the information given in the problem allows us to draw any conclusions about the relationship of r to p. AD is not necessarily an angle bisector.

6. (D) Since vertical angles are equal,

$$9x - 10 = 35$$
$$9x = 45$$
$$x = 5$$

7. (C) Ten cubes can be fitted across. Four cubes can be fitted along the depth. Only two cubes can be stacked along the height. Thus, $10 \times 4 \times 2 = 80$ cubes.

8. (E) Since the area of one face of a cube is 49, its edges must be each 7 (as each face is a perfect square). Knowing each edge is 7, you may now figure its volume using V = length times width times height, or $7 \times 7 \times 7 = 343$.

9. (C) Since the radius of circle O is $\sqrt{2}$, its diameter is $2\sqrt{2}$, which is also the diagonal of the square. The side of a square and its diagonal are always in a 1 to $1\sqrt{2}$ ratio. Therefore, if the diagonal is $2\sqrt{2}$, a side of the square must be 2. Hence its area is 2 times 2, or 4.

10. (D) First find the total interior degrees in a pentagon.

$$\text{total interior degrees} = (\text{number of sides} - 2)(180°)$$
$$= (5 - 2)(180°)$$
$$= 3(180°)$$
$$= 540°$$

Now, let the angles equal x, 2x, 3x, 4x, and 5x. Their sum is 15x. Therefore

$$15x = 540°$$
$$x = 36°$$

Therefore, the largest angle, 5x, is $5(36) = 180°$.

11. (E) Since angle POQ is marked a right angle, triangle POQ is a right triangle with hypotenuse 13 and one leg 5 (the radius of circle O). Therefore, the other leg, OQ, must be 12 (a 5-12-13 right triangle). Since line segment OK is a radius of circle O, it equals 5, leaving a distance of 7 for KQ, the radius of circle Q. Thus the area of circle Q is

$$A = \pi r^2$$
$$A = \pi(7)^2$$
$$A = 49\pi$$

12. (B) Since we know the area of circle O, we may find its radius.

$$A = \pi r^2$$
$$36\pi = \pi r^2$$
$$36\not{\pi} = \not{\pi} r^2$$
$$6 = r$$

Now that we know the radius of the circle is 6, we can see that each side will be twice 6, or 12. Thus, its perimeter is 4(12), or 48

13. (B) The volume of the cylindrical tank is

$$V = \pi r^2 h$$
$$V = \pi(6)^2(9)$$
$$V = \pi 36(9)$$
$$V = 324\pi$$

However, the tank must be filled only 2/3. Therefore,

$$\frac{2}{3}(324\pi) = 216\pi$$

14. (A) To find the area of the shaded region, first find the area of the larger triangle. Then subtract the area of the smaller, unshaded triangle. The area of the large triangle is ½bh, or ½(10)5 = 25. Now find the area of the small, unshaded triangle.

$$A = \tfrac{1}{2}bh$$
$$A = \tfrac{1}{2}(5)(4)$$
$$A = 10$$

Subtracting, 25 − 10 = 15, the area of the shaded region.

15. (C) The larger triangle is actually two 30-60-90 degree trian-gles, whose sides are in the ratio 1-$\sqrt{3}$-2. Therefore, p = 1, and q = 2. Their product is (1)(2) = 2.

16. (E) Since the rectangle's sides are 2 and 16, its perimeter is 2 + 2 + 16 + 16 = 36. Therefore, a square with the same perimeter, 36, has sides of 9 each. Therefore, the area of the square is 9 × 9 = 81.

17. (E) The hexagon is composed of six individual equilateral triangles, each having a base of 10. If a height is constructed within one of these triangles, then the height divides the triangle into equal 30-60-90 degree triangles. Thus, the height may be quickly calculated, using the relationship of the sides of any 30-60-90 degree triangle. 1, $\sqrt{3}$, 2. The area of one triangle is therefore ½bh, or ½(10)(5 $\sqrt{3}$) = 25 $\sqrt{3}$. The area of the hexagon is 6 times this, or 150 $\sqrt{3}$.

18. (B) If z equals 100°, x + v = 80°, since x, v, and z together equal 180° (a straight angle). Since line$_2$ bisects the angle composed of x and v, each must equal 40°.

19. (D) Since RP passes through center O, chord ROP is a diame-ter. Thus, inscribed angle RSP intercepts 180° of arc. Angle RSP therefore measures 90°. Triangle RSP is therefore a right triangle with hypotenuse of 10 (its diameter) and one leg 6 and is a 3-4-5 right triangle. The other side must be 8.

20. (C) Triangle ABC is a 3-4-5 right triangle. Since AB = 6 and BC = 8, then AC = 10. Notice that triangle ADC is a 30-60-90 degree triangle. Its sides are always in the ratio of 1:$\sqrt{3}$:2. Therefore, since the "2 side" is

here 10, each side is actually
multiplied by 5. Hence the other
two sides are 5 and 5 $\sqrt{3}$.
Now the area of triangle ADC
may be computed.

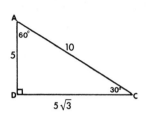

$A = \frac{1}{2}bh$

$A = \frac{1}{2}(5 \sqrt{3})(5)$

$A = \frac{25 \sqrt{3}}{2}$

21. (D) Using the coordinates of the
points given, a right triangle may
be constructed as shown. Notice
that the horizontal length of the
triangle is 6; its vertical leg
is 8. Therefore, it is a 3-4-5
right triangle. Its hypotenuse
(side AB) must be 10.

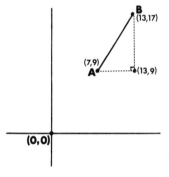

22. (B) Since FG = 16 feet, EH = 16 feet
(opposite sides of a parallelogram
are equal). Since BD is an altitude,
ED = DH = 8 feet (the altitude of an
isosceles triangle is also the median).
$(EB)^2 = (BD)^2 + (ED)^2$ (right triangle)
$(EB)^2 = 6^2 + 8^2 = 100$; EB = 10 feet
AB = BE + EA (given: EA = 1 foot)
Therefore, AB = 11 feet.

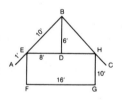

23. (A) This figure represents both a rectangle and a semicircle.
Use the following formulas:

area of a rectangle = 1(length) × w(width) or lw or wl

area of a semicircle = $\frac{\pi r^2}{2}$

area of this figure = wl + $\frac{\pi r^2}{2}$

24. (D) Given that r = width of the ring (shaded portion) and r = radius of the inner circle, therefore, 2r = radius of the entire circle. The area of a circle = πr^2. The area of the entire circle minus the area of the inner circle equals the area of the shaded portion. By substitution, then,

$(2r)^2$ or $4\pi r^2$ minus $\pi(r)^2$ or $\pi r^2 = 3\pi r^2$ (area of shaded portion)

$$\frac{\text{area of the shaded portion}}{\text{area of the entire circle}} = \frac{3\pi r^2}{4\pi r^2} = \frac{3}{4} = 75\%$$

25. (D) The area of a circle = πr^2. If x = radius of the original circle, then 2x = radius of the new circle. The area of the original circle = πx^2. The area of the new circle = $\pi(2x)^2 = 4\pi x^2$. Therefore, the area of the original circle has been multiplied by 4.

Procedure Problems

1. (E) Since the steering wheel grip cost three times the seat cushion, let's call the seat cushion x, and the steering wheel grip will then be 3x. Now notice that we do not have any other information except the price of the floor mat with tax. We have no way of determining in terms of dollars any of the statements, I, II, III, or IV. Deriving an answer in terms of an unknown (for example, 3x) is not determining a value.

2. (D) The only concrete piece of information from which we can begin is that Sue's car is a 1983 model. Therefore, we can first determine the approximate age of Sue's car (by subtracting 1983 from the year it is now). Once we know the age of Sue's car, we can find the age of John's car, since statement one says that his car is a year older than Sue's car. We can then find the age of Maria's truck, since statement two says it is one year newer than John's car. So we can determine the approximte age of Sue's car, Maria's truck, and John's car.

3. (D) Statements I and II are equations finding a balance by subtracting 5 from 10. In statement I, since the current balance is $5 less than last year's balance, $10, then the current balance equals $10 − $5. In statement II, the same equation will also

work to calculate last year's balance. Statement III cannot be calculated by $10 - 5$, as ten *percent* equals .10.

4. (E) To find the average of a number of items, you must find the sum of the items and then divide by the number of items. Note that since test 4 is weighted double, it will actually count as *two* scores (hence, as test 4 and 5). So, setting up the equation

$$\frac{\text{sum of the scores}}{\text{number of scores}} = \text{average}$$

$$\frac{83 + 85 + 100 + ? + ?}{5} = 90$$

Note that since test 4 is weighted double, the number of scores is 5, not 4.

5. (C) Since 845 equals Q, then 846 equals $Q + 1$. Therefore, 27,456 times 846 may be expressed as $(P)(Q + 1)$.

6. (C) To check $(x + 1)((x + 2) = x^2 + 3x + 2$, Francisco merely has to plug in any positive value for x. If the equation balances, it is correct. For example, using 1 for x

$$(x + 1)(x + 2) = x^2 + 3x + 2$$
$$(1 + 1)(1 + 2) = 1^2 + 3(1) + 2$$
$$(2)(3) = 1 + 3 + 2$$
$$6 = 6$$

The equation balances. Plugging in 1 enables Francisco to check his answer.

7. (D) The word *sum* indicates addition. The sum of two numbers is therefore $x + y$. If this sum equals one of the numbers, then the equation will be either $x + y = x$ or $x + y = y$.

8. (C) If Jorge is ten years old now, then last year he was $10 - 1$. The question states that Jorge's age last year (9) is three years less than twice Teresa's age now. Therefore, letting T equal

Teresa's age now, three years less than twice T can be represented as $2T - 3$. Thus,

$$10 - 1 = 2T - 3$$
$$9 = 2T - 3$$

9. (E) If a tie cost T dollars, then each tie $= T$. If a suit jacket cost four times the price of a tie, then each suit jacket $= 4T$. Hence, the cost of two ties and three suit jackets is $2(T) + 3(4T)$.

10. (C) To determine the area of a square that has the same perimeter as a rectangle 18 by 22, Rossanna must

   a. first find the perimeter of the rectangle by adding 18 and 22 and then doubling that sum
   b. divide the result by 4 to find the side of a square of the same perimeter
   c. square that to find the area

QUANTITATIVE COMPARISON

QUANTITATIVE COMPARISON STRATEGIES

This unique problem type appears on the SAT, PSAT, and the GRE, among others. It tests your ability to compare two given quantities using your knowledge of mathematics.

Complex computation is not required. In fact, mathematical insight allows this problem type to be solved more quickly than the more common math ability problem type.

Directions

In this section you will be given two quantities, one in column A and one in column B. You are to determine a relationship between the two quantities and mark—

- (A) if the quantity in column A is greater than the quantity in column B.
- (B) if the quantity in column B is greater than the quantity in column A.
- (C) If the two quantities are equal.
- (D) if the comparison cannot be determined from the information given.

Analysis

The purpose here is to make a comparison; therefore, exact answers are not always necessary. (Remember that you can tell whether you are taller than someone in many cases without knowing that person's height. Comparisons such as this can be made with only partial information—just enough to compare.) (D) is not a possible answer if there are *values* in each column, because you can always compare values.

If you get different relationships, depending on the values you choose for variables, then the answer is always (D). Notice that there are only four possible choices here. *Never* mark (E) on your answer sheet for Quantitative Comparison.

Suggested Approach with Examples

This question type emphasizes shortcuts, insight, and quick techniques. Long and/or involved mathematical computation is unnecessary and is contrary to the purpose of this section.

Cancel out Equal Amounts

Note that you can add, subtract, multiply, and divide both columns by the same value and the relationship between them will not change. EXCEPTION: You should *not* multiply or divide each column by negative numbers because then the relationship reverses. Squaring both columns is permissible, as long as each side is positive.

Column A	Column B
$21 \times 43 \times 56$	$44 \times 21 \times 57$

Canceling (or dividing) 21 from each side leaves

43×56	44×57

The rest of this problem should be done by inspection because it is obvious that column B is greater than column A without doing any multiplication. Each number in B is larger than the corresponding number in A. You could have reached the correct answer by actually multiplying out each column, but you would then not have enough time to finish the section. The correct answer is (B).

Make Partial Comparisons

The use of partial comparisons can be valuable in giving you insight into finding a comparison. If you cannot simply make a complete comparison, look at each column part by part. *For example:*

Column A	Column B
$\dfrac{1}{3} - \dfrac{1}{65}$	$\dfrac{1}{58} - \dfrac{1}{63}$

Since finding a common denominator would be too time consuming, you should first compare the first fraction in each column (partial comparison). Notice that $\frac{1}{3}$ is greater than $\frac{1}{58}$. Now compare the second fractions and notice that $\frac{1}{65}$ is less than $\frac{1}{63}$. Using some common sense and insight, if you start with a larger number and a smaller number, it must be greater than starting with a smaller number and subtracting a larger number, as pointed out below

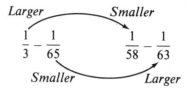

The correct answer is (A).

Keep Perspective

Always keep the column in perspective before starting any calculations. Take a good look at the value in each column before starting to work on one column. *For example:*

Column A	**Column B**
7^2	2^8

After looking at each column—note that the answer cannot be (D) because there are values in each column—compute the value on the left. $7^2 = 49$. There is no need to take 2 out to the 8th power. Just do as little as necessary: $2^2 = 4$, $2^3 = 8$, $2^4 = 16$, $2^5 = 32$. STOP. It is evident that 2^8 is much greater than 49. The correct answer is (B). Approximating can also be valuable while remembering to keep the columns in perspective.

Plug In 0, 1, −1

If a problem involves variables (without an equation), substitute in the numbers 0, 1, and −1. Then try $\frac{1}{2}$, and 2 if necessary. Using 0, 1, and −1 will often tip off the answer. *For example:*

Column A	**Column B**
$a + b$	ab

Substituting 0 for a and 0 for b gives

	$0 + 0$		$0(0)$
Therefore	0	$=$	0

Using these values for a and b gives the answer (C). But anytime you multiply two numbers, it is not the same as when you add them, so try some other values.

Substituting 1 for a and -1 for b gives

	$1 + (-1)$		$1(-1)$
Therefore	0	$>$	-1

and the answer is now (A).

Anytime you get more than one comparison (different relationships), depending on the values chosen, the correct answer must be (D) (the relationship cannot be determined). Notice that if you had substituted the values a = 4, b = 5; or a = 6, b = 7; or a = 7, b = 9; and so on, you would repeatedly have gotten the answer (B) and might have chosen the incorrect answer.

Simplify

Often simplifying one or both columns can make an answer evident. *For example:*

Column A	Column B
a, b, c, all greater than 0	
$a(b + c)$	$ab + ac$

Using the distributive property on column A to simplify, gives ab and ac; therefore, the columns are equal.

Look for a Simple Way

Sometimes you can solve for a column in one step, without solving and substituting. If you have to solve an equation or equations to give the columns values, take a second and see if there is a very simple way to get an answer before going through all of the steps. *For example:*

Column A   Column B

$$4x + 2 = 10$$

2x + 1   4

Hopefully, you would spot that the easiest way to solve for $2x + 1$ is directly by dividing $4x + 2 = 10$, by 2, leaving $2x + 1 = 5$.

Therefore   5   >   4

Solving for x first in the equation, and then substituting, would also have worked, but would have been more time consuming. The correct answer is (A).

Mark Diagrams

Marking diagrams can be very helpful for giving insight into a problem. Remember that figures and diagrams are meant for positional information only. Just because something "looks" larger is not enough reason to choose an answer. *For example:*

Column A   Column B

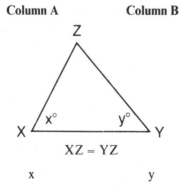

XZ = YZ

x   y

Even though x appears larger, this is not enough. Mark in the diagrams as shown.

Notice that you should mark things of equal measure with the same markings, and since angles opposite equal sides in a triangle are equal, x = y. The correct answer is (C).

Use Easier Numbers

If you are given information that is unfamiliar to you and difficult to work with, change the number slightly (but remember what you've changed) to something easier to work with. *For example:*

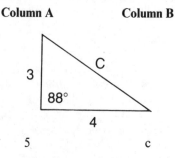

Column A   **Column B**

Since the 88° shown in the figure is unfamiliar to work with, change it to 90° for now, so that you may use the Pythagorean theorem to solve for c.

$$a^2 + b^2 = c^2$$

Solving for c $(3)^2 + (4)^2 = c^2$
$$9 + 16 = c^2$$

Therefore $5 = c^2$

But since you used 90° instead of 88°, you should realize that the side opposite the 88° will be slightly smaller or less than 5. The correct answer is then (A), 5 > c. (Some students may have noticed the 3:4:5 triangle relationship and have not needed the Pythagorean theorem.)

A PATTERNED PLAN OF ATTACK

Quantitative Comparison

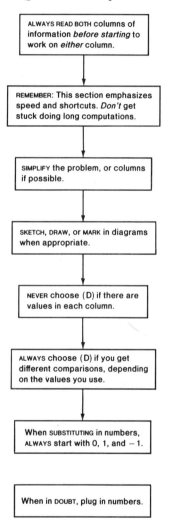

ALWAYS READ BOTH columns of information *before starting* to work on *either* column.

REMEMBER: This section emphasizes speed and shortcuts. *Don't* get stuck doing long computations.

SIMPLIFY the problem, or columns if possible.

SKETCH, DRAW, or MARK in diagrams when appropriate.

NEVER choose (D) if there are values in each column.

ALWAYS choose (D) if you get different comparisons, depending on the values you use.

When SUBSTITUTING in numbers, ALWAYS start with 0, 1, and −1.

When in DOUBT, plug in numbers.

QUANTITATIVE COMPARISON PRACTICE

DIRECTIONS

In this section you will be given two quantities, one in column A and one in column B. You are to determine a relationship between the two quantities and mark
  (A) if the quantity in column A is greater than the quantity in column B
  (B) if the quantity in column B is greater than the quantity in column A
  (C) if the quantities are equal
  (D) if the comparison cannot be determined from the information that is given

Common Information:
  Information centered above both columns refers to one or both columns.
  All numbers used are real numbers.
  Figures are intended to provide useful positional information, but are not necessarily drawn to scale and should not be used to estimate sizes by measurement.
  Lines that appear straight can be assumed to be straight.

Arithmetic

Questions

	Column A	Column B
1.	$\dfrac{2}{5} \times \dfrac{1}{9} \times \dfrac{3}{8}$	$\dfrac{2}{11} \times \dfrac{2}{5} \times \dfrac{3}{8}$
2.	$\dfrac{1}{8} \times \dfrac{1}{4} \times \dfrac{1}{9}$	$.125 \times .25 \times .1$
3.	The average of 12, 14, 16, 18, 20, 22	The average of 11, 13, 15, 17, 19, 21

	Column A	**Column B**
4.	The average speed of a car that travels 8 miles in 15 minutes	30
5.	.004	.04%
6.	$\dfrac{1}{79} - \dfrac{1}{81}$	$\dfrac{1}{71} - \dfrac{1}{80}$
7.	The percentage of increase from $400 to $500	20%
8.	The price of 2 lbs. of candy at 42¢ per lb.	The price of 3 lbs. of candy at 32¢ per lb.
9.	4% interest on $2,000 for 1 year	8% interest on $1,000 for 2 years
10.	$9^5 - 9^4$	9^4
11.	$7\sqrt{3}$	$3\sqrt{7}$

12.

12.	1	$\dfrac{1}{x}$

13.	$9^2 + 8 \times 10^4 - 6^{10}$	$9^2 + 8 \times 10^4 + 6^{10}$

	Column A	Column B
14.	$\dfrac{8 \times 10^4}{2 \times 10^2}$	400

A hat contains 3 blue pegs
2 red pegs, and 1 white peg.

15.	The probability of randomly picking a blue peg	The probability of randomly picking other than a blue peg

Algebra

Questions

	Column A	Column B
		$x > 2$
1.	$3x + 2$	$2x + 3$

$$\dfrac{2x}{7} = 8$$

$$3y = 87$$

2.	x	y

$$\dfrac{s}{r} > \dfrac{3}{5}$$

3.	s	r

x is a negative fraction

4.	$\dfrac{1}{x}$	$-x$

5.	$-(r - s)$	$-r + s$

	Column A	**Column B**
6.	$(a^4 + b^3)^2$	$(a^3b^6)^3$

$$x < 4 < y$$

7.	$x + 4$	$y - 4$

$$x \neq y$$
$$y \neq 0$$

8.	$1 + \dfrac{x}{y}$	$\dfrac{x + y}{y}$

$$y > 0$$

9.	The average of 3y, 5y, 3, and 5	The average of 2y, 6y, 4, and 10

$$0 < y < x$$

10.	$(x + 2)(y + 3)$	$(x + 3)(y + 2)$

---

15 is 30% of x
12 is 25% of y

11.	x	y

$$m > 0$$

12.	m^3	$2m^2$

$$\frac{r}{3} = \frac{s}{5}$$

13.	$5r$	$3s$

	Column A	Column B

$$x > 0, y > 0$$

| 14. | $\sqrt{x + y}$ | $\sqrt{x} + \sqrt{y}$ |

$$x + 3y = 7$$
$$4x + 12y = 28$$

| 15. | x | y |

Geometry

Questions

	Column A	Column B

1 and 1¹ are parallel lines

| 1. | x | y |

| 2. | The circumference of a semicircle with radius 4″ | The perimeter of a pentagon with each side 4″ long |

Questions 3, 4, and 5 refer to this diagram.

AB is a diameter.
△ABC is an isosceles right triangle.

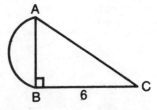

	Column A	Column B
3.	Area of semicircle	Area of triangle
4.	$\overset{\frown}{AB}$	AC
5.	∠A	45°

Questions 6 through 9 refer to this diagram.

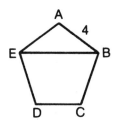

ABCDE is a regular pentagon.

6.	AB	EB
7.	Sum of interior angles of pentagon ABCDE	360°
8.	∠AEB	∠ABE
9.	∠D + ∠C	180°

| Column A | Column B |

Questions 10, 11, and 12 refer to this diagram.

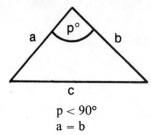

$p < 90°$
$a = b$

	Column A	Column B
10.	$b + c$	a
11.	c^2	$a^2 + b^2$
12.	a	$c - b$

Questions 13, 14, and 15 refer to this diagram.

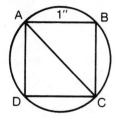

Vertices of square ABCD lie on the circle.

	Column A	Column B
13.	$\angle DAC$	$\angle BCA$
14.	Radius of circle	$\dfrac{\sqrt{2}}{2}$

Column A	Column B
15. 2 × area of square ABCD	Area of circle

ANSWER KEY FOR QUANTITATIVE COMPARISON PRACTICE

The first page number following each answer will direct you to the complete explanation for that specific problem. *Read this explanation first.* The page numbers in parentheses refer to the suggested basic review section.

Arithmetic

1. (B) p. 390 (42)
2. (A) p. 390 (42, 48)
3. (A) p. 390 (76)
4. (A) p. 390 (274)
5. (A) p. 390 (53)
6. (B) p. 391 (34)
7. (A) p. 391 (59)
8. (B) p. 391

9. (B) p. 391 (264)
10. (A) p. 391 (63)
11. (A) p. 391 (69)
12. (B) p. 391 (21)
13. (B) p. 392 (19)
14. (C) p. 392 (62)
15. (C) p. 392 (70)

Algebra

1. (A) p. 392 (110)
2. (B) p. 392 (113)
3. (D) p. 393 (116, 159)
4. (B) p. 393 (110)
5. (C) p. 393 (23)
6. (D) p. 393 (110, 129)
7. (D) p. 393 (110)
8. (C) p. 394 (154)

9. (B) p. 394 (128, 129)
10. (A) p. 394 (110, 130)
11. (A) p. 395 (55)
12. (D) p. 395 (110)
13. (C) p. 396 (120)
14. (B) p. 396 (172)
15. (D) p. 396 (122)

Geometry

1. (A) p. 396 (212)
2. (B) p. 396 (216, 237)
3. (B) p. 396 (225, 237)
4. (A) p. 397 (225, 236)
5. (C) p. 397 (225)
6. (B) p. 397 (220, 231)
7. (A) p. 398 (231)
8. (C) p. 398 (220)

9. (A) p. 398 (231)
10. (A) p. 398 (220)
11. (B) p. 398 (223)
12. (A) p. 398 (220)
13. (C) p. 399 (239)
14. (C) p. 399 (225, 239)
15. (A) p. 399 (232, 237)

QUANTITATIVE COMPARISON ANSWERS AND EXPLANATIONS

Arithmetic

1. (B) Dividing out equal fractions from both sides ($\frac{2}{5}$ and $\frac{3}{8}$), leaves column A with $\frac{1}{9}$ and column B with $\frac{2}{11}$. Cross multiplying up

Since the larger product is always over the larger fraction, column B is greater.

2. (A) Changing the decimals in column B to fractions

$$\frac{125}{1,000} \times \frac{25}{100} \times \frac{1}{10}$$

and reducing to simplest form gives this comparison:

$$\frac{1}{8} \times \frac{1}{4} \times \frac{1}{9} \qquad \frac{1}{8} \times \frac{1}{4} \times \frac{1}{10}$$

Canceling out the $\frac{1}{8}$ and $\frac{1}{4}$ from each side leaves

$$\frac{1}{9} > \frac{1}{10}$$

3. (A) The fastest way to determine which average is greater is to notice that each of the numbers in column A is one larger than its corresponding number in column B. Therefore column A's average must be greater than column B's average.

4. (A) To find the average speed of the car in miles per hour multiply 8 miles by 4, since 15 minutes is $\frac{1}{4}$ of an hour.

$$8 \times 4 = 32$$

32 miles per hour is the average speed and $32 > 30$.

5. (A) Expressed as a percent, column A equals .4%, which is greater than column B.

6. (B) This problem is best solved by inspection. Notice that the values in column A are very close together. Therefore, their difference would be very small. Column B's values are farther apart, therefore having a greater difference.

7. (A) To find percent increase use the formula

$$\frac{change}{starting\ point} = percent\ change$$

$$\frac{500 - 400}{400} = \frac{100}{400} = \frac{1}{4} = 25\% \text{ and } 25\% > 20\%$$

8. (B) Column A equals two times 42¢, or 84¢. Column B equals three times 32¢, or 96¢. Therefore, Column B is greater.

9. (B) The interest in column A equals $2,000 times .04 times 1 year, or $80. The interest in column B equals $1,000 times .08 times 2 years, or $160. Therefore, column B is greater.

10. (A) 9^5 is 9×9^4, so if 9^4 is subtracted from 9^5, the remainder is obviously must greater than 9^4. Following is an alternate method.

$$\overbrace{9^5}\qquad - \qquad\overbrace{9^4}$$

$$\underbrace{(9 \times 9 \times 9 \times 9 \times 9)} - \underbrace{(9 \times 9 \times 9 \times 9)} = 52,488$$

$$59,049 \qquad - \qquad 6,561$$

$$52,488 > 6,561$$

11. (A) The fastest and most accurate way to compare two terms, each of which contains a square root, is to change each term to a single term under a radical. For example,

$$7\sqrt{3} = \sqrt{3 \times 49} = \sqrt{147} \qquad 3\sqrt{7} = \sqrt{7 \times 9} = \sqrt{63}$$

Since $\sqrt{147}$ is greater than $\sqrt{63}$, column A is greater.

12. (B) On the number line, x is between 0 and 1. Therefore, x is a positive fraction less than 1. Plugging in a simple value for x (use ½, an easy-to-work-with fraction less than 1), we find column B equals

$$\frac{1}{\frac{1}{2}} \text{ which equals } 2$$

Every other fraction less than 1 will also make column B greater than 1. Therefore, column B is greater than column A.

13. **(B)** Note that the only difference in the two columns is the signs of the last values, 6^{10}. Since column B is positive $(+6^{10})$ and column A is negative (-6^{10}), column B is greater than column A. Actually calculating the numerical values is a waste of time and not necessary.

14. **(C)** Canceling column A gives

$$\frac{8 \times 10^4}{2 \times 10^2} \qquad\qquad 400$$

$$4 \times 10^2 \qquad\qquad 400$$
$$4 \times 100 \qquad\qquad 400$$
$$400 \qquad\qquad 400$$

The columns are equal.

15. **(C)** In column A, the probability of randomly selecting a blue peg is 3 out of a total of 6, or 3/6 or 1/2. In column B, the probability of randomly selecting a color other than blue is $2 + 1$ out of 6, or, again, 3/6, or 1/2. The columns are equal.

Algebra

1. **(A)** First subtracting 2 from both sides gives 3x in column A and $2x + 1$ in column B. Since $x > 2$, start by plugging in values greater than 2 for x. Trying 2.1, then 3, then, say, 10, you'll find that column A will always be larger.

2. **(B)** Solving each equation

$$\frac{2x}{7} = 8 \qquad\qquad 3y = 87$$

$$\frac{7}{2} \times \frac{2x}{7} = \frac{8}{1} \times \frac{7}{2} \qquad\qquad \frac{3y}{3} = \frac{87}{3}$$

$$x = 28 \qquad\qquad y = 29$$

$$28 < 29$$

3. **(D)** Trying some values in the equation gives different outcomes, such as

$$s = 4, r = 5 \qquad \frac{4}{5} > \frac{3}{5}$$

$$s < r$$

$$s = -4, r = -5 \qquad \frac{-4}{-5} > \frac{3}{5}$$

$$s > r$$

No determination is possible.

4. **(B)** Substituting a value for x and considering the given condition (x is a negative fraction) makes it evident that column B will always be positive and column A negative. Let $x = -\frac{1}{2}$.

$$\frac{1}{-\frac{1}{2}} \qquad\qquad -\left(\frac{-1}{2}\right)$$

$$-2 < +\frac{1}{2}$$

5. **(C)** This is really an example of the distributive property and can be solved by inspection. Or using an alternate method, let $r = 3$ and $s = 2$. Then

$$\begin{array}{ccc} -(3 - 2) & & -3 + 2 \\ -1 & = & -1 \end{array}$$

6. **(D)** Let $a = 0$ and $b = 0$. Then both columns are obviously equal. If $a = 1$ and $b = 0$, then column A is greater than column B. Therefore, the answer cannot be determined.

7. **(D)** Since x must be less than 4, column A $(x + 4)$ can equal any value less than 8. Since y must be more than 4, column B $(y - 4)$ can be any value more than 0. Therefore, between the range of 0 and 8, column A and column B could be equal or one column could be greater than the other. Therefore, no relationship can be determined.

8. (C) By changing the value of 1 in column A to equal

$$\frac{y}{y}$$

column A can also equal $\frac{y}{y} + \frac{x}{y}$

which combined into one fraction equals $\frac{y + x}{y}$

Therefore, the two columns are equal. Likewise, column B could have been broken into two fractions.

$$\frac{x}{y} + \frac{y}{y}$$

which is the same as $\frac{x}{y} + 1$

and thus equal to column A.

9. (B) Simplifying:

$$\frac{3y + 5y + 3 + 5}{4} \qquad\qquad \frac{2y + 6y + 4 + 10}{4}$$

$$\frac{8y + 8}{4} \qquad\qquad\qquad \frac{8y + 14}{4}$$

$$\frac{8y}{4} + \frac{8}{4} \qquad\qquad\qquad \frac{8y}{4} + \frac{14}{4}$$

$$2y + 2 \qquad\qquad\qquad 2y + \frac{14}{4}$$

Subtracting 2y from both

$$2 < \frac{14}{4}$$

10. (A) Simplifying each column leaves

$$xy + 3x + 2y + 6 \qquad\qquad xy + 2x + 3y + 6$$

Subtracting xy, 2x, 2y, and 6 from both sides leaves

$$x > y$$

from the condition given, $0 < y < x$.

11. (A) Solving each problem, first for x: 15 is 30% of x

$$\frac{30}{100} = \frac{15}{x}$$

$$\frac{3}{10} = \frac{15}{x}$$

Cross multiplying

$$3x = 150$$
$$x = 50$$

Solving for y: 12 is 25% of y

$$\frac{25}{100} = \frac{12}{y}$$

$$\frac{1}{4} = \frac{12}{y}$$

Cross multiplying

$$y = 48$$
and $$50 > 48$$

12. (D) Trying the value m = 1 gives

$$(1)^3 \qquad\qquad 2(1)^2$$

$$1 < 2$$

Now letting m = 2 gives

$$(2)^3 \qquad\qquad 2(2)^2$$

$$8 = 8$$

No solution can be determined because different values give different answers.

13. **(C)** Cross multiply the given equation.

$$\frac{r}{3} = \frac{s}{5}$$

leaves $5r = 3s$

14. **(B)** Substituting x = 1, y = 1 gives

$$\frac{\sqrt{1 + 1}}{\sqrt{2}} \qquad\qquad \frac{\sqrt{1} + \sqrt{1}}{1 + 1}$$

$$1.4 < 2$$

Trying other values gives the same result.

15. **(D)** By inspection, the two given equations are the same: x + 3y = 7 and 4x + 12y = 28 if the second equation is simplified by dividing by 4. Since the two equations are equivalent, no definite values for x and y can be determined.

Geometry

1. **(A)** That y = 80° is evident by the diagram and the rules of a transversal through parallel lines. x = 100° because x and 80 must equal a straight line of 180°, or 180° − 80°. Therefore, 100° > 80°.

2. **(B)** Since the circumference of a circle equals $2\pi r$, the circumference of the semicircle in column A equals $\frac{1}{2}(2\pi r)$, or $(\pi)4''$. Since π equals about 3, column A equals approximately 12″. In column B, if each side of a pentagon equals 4″, its perimeter equals 5 times 4″, or 20″. Therefore, column B is greater.

3. **(B)** AB = 6 because triangle ABE is isosceles. The radius of the semicircle is $\frac{1}{2}$AB, or 3. Using the area formula for the circle

$A = \pi r^2$
$A = \pi(3)^2$
$A = \pi(9)$
$A \approx 28$

Taking $\frac{1}{2}$ of this leaves the area of the semicircle as approximately 14. Now, using the area formula for the triangle

$$A = \tfrac{1}{2}bh$$
$$A = \tfrac{1}{2}(6)(6)$$
$$A = \tfrac{1}{2}(36)$$
$$A = 18$$
and $14 < 18$

4. **(A)** Using the circumference formula for a circle of diameter 6

$$C = \pi d$$
$$C = \pi(6)$$
$$C \cong 18$$

Taking $\tfrac{1}{2}$ of this leaves 9 as the length. Now, using the Pythagorean theorem to find AC

$$(AB)^2 + (BC)^2 = (AC)^2$$
$$(6)^2 + (6)^2 = (AC)^2$$
$$36 + 36 = (AC)^2$$
$$72 = (AC)^2$$
$$\sqrt{72} = AC$$

Since $\sqrt{72}$ is approximately 8.5, $9 > \sqrt{72}$.

5. **(C)** Since $\triangle ABC$ is an isosceles right triangle, $\angle A = \angle C$ and $\angle B = 90°$. This leaves $90°$ to be divided evenly between $\angle A$ and $\angle C$. Therefore, $\angle A$ is $45°$.

6. **(B)** Any diagonal of a regular pentagon is greater than any of the sides. Using an alternate method, use the formula for finding the interior degrees of a polygon—$180(N - 2)$ using 5 for N (number of sides of a pentagon).

$$180(N - 2)$$
$$180(5 - 2)$$
$$180(3)$$
$$540$$

There are $540°$ in the interior of the pentagon. Dividing this by 5 for the number of equal angles, leaves $108°$ in each angle. Angle A is $108°$ in triangle ABE and therefore is the greatest angle in the triangle. The longest side of a triangle is across from the largest angle, so $AB < EB$.

7. **(A)** As we know from the previous problem, the sum of the interior angles of pentagon ABCDE is 540° and 540° > 360°. Using an alternate method, the sum of the interior degrees of a pentagon can be derived by dividing the pentagon into triangles as shown.

   Since there are three triangles and 180° in a triangle, there are 3 × 180°, or 540°, in the pentagon.

8. **(C)** Since the pentagon is equilateral, side AB = side AE, and therefore ∠AEB = ∠ABE, as angles opposite equal sides in a triangle are equal.

9. **(A)** As shown in the previous problems, each angle of the pentagon is 108°. Therefore,

$$108° + 108° = 216°$$
$$216° > 180°$$

10. **(A)** The sum of any two sides of a triangle is greater than the third side.

11. **(B)** If $p = 90°$, then $c^2 = a^2 + b^2$, but since $p < 90°$, the opposite side, C, gets smaller. Therefore, $c^2 < a^2 + b^2$.

12. **(A)** The sum of any two sides of a triangle is greater than the third side. Therefore, the difference of any two sides of a triangle is less than the third side. Solving algebraically

$$a + b > c$$

Subtracting b from both sides leaves $a > c - b$.

13. (C) Since all sides of a square are equal, AD = DC. Angles opposite equal sides in a triangle are equal. Therefore, $\angle DAC = \angle BCA$.

14. (C) Using the Pythagorean theorem to find the length of diameter AC gives.

$(AB)^2 + (BC)^2 = (AC)^2$
$(1)^2 + (1)^2 = (AC)^2$.
$1 + 1 = (AC)^2$
$2 = (AC)^2$
$\sqrt{2} = AC$

Since the radius is $\frac{1}{2}$ of the diameter,

$\frac{1}{2}$ of $\sqrt{2}$ is $\dfrac{\sqrt{2}}{2}$

and $\dfrac{\sqrt{2}}{2} = \dfrac{\sqrt{2}}{2}$

15. (A) Using the proper formulas

$$A = s \times s \qquad A = \pi r^2$$

and substituting s = 1 and r = $\dfrac{\sqrt{2}}{2}$ from an earlier problem,

$$A = (1) \times (1) \qquad A = \pi \left(\dfrac{\sqrt{2}}{2}\right)^2$$

$$2(1) \qquad\qquad = \pi \times \dfrac{2}{4}$$

$$= 3.14 \times \tfrac{1}{2}$$

$$2 > 1.57$$

DATA SUFFICIENCY

DATA SUFFICIENCY STRATEGIES

Data Sufficiency is another unique problem type. It appears on the GMAT. Data Sufficiency problems test your ability to determine if enough information is present in order to solve given questions. These problems usually require no complex calculations.

Directions

Each of the problems below consists of a question and two statements, labeled (1) and (2), in which certain data are given. You must decide whether the data given in the statements are *sufficient* to answer the question. Using the data given in the statements *plus* your knowledge of mathematics and everyday facts (such as the number of days in July or the meaning of *counterclockwise*), you are to blacken space

- (A) if statement (1) ALONE is sufficient, but statement (2) alone is not sufficient to answer the question asked;
- (B) if statement (2) ALONE is sufficient, but statement (1) alone is not sufficient to answer the question asked;
- (C) if BOTH statements (1) and (2) TOGETHER are sufficient to answer the question asked, but NEITHER statement ALONE is sufficient;
- (D) if EACH statement ALONE is sufficient to answer the question asked;
- (E) if statements (1) and (2) TOGETHER are NOT sufficient to answer the question asked, and additional data specific to the problem are needed.

Analysis

The purpose here is to determine whether information given is *sufficient* to answer the question; therefore, *do not solve the problem* unless it is absolutely necessary.

The memory aid 12TEN will simplify the directions, making them easier to memorize and/or refer to. 12TEN stands for:

1 *First* statement ALONE is sufficient, not the second. CHOOSE (A).
2 *Second* statement ALONE is sufficient, not the first. CHOOSE (B).
T *Together* is the only way they are sufficient. CHOOSE (C).
E *Either* statement ALONE is sufficient. CHOOSE (D).
N *Neither* statement, TOGETHER or ALONE, is sufficient. CHOOSE (E).

REMEMBER: ONE TWO, TOGETHER, EITHER, NEITHER, or 12TEN. (Note: *Either* means choose answer (D) *not* (E).)

Because of the structure of this type of question, you should always be able to eliminate some of the choices. If statement (1) ALONE is sufficient to answer the question, then the answer *must* be (A) or (D). If statement (1) ALONE is *not* sufficient to answer the question, then the answer *must* be (B), (C), or (E). If statements (1) or (2) ALONE are *not* sufficient, then the answer *must* be (C) or (E).

If statements (1) or (2) ALONE *are* sufficient, then you *never* try them TOGETHER.

Sometimes geometric figures are included; they should be used only for positional value, and are not to be measured as they are not necessarily drawn to scale.

Suggested Approach with Examples

Determine Necessary Information

Quickly decide what is the necessary basic information to answer the question. Then see if the data supplies that information. *For example:*

What is the area of circle O?
(1) The circumference is 12π.
(2) The diameter is 12.

The find the area of a circle, it is necessary to have the radius. (1) gives enough information to find the radius by substituting into the circumference formula. $C = 2\pi r$, and getting $12\pi = 2\pi r$. Then simply solve for r, which is 6. Thus this area is 36π. None of this solving was necessary, only knowing that you needed the radius and could find it from the information given. (2) also gives enough information to find the radius; therefore the answer is (D), either will be sufficient.

Don't Solve Unless Necessary

Don't solve unless it is absolutely necessary. *For example:*

What is the value of x?
(1) $83x + 12 = 360$
(2) $25x + 3y = 16$

This problem is most easily solved by inspecting the first bit of data and quickly noticing that (1) is enough to answer the question (one variable, one equation, solvable), (2) does not answer the question. This can also be determined by inspection (two variables, one equation, not solvable for a single value). The correct answer is (A), yet no actual solving had to be done.

Use a Simple Marking System

Use a simple marking system to assist you in making your decision. *For example:*

What is the average height of Tom, Bob, and Luke?
(1) Bob is 4 inches shorter than Luke, and Tom is 4 inches taller than Luke.
(2) Luke is 5 feet 6 inches tall.

(1) is not sufficient, since no actual height is given; therefore mark a slash through (1). Note that the answer is immediately narrowed to (B), (C), or (E). (2) by itself is also not sufficient, as the other two, Tom and Bob, aren't mentioned; therefore, a slash should be made through (2). Notice that the answer is now narrowed to (C) or (E). Your markings should look as follows:

What is the average height of Tom, Bob, and Luke?
(1̸) Bob is 4 inches shorter than Luke, and Tom is 4 inches taller than Luke.
(2̸) Luke is 5 feet 6 inches tall.

Now trying them together, they are sufficient. The answer is (C). In marking the data, if you are in doubt whether it is sufficient or not, put a question mark by the data and try the next bit of data. Don't waste time trying one bit of data for over about 30 seconds.

Use Only Common Knowledge

Don't read in specialized knowledge. Use only the information given and general, or common, knowledge.

What is the runner's average speed in running around the track?
(1) One lap took 49 seconds.
(2) He ran 5 seconds faster than his previous best time.

Someone familiar with track and field might quickly assume that one lap is the standard 440 yards and would then *incorrectly answer* (A). This sort of assumption cannot be made as it is from specialized knowledge in the area and therefore is not general knowledge. The correct answer is (E) as the distance around the track is not given in either bit of data.

Mark Diagrams

If a geometric figure is involved in the question, mark the figure with the information and circle what you are look for. *For example:*

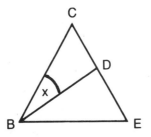

In the equilateral triangle above, what is the measure of angle x?
(1) BD is a median.
(2) Angle BDE is 90°.

Notice the markings from the information given:

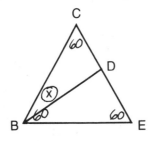

Mark in information given in data (1) as you read it, *but remember to erase that information before you try data* (2). (1) If BD is a median in an equilateral triangle, then it is also an angle bisector, making angle x equal to 30°. (Once again, the answer is not necessary, just the knowledge that it could be found.) (2) also gives enough information because if angle BDE is 90°, then angle BDC is 90°, and angle x is 30°, as there are 180° in a triangle. Marking the diagram makes the problem easier to solve.

Draw Diagrams

If a geometric diagram is discussed but no figure given, draw a simple diagram. *For example:*

If the legs of a trapezoid are equal, what is the area?
(1) The smaller base is 8 inches and the legs are 6 inches.
(2) The height is 5 inches.

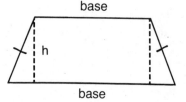

Drawing the diagram helps give important insight into what is needed to answer the question.

Now consider what is needed to find the area height and length of each base since the area formula is ½ h(b₁ + b₂) or h(b₁ + b₂)/2.

(1) does not give sufficient information to find the larger base or the height. (2), by itself, does not give enough information to find the bases. (1) and (2) together give enough information to find the bases and the height. The answer is (C). The Pythagorean theorem would be necessary to find the length of the difference between the smaller and larger bases. Adding this difference to the length of the shorter base would give the longer base. You now have the necessary information. Notice the markings on the diagram below, to assist you in deciding what you have to work with.

A PATTERNED PLAN OF ATTACK

Data Sufficiency

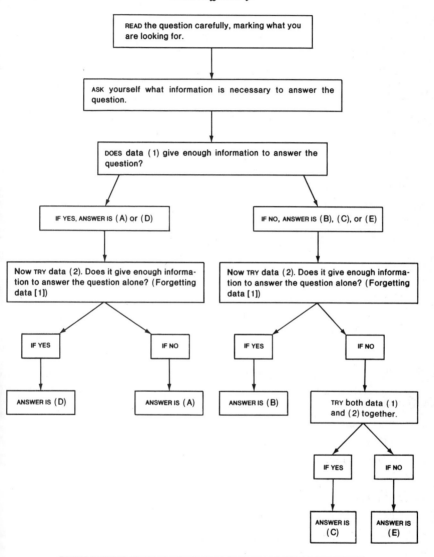

KEEP THE FOLLOWING TIPS IN MIND.
1. Don't solve unless it is absolutely necessary.
2. Use a simple marking system (slashes, question marks, etc.).
3. Don't read in specialized knowledge. Use only common information.
4. Mark in or draw geometric figures when appropriate.

DATA SUFFICIENCY PRACTICE

DIRECTIONS

Each of the problems below consists of a question and two statements, labeled (1) and (2), in which certain data are given. You must decide whether the data given in the statements are *sufficient* to answer the question. Using the data given in the statements *plus* your knowledge of mathematics and everyday facts (such as the number of days in July or the meaning of *counterclockwise*), you are to blacken space

- (A) if statement (1) ALONE is sufficient, but statement (2) alone is not sufficient to answer the question asked;
- (B) if statement (2) ALONE is sufficient, but statement (1) alone is not sufficient to answer the question asked;
- (C) if BOTH statements (1) and (2) TOGETHER are sufficient to answer the question asked, but NEITHER statement ALONE is sufficient;
- (D) if EACH statement ALONE is sufficient to answer the question asked;
- (E) if statements (1) and (2) TOGETHER are NOT sufficient to answer the question asked, and additional data specific to the problem are needed.

Arithmetic

Questions

1. The product of two integers is 6. What are the integers?
   - (1) Both integers are positive.
   - (2) One integer is 2.

2. How far did the airplane travel?
   - (1) It flew from east to west for 9 hours.
   - (2) It flew at a rate of 300 miles per hour for the first 8 hours.

3. The average of two numbers is 5. What are the numbers?
   - (1) 1 is one of the numbers.
   - (2) 3 is one of the numbers.

4. What must Maria's salary increase be in order to meet a 6% cost of living increase?
   (1) Maria's current salary is $15,000.
   (2) Maria's new salary will be $15,900 if her raise meets the increase in the cost of living.

5. John can jump half his height. How tall is he?
   (1) John is shorter than his brother.
   (2) John's brother can jump 5 feet.

6. What two fractions add to one?
   (1) The fractions are equal.
   (2) The reciprocal of the first fraction is 2.

7. How many people at the party are men?
   (1) There are twice as many men at the party as women.
   (2) There are 9 women at the party.

8. How many ounces does a full water bottle hold if 12 ounces of water remain?
   (1) The full bottle holds an even number of ounces.
   (2) 25% of the bottle has been used.

9. Bob can read 25 pages an hour. How long will it take him to finish the book?
   (1) Bob has read half the book by midnight.
   (2) Bob reads consistently from 8 P.M. until he finishes the book.

10. How much taller is Alice than her brother?
    (1) Her brother is 5 feet, 4 inches tall.
    (2) Alice is 180 centimerters tall. (1 inch = 2.54 cm)

11. How many miles per gallon did Bruce get on his 300 mile trip?
    (1) He used 3/4 of a tank of gas.
    (2) The tank holds 12 gallons.

12. Two integers are in the proportion 1 to 5. What is the larger number?
    (1) The smaller integer is one digit and prime.
    (2) The larger integer is greater than 30.

13. What is Hal's average weekly salary?
    (1) Hal's monthly salary is over $800.
    (2) Hal's average daily salary is $40.

14. What is the annual rate of simple interest in Arlene's bank?
    (1) Arlene receives $36 interest for two years on savings of $120.
    (2) If Arlene were to open an account of $50, after one year she would receive $7.50 interest.

15. If the volume of a mixture doubles every 20 minutes, at what time was its volume one cubic meter?
    (1) At 8 P.M. its volume was 64 cubic meters.
    (2) Twenty minutes ago its volume was 16 cubic meters.

Algebra

Questions

1. What is the value of a if $3a - 2b = 4$?
    (1) $a = 2b$
    (2) a and b are integers.

2. John is twice as old as his brother, who is older than his sister. How old is John?
    (1) John's brother is two years older than their sister.
    (2) Their sister is three years old.

3. What is the value of x?
    (1) The square of x is three more than twice x.
    (2) x is negative

4. If $a^n a^m = a^{15}$, what is the value of n?
    (1) n is even and m is 3.
    (2) n is four times as large as m.

5. What is the value of p?
    (1) $p + 3h = 10$
    (2) $9 + h = 15 - h$

6. If $\sqrt{ab} = 4$ and $a > 0$, what is the value of a?
    (1) $ab = 16$ and b is even.
    (2) $a = b$

7. John's first long jump was one foot short of the school record. His second jump exceeded the school's record by a foot. What was the old record which John broke by one foot?
   (1) The average of John's two jumps was 18 feet.
   (2) The sum of John's two jumps was 36 feet.

8. John has x dollars and Mary has y dollars. Together they can buy a $45 ticket. How much money does John have?
   (1) After the purchase, they have a total of $3 left.
   (2) John started with less money than Mary.

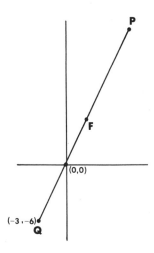

9. In the figure above, what are the coordinates of point P?
   (1) The midpoint of line QP is at point F (2, 4).
   (2) Line QP passes through origin (0, 0)

10. For all integers a and b, the operation ⊙ is defined by $a \odot b = \dfrac{a}{b}$ where $b \neq 0$. If x and y are integers, is $x \odot y$ an integer?
    (1) $x^2 = y^2$
    (2) $x = 0$

11. What is the average of a, b, and c if $a + c = 20$?
    (1) $a - c = 12$ and $a + b = 18$
    (2) $b = 2$

12. How tall is Larry?
    (1) Three years ago Larry was four inches shorter than his brother, Bill.
    (2) Larry has grown three inches in the last three years. Bill has grown only two inches.

13. Is $y > \frac{1}{y}$?
    (1) $y > 0$
    (2) $y > 1$

14. If x is an integer multiple of 7, what is the value of x?
    (1) $x = 5y$, where y is an integer
    (2) $27 < x < 43$

15. What is the value of $xy - 8$?
    (1) $x + y = 5$
    (2) $xy - 10 = 22$

Geometry

Questions

1. In parallelogram ABCD, what is the length of AE?
   (1) $AB = 10$ and $\angle AEB = 90°$
   (2) $AC = 12$

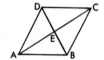

2. Are lines ℓ_1 and ℓ_2 parallel?
   (1) $\angle 1 = \angle 2$
   (2) $\angle 1 + \angle 3 = 180°$

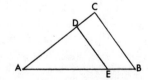

3. Is triangle AED similar to triangle ABC?
   (1) $\angle ACB = 90°$
   (2) $DE = \frac{2}{3} CB$

4. Is the triangle ABC an isosceles triangle?
   (1) CD is perpendicular to AB.
   (2) ∠ACB is bisected by CD.

5. What is the measure of ∠ACB in the circle with center O?
   (1) CA = CB
   (2) The arc AB is ⅕ the circumference of the circle.

6. What is the area of triangle ABC?
   (1) AC = 6
   (2) BD = 10

7. What is the measure of ∠x?
   (1) ∠y is twice ∠x.
   (2) ∠x = ∠z

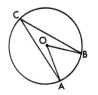

8. What is the measure of ∠DBC?
   (1) ∠ADB = 100°
   (2) AD = DB

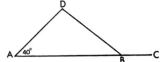

9. The small circle with center B is tangent to the large circle with center D. What is the area of the small circle?
   (1) The large circle has area 9π and CD = 1.
   (2) BD = 2

10. What is the area of the shaded portion?
    (1) ABCD is a square and DB is an arc of a circle with center A.
    (2) AD = 2

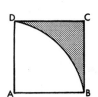

11. The volume of a box is 216 cubic inches. What are the dimensions of the box?
    (1) Length, width, and height are equal.
    (2) The length and width are each 6".

12. What is the length of the hypotenuse of a 45°–45°–90° triangle?
    (1) The area is 8.
    (2) The perimeter equals $8 + 4\sqrt{2}$.

13. What is the volume of the right circular cylinder?
    (1) The height is 4.
    (2) The radius is an integer which is less than the height.

14. The circle centered at O has AD passing through O. What is the radius of the circle?
    (1) AB = 1
    (2) BD = 2

15. Does AB = CD?
    (1) C is the midpoint of AE.
    (2) BC = CD

ANSWER KEY FOR DATA SUFFICIENCY PRACTICE

The first page number following each answer will direct you to the complete explanation for that specific problem. *Read this explanation first.* The page numbers in parentheses refer to the suggested basic review section.

Arithmetic

1. (B) p. 414 (13)
2. (E) p. 414 (274)
3. (D) p. 414 (76)
4. (D) p. 414 (55)
5. (E) p. 414
6. (D) p. 414 (34)
7. (C) p. 414
8. (B) p. 415 (55)

9. (C) p. 415 (270)
10. (C) p. 415 (83)
11. (C) p. 415 (42)
12. (C) p. 415 (13)
13. (E) p. 416 (76)
14. (D) p. 416 (264)
15. (A) p. 416

Algebra

1. (A) p. 416 (122)
2. (C) p. 416 (285)
3. (C) p. 416 (110)
4. (D) p. 417 (63, 110)
5. (C) p. 417 (122)
6. (B) p. 417 (170)
7. (D) p. 417 (109, 113)
8. (E) p. 417

9. (A) p. 418 (163)
10. (D) p. 418 (176)
11. (D) p. 418 (122)
12. (E) p. 418
13. (B) p. 419 (110)
14. (C) p. 419 (32)
15. (B) p. 419 (113)

Geometry

1. (B) p. 419 (223, 229)
2. (B) p. 419 (212)
3. (E) p. 420 (241)
4. (C) p. 420 (217)
5. (B) p. 420 (236, 239)
6. (E) p. 420 (232)
7. (A) p. 420 (207)
8. (D) p. 420 (220)

9. (A) p. 420 (237)
10. (C) p. 421 (232, 237)
11. (D) p. 421 (241. 242)
12. (D) p. 421 (225)
13. (E) p. 421 (242)
14. (C) p. 421 (223, 235)
15. (E) p. 422 (210)

DATA SUFFICIENCY ANSWERS
AND EXPLANATIONS

Arithmetic

1. (B) 6 is the product of 6 and 1, 2 and 3, -6 and -1, and -2 and -3. Statement (1) says that both integers are positive, but that still leaves two choices. Statement (2) says that one of the integers is 2. Therefore, the other must be 3. Statement (2) suffices.

2. (E) Without our knowing the rate at which the airplane flew, statement (1) does not suffice. Statement (2) provides more information but does not say how long the total travel time was or the speed after 8 hours. The statements together do not provide sufficient data to answer the question, as we do not know the speed for the final hour.

3. (D) Knowing that the two numbers average 5, we can use either statement alone to determine both numbers. For example, using statement (1) that 7 is one of the numbers, we can determine that the other number must be 3, as the average of the two numbers is 5. The same process works for statement (2) alone.

4. (D) Statement (1) is sufficient to determine an answer. Just multiply $15,000 by .06. Statement (2) is also sufficient to determine an answer. Just divide $15,900 by 1.06.

5. (E) John's being shorter than his brother has nothing to do with John's jump; so statement (1) alone does not solve the problem. Since no information is given about how John's jump compares to his brother's jump, statement (2) is not useful either.

6. (D) Statement (1) implies that the fractions are both ½. Statement (2) implies that the first fraction is ½; therefore, the second is ½. Each statement is separately sufficient.

7. (C) Statement (1) gives the proportion of men to women, but since no numbers are given, it is insufficient to determine the

number of men. Statement (2) alone is insufficient to determine the number of men. If we take them together, however, we know that the number of men is twice the number of women, 9. Therefore, there are 18 men at the party.

8. **(B)** Statement (1) tells us nothing of value for this problem. Statement (2) suffices. Since 75% of the total is 12 ounces, then $175T = 12$, or $T = 12/.75$.

9. **(C)** Statement (1) tells us that Bob has read half the book by midnight. But since we do not know when he started or how long he has been reading, we cannot calculate when he will finish. Statement (2) alone is also insufficient. But together with statement (1) it allows us to calculate that it takes Bob 4 hours to read half the book; therefore, he will finish in 4 more hours. The answer is (C). Note that our knowledge of Bob's reading speed is useless, as we do not know the page length of the book.

10. **(C)** Statement (1) gives the brother's height in feet and inches. Statement (2) gives Alice's height in centimeters. Neither statement alone will suffice. Converting centimeters to feet and inches and subtracting the height in statement (1) from that in statement (2) shows the answer is (C).

11. **(C)** To answer the question, we need to know how much gas was used. Statement (1) says how much of the tank was used but not how much gas. Statement (2) says how much gas is in a full tank. Neither alone is enough, but taking the statements together, we find that Bruce used 9 gallons. We can then divide 300 miles by 9 gallons of gas.

12. **(C)** From statement (1), we know that the smaller integer must be 2, 3, 5, or 7, as they are the only one-digit prime numbers. This statement alone is insufficient. From statement (2), we know that 5 times the smaller integer will give the second integer, greater than 30. Statement (2) alone is insufficient. Together, however, the statements provide the information that only 7 could be the smaller integer, as $5 \times 7 > 30$.

13. (E) Since we know only that Hal's salary is *over* $800 per month, no precise average weekly salary may be determined from statement (1). Statement (2) is also insufficient, as we do not know how many days each week Hal works.

14. (D) By using the simple interest formula ($I = prt$), either statement alone will suffice to determine rate of interest (15% in this case).

15. (A) Statement (1) alone allows us to extrapolate back 20 minutes at a time to determine when volume was 1 cubic meter. (Each previous 20 minutes the mixture is halved.) Statement (2) is insufficient as we are not given any information regarding what the *present* time is.

Algebra

1. (A) The problem states that $3a - 2b = 4$. Statement (1) gives $a = 2b$, resulting in two equations in two unknowns, which will lead to a unique solution. Statement (2) does not lead to a unique solution, however, since many pairs of integers a, b, will satisfy $3a - 2b = 4$.

2. (C) Let x = John's brother's age, then $2x$ = John's age. Statement (1) tells us that John's brother is two years older than their sister. Hence, $x - 2$ = sister's age. But we have no value for x. Thus, statement (1) alone is insufficient. Statement (2) tells us the sister's age, three years old, but we have no exact relationship between the sister and either of her brothers. So statement (2) alone is insufficient. Taking the statements together we have

x = John's brother
$2x$ = John
$x - 2 = 3$ = sister

Thus, we can solve for x (5 years) and find John's age, 10.

3. (C) Statement (1) says that $x^2 = 3 + 2x$; so $x^2 - 2x - 3 = 0$, which factors to give $(x - 3)(x + 1) = 0$. This has two answers, $x = 3$ or $x = -1$, which in Data Sufficiency problems does not constitute a solution. Statement (2) says that the answer is

negative, which alone does not suffice. However, taken together, the data are sufficient to determine a unique solution, $x = -1$.

4. (D) Since $a^n a^m = a^{15}$ and we know that $a^n a^m = a^{n+m}$, we have $n + m = 15$. Statement (1) says that n is even and m is 3, which results in $n + 3 = 15$, or $n = 12$, a solution. Statement (2) says $n = 4m$. This together with $n + m = 15$ gives two equations in two unknowns which lead to a solution also.

5. (C) Statement (1) alone is not sufficient as it is an equation with two unknowns. Statement (2) allows us to solve for the unknown, h, which we may then plug into statement (1) to determine the value of p. Both statements taken together will answer the question.

6. (B) The fact that $\sqrt{ab} = 4$ implies that $ab = 16$. Statement (1) says $ab = 16$ and b is even. This does not allow us to find a, since several choices are possible: (2)(8), (4)(4), etc. If statement (2) is used, we have $a^2 = 16$, and there is only one positive integer solution, 4.

7. (D) If we let x represent the original school record, then John's first jump was $x - 1$ feet and his second jump was $x + 1$ feet. Statement (1) says that the average of the two jumps was 18 feet. This means that

$$\frac{(x - 1) + (x + 1)}{2} = 18$$

$$\frac{2x}{2} = 18$$

$$x = 18$$

18 feet was the old record. Statement (1) will suffice. Statement (2) says that $(x - 1) + (x + 1) = 36$. Solving this for x gives 18 feet. So this too gives a solution.

8. (E) The question implies that $x + y$ must be 45 or larger. Statement (1) implies that $(x + y) - 45 = 3$. So $x + y = 48$, which does not allow us to find x. Statement (2) implies that

x < y, but neither this nor the previous piece of information allows us to determine x.

9. **(A)** Statement (1) alone is sufficient to determine the coordinates of point P. Since the coordinates are given for endpoint Q $(-3, -6)$, using the midpoint, we can derive coordinates for the other endpoint, P. (The midpoint coordinates are the averages of the endpoint coordinates. Thus, coordinates of point P are (7, 14). Statement (2) tells us nothing of value.

10. **(D)** Either statement (1) or (2) alone is sufficient to answer the question conclusively. Statement (1) tells us that x = y or x = −y. In either case, x ⊙ y (or $\frac{x}{y}$) will be an integer, as it will equal either 1 or −1. Statement (2) tells us that x = 0. Therefore, $\frac{x}{y}$ will equal 0, which is also an integer.

11. **(D)** The average of a, b, and c is

$$\frac{a + b + c}{3}$$

Statement (1) and the information in the question give us three equations.

$$a + c = 20$$
$$a - c = 12$$
$$a + b = 18$$

If we add the first two equations we obtain 2a = 32, so a = 16. This allows us to find b and c. So statement (1) is sufficient. Statement (2) says b = 2. So this together with a + c = 20 allows us to find a + b + c = 12 + 20 = 32. Thus, statement (2) will suffice.

12. **(E)** If we let x represent Larry's height three years ago and y represent Bill's height three years ago, statement (1) says x = y − 4. This does not allow us to find x or Larry's present height. Statement (2) gives no relationship between the heights. Putting both statements together allows us to write the second condition as

(x + 3) Larry's height now
(y + z) Bill's height now

Since Larry was four inches shorter, he is now only three inches shorter than Bill, so

$$(x + 3) = (y + z) - 3$$
$$x = y - 4$$

Thus, no new information is gained and the problem cannot be solved.

13. (B) Statement (1) alone is insufficient. Substituting 1 and 2 as values of y will result in a "no" then a "yes" answer for the original question. Statement (2), however, is alone sufficient. Any value of y greater than 1 will yield a consistent answer ("yes") to the question.

14. (C) Statement (1) allows us to know that x is a multiple of both 5 and 7. Thus x may be 35, 70, 105, etc. Since statement (2) alone tells us that x may be 28, 35, or 42 (all multiples of 7), it too is insufficient. Both statements taken together, however, will suffice to determine that x is 35.

15. (B) Statement (1) is insufficient, as it contains two unknowns. Statement (2) is sufficient alone. Although it contains two unknowns, notice that xy − 10 is simply two less than xy − 8. Therefore, if xy − 10 equals 22, xy − 8 equals 24.

Geometry

1. (B) The key here is that the diagonals of a parallelogram bisect each other. Statement (1) does not provide enough information to compute the length of AE. However, the fact that △AEB is a right triangle with hypotenuse 10 does not determine the lengths of AE or EB. Statement (2) allows us to determine AE at once.

2. (B) Although statement (1) allows us to conclude that both ∠1 and ∠2 are right angles, this does not suffice to conclude that ℓ_1 and ℓ_2 are parallel. We can conclude from statement (2), however, that ℓ_1 and ℓ_2 are parallel because ∠1 and ∠3 are supplementary angles.

3. (E) In order to conclude that the triangles are similar, we would need to know that DE and CB are parallel. Neither statement (1) nor statement (2) gives enough information to allow this conclusion.

4. (C) An isosceles triangle has two sides of equal length. To conclude this, the information provided in statement (1) does not suffice because no conclusions about the sides AC and BC can be drawn. Similarly, statement (2) alone is insufficient. The information combined, however, leads to the conclusion that $\triangle ACD$ and $\triangle BCD$ are congruent (angle-side-angle). Hence AC = BC.

5. (B) Angle ACB is an inscribed angle. Hence, its measure is equal to one-half of $\angle AOB$. Statement (1) gives no information about the number of degrees in $\angle ACB$. Statement (2), however, tells us that $\angle AOB$ is $\frac{1}{5}$ of 360°. This, together with our initial observation, is sufficient to answer the question.

6. (E) The area of a triangle is equal to one-half the product of a base and an altitude. Neither statement (1) nor statement (2) allows us to determine the altitude of the triangle.

7. (A) The key here is that $\angle x$ and $\angle y$ are supplementary angles. Thus, statement (1) implies that $\angle x$ is 60° and $\angle y$ is 120°. Statement (2) is always true (because vertical angles are equal).

8. (D) Angle DBC is an exterior angle of $\triangle ABD$ and hence it is equal to the sum of the angles BAD and ADB. Since $\angle BAD$ is given as 40° and statement (1) tells us that $\angle ADB$ is 100°, we can determine $\angle DBC$. Statement (2) tells us that the triangle ABD has two equal sides. Therefore, it is isosceles. Thus, $\angle BAD = \angle ABD$, and because $\angle ABD$ and $\angle DBC$ are supplementary, we can determine $\angle DBC$ based on statement (2) alone.

9. (A) We would need either the radius or the diameter of the small circle to find its area. Statement (1) tells us that the radius of the large circle (AD or DE) is 3 (because the area is π times the square of the radius). Because AE must therefore be 6 and CE = CD + DE = 1 + 3 = 4, we know AC = 2, and we can find

the area of the small circle. Statement (2) does not give us any information about the relationship between BD and the other parts of the circle.

10. (C) Statement (1) tells us that if we knew the radius of the circle (or equivalently the length of the side of the square), we could find the area of the shaded portion by subtracting the area of one-quarter of the circle from that of the square. However, statement (1) does not alone suffice. Statement (2) alone is of little use, since we know nothing of the nature of the geometric figures. We need both statements to solve the problem.

11. (D) Statement (1) tells us that our box is a cube. From the known volume, the length of its edge can be found. So statement (1) is sufficient. Statement (2) tells us that $(6)(6)(h) = 216$. Thus we can find the third dimension, height.

12. (D) The right triangle is isosceles and thus its sides are in the proportion of $1:1:\sqrt{2}$. Statement (1) tell sus that if we multiply one-half the length of a base times the altitude, we get 8. Because the legs in this case give us a base and an altitude, we can solve for the length of a leg and hence find the hypotenuse.

$$\tfrac{1}{2}(s)(s) = 8$$
$$s^2 = 16$$
$$s = 4$$
$$\text{hypotenuse} = 4\sqrt{2}$$

Using statement (2), we know that $s + s + 4\sqrt{2} = 8 + 4\sqrt{2}$. Thus, $s = 4$ and, again, hypotenuse $= 4\sqrt{2}$.

13. (E) The volume of a right circular cylinder is $\pi r^2 h$, where r is the radius of the base and h is the height. Hence, statement (1) does not give sufficient information to compute the volume. Statement (2) does not specify the radius.

14. (C) Because AD is a diameter, the triangle ABD is inscribed in a semicircle and is therefore a right triangle, as $\angle ABD = 90°$. We can find the radius OA if we can determine AD (the diameter).

Statement (1) gives us one leg of the right triangle. Statement (2) gives us the second leg. The Pythagorean theorem allows us to find AD and hence the radius.

15. (E) Although statement (1) shows us that AC = CE, even taken with statement (2), no relationship may be derived between AB and CD. Note that with both pieces of data, a diagram may be drawn as follows.

FINAL SUGGESTIONS

Now that you have completed this guide you should
1. Obtain the *Cliffs Preparation Guide* for your specific test. This guide will key in on your specific math problem types, offer more practice problems, and prepare you for the nonmathematical questions on your exam.
2. Practice working problems under time pressure. Now that you've reviewed the basic skills, the next hurdle is being comfortable using them under timed test pressure.
3. Use this guide as a reference should problems arise.